EMPLOYEE
INVOLVEMENT

EMPLOYEE INVOLVEMENT

Methods for Improving Performance and Work Attitudes

John L. Cotton

SAGE Publications
International Educational and Professional Publisher
Newbury Park   London   New Delhi

For information address:

SAGE Publications, Inc.
2455 Teller Road
Newbury Park, California 91320

SAGE Publications Ltd.
6 Bonhill Street
London EC2A 4PU
United Kingdom

SAGE Publications India Pvt. Ltd.
M-32 Market
Greater Kailash I
New Delhi 110 048 India

Printed in the United States of America

Library of Congress Cataloging-in-Publication Data

Cotton, John L.
    Employee involvement: methods for improving performance and work
attitudes / John L. Cotton.
        p.   cm.
    Includes bibliographical references (pp. 246-287) and index.
    ISBN 0-8039-4532-9 (cloth).—ISBN 0-8039-4533-7 (pbk.)
        1. Management—United States—Employee participation.
    2. Personnel management—United States.   3. Employee motivation—
United States.   4. Quality circles—United States.   I. Title.
HD5660.U5C68   1993
658.3'14—dc20   92-40084

93 94 95 96 10 9 8 7 6 5 4 3 2

Sage Production Editor: Diane S. Foster

Contents

Foreword

We are living in a world of organizational turmoil. Faced with severe competitive pressures and rapidly changing markets and technologies, private-sector firms are seeking ways to make themselves more flexible, adaptive, and competitive. Asked to do more and more with less and less, pubic-sector organizations are trying to make themselves more efficient and responsive to public needs. This search to succeed, and in some cases, even to survive in today's demanding environment has spawned a host of organizational innovations, some rather radical by traditional bureaucratic standards. We have seen organizations drastically downsize themselves while adopting the latest technologies, techniques, and practices. We have witnessed a virtual organizational revolution with leaner, more flexible structures replacing rigid bureaucracies. We have seen unprecedented attention to quality, customer service, and continuous improvement.

In the midst of all of this innovation, organizations are discovering, or rediscovering in some instances, that people really are their most important asset. Traditionally organizations structured themselves to maximize employee control. They tended to underutilize employees, relegating them to narrow jobs requiring limited capability. In today's competitive environment, however, success depends on using the workforce's entire capacity to generate new ideas and ways of working and to make relevant and timely decisions. Consequently organizations are increasingly structuring themselves to promote high levels of employee involvement. Moreover, a highly involved workforce is essential to implementing many of the new technologies, techniques, and practices used in organizations today. Employees must be involved if they are to understand the need for the innovations and how they operate; they must by involved if they are to be committed to changing their behaviors to work in new, improved ways.

Getting employees involved, however, is more easily said than done. Organizations are discovering that employee involvement is far more complex and difficult than previously imagined. Organizations are discovering that employee involvement is not just one thing but can take a variety of forms. The different approaches vary in the kinds of organizational changes that are required, the amount of influence that is afforded workers, and the results that can be expected. Organizations also are learning that employee involvement must be tailored to fit the particular situation. Its success depends on a variety of situational factors, such as the organization's technology, environment, and culture. Finally, organizations are discovering that implementing employee involvement efforts goes far beyond rolling out a traditional change program. Employee involvement generally requires fundamental changes in leadership practices, skills, and abilities, information sharing, and rewards. These changes go to the core of the organization's values, beliefs, and norms about work behavior.

Given these complexities inherent in employee involvement, organizations and researchers alike are searching for answers to the following kinds of questions:

1. What are the different forms of employee involvement? How do they work and what results can be expected?
2. What situational contingencies affect whether these results will occur in different organizational contexts?
3. How can the different forms of employee involvement be implemented practically.

Unfortunately, coherent answers to these questions are not readily available. Although there is a vast literature on employee involvement, it does not form a clear pattern of knowledge. Much of the material is highly normative offering practical advice about how employee involvement efforts should be implemented. This information has some practical utility but is open to question about its underlying validity and general applicability. The scientific literature on employee involvement attempts to overcome these problems. It offers a diversity of findings on a variety of employee involvement techniques. However, it is difficult to compare and contrast the different methods and to draw concise answers to the kinds of questions mentioned above.

John Cotton's book represents a major step toward remedying these problems and providing the necessary knowledge to understand and implement employee involvement efforts. It brings together a vast array of scientific findings and practical advice on the different forms of employee involvement that are available today. The book reviews and integrates this enormous literature and provides comprehensive knowledge about the different approaches—how they work, their expected results, their general applicability, and their methods of implementation. What makes this book all the more impressive is that it pulls no punches about what we know and do not know about employee involvement. Moreover, Cotton's book offers none of the quick fixes or easy steps to success that are so prevalent in the popular literature on employee involvement. Rather, it provides a scientific and realistic appraisal about what is needed to involve employees meaningfully in their work. Such knowledge is the cornerstone of practical wisdom about employee involvement in modern organizations.

Thomas G. Cummings
University of Southern California

Acknowledgments

I would like to thank the many reviewers who corrected my earlier mistakes, including Thomas Cummings, Donald Gardner, Tove Hammer, Thomas Head, Joan Kaspin, Jon Pierce, and Susan Rhodes. The failings that still remain are my own.

Most of all, I want to thank Laura, for her patience, her assistance, and her love.

1 The Need for Employee Involvement

Even the casual reader of business today is aware of American management problems in the global marketplace. American businesses have been pushed out of industries that they created. American productivity has been growing only 1% a year for the last 15 years, significantly below the 2.7% of the previous 15 years (Blinder, 1989; 1989/1990). Our products are too costly, our quality is too low, and we take too long to develop new products and services.

The thesis of this book is that by involving employees more, some of these negative outcomes may be avoided or at least minimized. In the past, American management has concentrated on portfolio strategies, investment in automation, offshore manufacturing, and other approaches that ignore human capital. As these have proven unsuccessful, managers have been forced to look at people as a resource to be improved and used.

Consider these specific items about how people are managed in American business:

> According to a recent Grant Thornton survey of 250 mid-size manufacturing companies, more than two thirds of the companies said they had a productivity problem. More than half of those considered the problem a minor one because it was caused by people, who could be replaced by machines. (Washington Post Service, 1990, p. D5)

However, we are beginning to reach the point of diminishing returns in the substitution of capital for labor. (Donahue, 1981, p. 111)

Many companies have already cut the layers of management between the chief executive and front-line supervisors from a dozen to six or fewer. This means that the span of control has broadened, with the number of people reporting to each manager expanding dramatically. It's fine to say tomorrow's manager should oversee the efforts of 300 people rather than 30, but how is he to keep in touch with all of them? (Dumaine, 1989, p. 50)

Just because Americans show up for work doesn't mean their heart is in it—that they are finding fulfillment in labor or doing their best. Interviews with workers around the country turn up a lot of disenchantment among people who feel abused by their employers and by society at large. Yes, the work ethic may be slipping. But laziness isn't the reason; alienation is. (Davis & Milbank, 1992, p. 1)

Hourly workers and supervisors indeed agree that "we're all in this together." But what "we're in" turns out to be a frame of mind that mistrusts senior management's intentions, doubts its competence, and resents its self-congratulatory pay. (Farnham, 1989, p. 56)

What can be done about the problems in American business? The data presented in this book indicate that one possibility is employee involvement. By getting employees involved, a variety of positive effects can occur. Here are some examples:

Before Christmas last year some experts brought new computers into one mill [of America Steel and Wire] for inventory control, set them up, and began to teach a steelworker the program to run the machine. But the experts ran out of time, saying they would return the next day. That night, the worker went home, sat down with his kids at a computer, and figured the program out. The next morning he went in and taught it to other workers. By the time the computer experts came back to complete the training, the guys in the mill already had the system up and running. (Dumaine, 1989, p. 54)

A Blacksburg team, made up of workers with interchangeable skills, can retool a line to produce a different type of filter in only 10 minutes, six times faster than workers in a traditional filter plant. This is crucial for a plant that must constantly change product lines, and it's one reason why Blacksburg turned a $2 million profit in its first 8 months of production, instead of losing $2.3 million as projected for the start-up period. (Hoerr, 1990, p. 72)

Two years ago, as part of a company-wide push to convert to teams, Fedex organized its 1,000 clerical workers into superteams of five to ten people, and gave them the training and authority to manage themselves. With the help of its teams, the company cut service glitches, such as incorrect bills and lost packages, by 13% in 1989. (Dumaine, 1990, p. 54)

[American Express's] customer-service center in Phoenix began a crusade in January to boost service. . . . Until this year, each representative performed a separate function in the complaint-handling chain— one person opened mail, another wrote back to the customer, still a third might track down copies of receipts on microfiche. Now that one representative handles a card member's complaint straight through, most issues are cleared up in 6 days on average instead of 35, and customer satisfaction has shot up. Moreover, employee turnover has declined about 30% in just 3 months. (Sellers, 1990, p. 59)

However, employee involvement should not be portrayed as the savior of American business, nor is it a technique that always has positive effects. It is a process that has the *potential* to improve productivity, quality, and employee attitudes. It is not a magic wand that solves all problems.

In Chapter 2, I review the various theories and models designed to describe and explain employee involvement. To get started, however, let me define *employee involvement* (borrowing somewhat from Lawler & Mohrman, 1989) as "a participative process to use the entire capacity of workers, designed to encourage employee commitment to organizational success." This process typically comes about by giving employees some combination of information, influence, and/or incentives. *Employee involvement* in this book is not a true unitary scientific concept; rather, it is a general label for a variety of techniques designed to achieve the objectives above. These various techniques are described in Chapters 3 through 9.

In this chapter I focus on how the concept of *employee involvement* has developed, giving a historical and philosophical perspective. The rest of this book is primarily a scientific treatise describing various ways to increase employee involvement, reviewing the available theory and research, and discussing issues of implementing these approaches in organizations.

History and Development
of Employee Involvement

If you asked any manager, or for that matter, any person off the street, to design a manufacturing facility, he or she probably would come up with a typical factory. There would be an engineering department to design the product and the production process, managers to oversee the process, and production employees to actually build the product. There probably also would be an assembly line, with the products moving past each employee, who would perform some small part of the process.

So omnipresent is this approach to work that people often forget this is only *one* way to design work. In fact, it is a relatively recent way. Back in the middle of the 19th century, if you were to buy a chair, you probably would buy it from a furniture maker, who would cut the wood, shape it into a unique design, finish the wood, assemble the chair, and sell it to you. The same crafter would fill all of these roles.

This approach provided beautiful chairs, but they were expensive and slow to manufacture. In the latter part of the 19th century and the beginning of the 20th, a number of factors began to change this process. First, there were large migrations of workers to cities in America—unskilled workers off of farms that no longer needed them, and workers from Eastern Europe who often spoke little or no English. In addition, the development of the internal combustion engine made it possible to deliver mechanical power easily to any factory that might need it. Finally, engineers and managers began to develop the ideas that eventually evolved into scientific management (Taylor, 1911).

Scientific Management

Frederick W. Taylor often is named as the father of scientific management and modern industrial engineering. This mechanical engineer strived in the early part of the 20th century to develop ways of improving the efficiency of employees.

Although scientific management contains many rules and examples, three core principles can be found in Taylor's writings (Taylor, 1947). First, Taylor assumed that it is possible to "gather together all of the traditional knowledge which in the past has been possessed by the workman and then classifying, tabulating, and reducing this knowledge to rules, laws, and formulae which are immensely helpful to the workmen in doing their daily work" (p. 36). In this way the industrial engineer (and the manager) learns the *best* way for a job to be performed.

Second, the work of every individual employee "is fully planned out by the management at least one day in advance . . . describing in detail the task which he is to accomplish as well as the means to be used in doing the work" (p. 39). If management understands the process by which the work is done, it should be possible to plan out the work in the smallest detail before the employee even shows up. In this way the manager and engineer know *exactly* how the work will be accomplished.

Third, "the science which underlies each workman's act is so great and amounts to so much that the workman who is best suited to actually do the work is incapable (either through lack of education or through insufficient mental capacity) of understanding this science" (p. 41). If management understands the best, most efficient way for a job to be accomplished, and if this is planned out in advance, no mental contribution is necessary from the worker.

An interesting example of this third assumption comes from a novel idea developed by an industrial/organizational psychologist in the late 1920s (Landy, 1989). The psychologist J. D. Houser suggested a revolutionary idea for assessing worker morale: Why not *ask workers* how they feel about their jobs? Up to this point, when people were interested in workers' morale, they would ask the workers' supervisors. Apparently it was felt that the supervisor would be more knowledgeable than the workers about how they felt about their jobs.

The scientific management approach was extremely successful in the first half of the 20th century. American managers applied this approach to all forms of business, from the manufacturing of automobiles to the serving of hamburgers. Rather than the haphazard, variable approach of the crafter, we were well served by the predictable, efficient, consistent production of the assembly line. However, as the problems described at the beginning of this

chapter indicate, the effectiveness of scientific management has
waned in recent years.

Limits on the Effectiveness
of Scientific Management

Although scientific management was undeniably effective for
more than 50 years, a number of factors suggest that its usefulness
is diminishing. First, production and/or service jobs are no longer
simple. Creating uncomplicated jobs was easy at the beginning of
the 20th century because the products and the manufacturing
processes were rudimentary and straightforward (e.g., carrying
iron ingots). This is not the case today. Even unskilled factory jobs
today require reading computer screens, working with numerical
tools, or using and/or making custom products and services. Jobs
are no longer simple.

Associated with this increase in job complexity, the technology
employed in both manufacturing and the service sector has increased in complexity, and these changes in technology are accel-
erating. The jobs of today also are changing more rapidly than in
the past. This swiftness makes it increasingly difficult for managers and engineers to gather all of the relevant information and to
develop rules. If the technology is changing daily, so are those
rules. By the time management understands the technology and
how it should best be used, the technology has changed.

Finally, products and services are changing at an ever more rapid
rate. Whereas Henry Ford could produce the Model T for nearly 20
years, today's cars need to be updated yearly, with major overhauls
every 2 or 3 years. H. Ross Perot said, "It takes five years to develop
a new car in this country. Heck, we won World War II in four years"
(quoted in Peters, 1988, p. 211). If we want to compete in the global
marketplace, speed has become a necessity (Dumaine, 1989).

Recent surveys of industrial engineers indicate that they are
aware of the limits of technology and scientific management. In
one survey of automotive manufacturing engineers (Arnholt, 1986),
71% felt that the productivity and quality benefits of advanced
technology (robots, lasers, etc.) had been overrated. When asked
"What will produce the biggest productivity gains in the next five
years?" the number one choice, with 65%, was "better use of
human resources" (p. 38).

At the Institute of Industrial Engineers (1991), when a group of top engineering managers was asked what key opportunities and challenges their company faced, one response predominated. The number one answer to both questions was "empowering and motivating employees." As one executive said, "The opportunity and the challenge is to develop true employee involvement where all barriers to productivity, quality, and service are torn down, and everyone works together as a team to ensure survival in a global economy" (p. 3).

Jobs are more complicated, technology is more complex, and everything is constantly changing. Therefore, manufacturing and service processes, labor forces, and management need to become more flexible. How do we gain this greater flexibility? Through employee involvement.

The Move Toward Employee Involvement and Participation

Although the first direct criticisms against scientific management surfaced in the 1950s and 1960s in the writings of McGregor (1957) and Herzberg (1966), earlier pioneers laid the groundwork for employee involvement.

Kurt Lewin

Kurt Lewin's contribution to employee involvement comes from several sources. First, he was one of the first psychologists to focus on the individual as a member of a group or within a social environment (Lewin, 1948, 1951). Instead of just describing the person as a collection of traits or responses to a variety of stimuli, Lewin took the individual out of the abstract and placed him or her into the everyday environment of social forces. This innovation led others to speculate on how the group could influence the individual (Asch, 1956), how nonphysical entities such as norms could affect behavior (Festinger, Schachter, & Back, 1950), and how groups behave (Janis, 1972). Lewin's contributions mark him as one of the forerunners of organizational behavior, as well as the father of social psychology.

Lewin's second contribution was to push theories out of the laboratory and into the real world (Lewin, 1947). His quote, "Nothing is so practical as a good theory" (Lewin, 1951, p. 169) has continued to remind academics to try their ideas about human behavior in real organizations. This perspective has led to the notion of *action research,* much of which has focused on employee involvement (Peters & Robinson, 1984).

The final contribution by Lewin was his research that directly studied the impact of involvement. Lewin and his students (Lewin, Lippitt, & White, 1939; Lippitt, 1940; White & Lippitt, 1960) carried out a series of classic experiments comparing authoritarian, democratic, and laissez-faire leaders of boys' groups. They found greater aggression, more discontent, and less individualistic behavior in the autocratic groups. In addition, although the groups acted similarly when the leader was present, groups with democratic leaders (those that involved the boys in decisions more) were more productive when the leader was not present.

In another series of classic studies, Lewin (1947, 1952) compared methods for persuading housewives to use foods such as beef hearts, kidneys, cod liver oil, and so on. Lewin found that a group discussion followed by a group decision was more effective than simply listening to a persuasive lecture. By involving rather than simply lecturing the housewives, their attitudes were more easily altered.

In short, Lewin could rightly be called the father of employee involvement. His ideas and research sparked many of the theories and studies reviewed in this volume. Although he never studied employee involvement in a business organization, his contributions can be seen in every quality circle, suggestion plan, or other involvement program.

Trist and Emery

Eric Trist and Fred Emery transformed many of Lewin's ideas into concepts and theories directly aimed at improving organizations. Trist and Emery's major contribution involved developing the notion of *sociotechnical systems* and applying it to organizations. These authors observed that to understand how people operate in an organization, it is necessary to understand both the social system (the interaction of people with each other) and the technical system (the tools and techniques employed in the work). A positive, productive work organization exists when these two systems (as well as other, external systems) operate synchronously, not at odds with each other.

A second major contribution of Trist and Emery is the promotion of self-directed work teams, as well as the careful testing of these types of interventions. As part of the Tavistock Institute for Human Relations in London, Trist and Emery have been great champions of self-directed work teams. They have implemented sociotechnical interventions in organizations around the world, including Britain (Trist, Higgin, Murray, & Pollock, 1963), the United States (Trist, Susman, & Brown, 1977), and Norway (Emery & Thorsrud, 1964/1969). These examples have served to stimulate others so that this is one of the most popular forms of employee involvement across national borders.

In addition to promoting self-directed work teams, Trist and Emery's research also has served as an example of how research studying such interventions *should* be designed. The careful studies describing the details of what was done in the organization, comparing their results to more traditional sites (control groups), and being candid about their difficulties have demonstrated the way such research should be conducted. If all of the research on employee involvement was this careful and complete, more decisive conclusions could be made.

Lawler

During the last 20 years there has been a massive spread of the concepts behind employee involvement. One of the leaders in this effort to explore and integrate employee involvement has been Edward E. Lawler.

Like Trist and Emery, Lawler has strived to make careful studies of the effectiveness of involvement, trying to be sure the data actually support his conclusions. Although some authors accept employee involvement as a philosophical necessity, regardless of effectiveness, Lawler has been honest in his evaluation and, at times, critical of certain forms of employee involvement (Lawler & Mohrman, 1985).

If employee involvement is to spread throughout business organizations, it needs practical motivation, not just religious fervor. Within the United States in particular, managers need to be convinced that involvement has a practical benefit and is not just an ideological goal. Lawler has been at the forefront of those demonstrating benefits and convincing managers.

In addition, Lawler has firmly tied employee involvement to other human resource management issues, such as compensation systems (Lawler, 1971) and performance appraisals (Mohrman, Resnick-West, & Lawler, 1989). If involvement is to be successful, it typically requires changes in other human resource systems. For example, many of the forms of involvement described in the following chapters entail changes in the pay system. Too many advocates of employee involvement have assumed that involvement could be simply "added on" to the current practices within the organization and so have failed. Additional changes that can serve to support the involvement need to be made to other systems in the organization.

Finally, Lawler has assisted directly in a number of employee involvement interventions through the Center for Effective Organizations at the University of Southern California. This center (which Lawler founded and heads) attempts to bridge the gap between academics interested in employee involvement and organizations attempting new approaches to how work is done.

Current Work on Employee Involvement

This historical review brings us to the present, where employee involvement has fragmented into different directions with separate audiences. *Human resource management* professionals examine gainsharing and employee stock ownership plans (ESOPs) as approaches to compensation. *Organizational development* professionals study self-directed work teams and other sociotechnical approaches as organizational interventions. *Industrial relations* authorities investigate quality of work life projects and representative participation in Europe through codetermination. Finally *organizational behavior* researchers examine quality circles and work enrichment.

The difficulty is that each of these approaches to employee involvement is studied in isolation. It is not possible to test these approaches comparatively, using a strong inference approach (Pfeffer, 1981; Platt, 1964); however, it is possible to compare and contrast them. With infrequent exceptions (such as Lawler, 1986), few have attempted to bring together these different perspectives. I have tried to do this here.

Assumptions, Aims, and Value of This Book

This book makes two somewhat contradictory assumptions. The first is that all of these forms of employee involvement are related; that is, they all operate, in some sense, by getting people involved. The second is that the different forms are indeed different and cannot be totalled together. It is more valuable to examine each independently than to try to tally them together like adding apples and oranges.

The aim of this book is to present the empirical knowledge about these different forms of involvement and to deduce which are effective, which are not, and what factors are involved. Too much about employee involvement and participation has been proselytizing, trying to convert others (Locke & Schweiger, 1979). I believe employee involvement can have positive effects and perhaps can help solve many of the problems outlined above. However, I believe that although some evidence shows how involvement can be effective, some evidence also demonstrates how it is not productive. All sides of the issues need to be presented, allowing the reader to draw his or her own conclusion.

One value of this book (I hope) is to bring together the current knowledge on a wide range of perspectives concerning employee involvement. This presentation should be of use to the academic who is focused on the details of one approach but knows little about the others. It also can be worthwhile for the student who should be learning all of the various ways that employees can be involved, not just one or two ways. Finally, this presentation may be of value to the sophisticated manager who is considering which approach to follow.

Summary and Conclusions

American business is in trouble, and it seems likely that, after considering offshore manufacturing, automation, or other approaches, employee involvement may be an effective response to some of these dilemmas (Long & Warner, 1987). I have traced very briefly the history of work in America during the 20th century, outlining how scientific management operated and why it is not as effective today. Over the last 50 years, a number of innovators have pioneered a variety of approaches to get employees more involved. The purpose of this book is to bring together the many far-flung approaches to employee involvement. In this way the academic, the student, and the professional manager can better appreciate and use employee involvement.

2 Empirical Research and Models of Employee Involvement

This book could just as easily have been titled, *Employee Participation: Methods for Improving Performance and Work Attitudes*. It also could have been called *Workplace Democracy, The Empowered Employee, Work Redesign,* or many other titles. All of these terms refer to the same general concept, yet all offer a slightly different flavor.

The notion is that, by involving workers, by having them participate in decision making, by making the workplace more democratic, and by empowering employees, certain outcomes (e.g., attitudes and productivity) may improve. The problem, by now apparent, is that this process, whatever it is, is fuzzy. When you consider that all the aforementioned terms are related and that all can refer to suggestion plans, to self-directed work teams, or to employee ownership, you can see that it is *very* fuzzy. We have numerous terms referring to a myriad of techniques, yet we argue that some central concept of involvement or participation underlies all of them.

These problems are why many individuals, managers, and academics have ignored employee involvement or, worse, have sneered at its supposed value. How can any worth be ascribed to such a hazy, indistinct, obscure concept?

In Chapter 1, I defined *employee involvement* as "a participative process to use the entire capacity of workers, designed to encourage employee commitment to organizational success." In this chapter I briefly summarize the major reviews and examine the numerous models of employee involvement. Ideally this coverage will serve to further elucidate the concept of *employee involvement*. Then I present a framework that describes the many *forms* that employee involvement may take. This framework then is used to introduce the chapters to follow, each summarizing a particular form of employee involvement.

Effectiveness of Employee Involvement

Among the first questions (and often the very first question) a manager has about employee involvement is, "Does it work?" That is, does employee involvement improve productivity or job attitudes or reduce costs or absenteeism or turnover? Although individuals have argued that employees should be involved for ethical reasons (Sashkin, 1984, 1986), many behavioral scientists have tried to establish its efficacy in attaining a wide variety of management goals.

Much of this book is taken up in reviewing the research for each form of employee involvement. It would be useful at the beginning, however, to see how others have attempted to review this wide-ranging literature. Most reviews have not employed the term *employee involvement* but have used the label *employee participation*. I use the term *involvement* rather than *participation* because participation describes a more limited process. As the definition in Chapter 1 indicates, employee involvement is more than simply taking part in decision making; it can include incentives (gainsharing), group behavior (quality circles), and training (self-directed work teams). Studies of participation attempt to "purify" the concept and ignore these factors. This abbreviation is suitable for studying participation, but not employee involvement. As I pointed out earlier, *employee involvement* is *not* a true scientific concept; rather, it is a useful catchall term.

In summarizing the reviews, I first focus on those articles concerned with the effectiveness of employee involvement. Then I briefly review the evidence concerning those factors that are assumed to affect the involvement process.

Locke and Schweiger (1979) presented probably the best-known review of employee participation. They divided the broad literature into four general subsections on the basis of methodology: laboratory studies, correlational field studies, multivariate experimental field studies, and univariate (controlled) experimental field studies.

The *laboratory studies* include studies that examined participation in an artificial situation. From a sample of 18 studies, Locke and Schweiger (1979) found no advantage for participation in terms of productivity or satisfaction when compared to an autocratic or more directive leadership. Of course, generalizability of these results is questionable. First, they primarily, but not exclusively, employed students as subjects. Second, the experiments employed a variety of tasks, including 20 questions, mechanical tasks, role plays, mazes, decision making, and problem solving. Third, the experiments were of short duration, so the participation lasted no more than an hour or so.

Locke and Schweiger's second group, *correlational field studies,* examined employee participation by correlating outcomes (such as productivity and satisfaction) with some measure of participation. Of the 25 studies in this category, Locke and Schweiger found no effect on productivity but did find a tendency for satisfaction to be higher when employee participation was greater. Of course, it is impossible to determine causality from these studies. One can ask, Are more involved employees more satisfied, or are more satisfied employees given more opportunities for participation?

Multivariate experimental field studies in the Locke and Schweiger review refers to experiments where participation was manipulated but additional factors also were varied. For example, if self-directed work teams were introduced into a factory, and if pay incentives also were changed, the study would fall into this category. Locke and Schweiger reviewed 12 studies that they classified in this way but do not summarize these results. Although they acknowledged that most of the studies demonstrated beneficial results, they correctly pointed out that it is impossible to determine whether the positive results were due solely to greater employee involvement.

The final category, *controlled experimental field studies*, includes studies that had some type of control or comparison. This format would allow the reader to conclude that any results would have been due to the employee participation. Of the 17 studies in this group, few effects were found for productivity, but increased satisfaction was found in a majority of the studies.

Overall, Locke and Schweiger found that employee participation had little consistent effect on productivity. However, about 60% of the studies they summarized did find more positive satisfaction with employee participation. Locke and Schweiger's results were not extremely positive, but neither were they as negative as sometimes portrayed. These authors also emphasized the need to examine contextual factors that may determine the effectiveness of employee participation.

Schweiger and Leana (1986) extended this review to compare laboratory and field research concerning employee participation. Their review found similar effects from both settings and overall results similar to Locke and Schweiger's (1979).

More positive findings were reported by Katzell and Guzzo (1983), who conducted a review of 207 studies employing one or more of 11 psychologically based methods of improving productivity. Their review found that 87% of the studies reported improvement in one or more measures of productivity.

In a later analysis Guzzo, Jette, and Katzell (1985) employed meta-analysis to examine the relative impact of 11 types of psychologically based organizational interventions in 98 studies. Guzzo et al. examined gainsharing programs, work redesign, and sociotechnical interventions (self-directed work teams), in addition to eight other types of interventions. These authors employed meta-analysis to compute average effect sizes for the various innovations. Meta-analysis (Glass, McGaw, & Smith, 1981; Guzzo, Jackson, & Katzell, 1987; Hunter, Schmidt, & Jackson, 1982) is a quantitative method for reviewing research studies. Using meta-analysis, the reviewer can determine whether the effects across the different studies are statistically significant or random. In addition, it is possible to test potential moderators across different studies.

Guzzo et al. (1987) determined that the different interventions did produce improvements in productivity, overall, about half of a standard deviation. Considerable differences also were found across the various types of programs. Sociotechnical interventions tended to show greater than average impact, followed by job redesign. Gainsharing programs, however, did not have a significant effect on productivity. Guzzo et al. pointed out that this lack of significance probably is due to the enormous variance in results across studies of financial incentives.

Guzzo et al. (1987) also found that the size of the organization, type of organization, and type of worker influenced the overall effects. Across the 11 types of psychological interventions, larger effects were found in smaller organizations, in government versus private and nonprofit organizations, and with sales and managerial workers versus blue-collar and clerical workers.

Spector (1986) presented a review and meta-analysis of 88 studies that examined the impact of employees' perceived control on a number of outcomes. He found that, in his sample of studies, employee participation was associated with an improvement in general satisfaction, as well as satisfaction with the work, supervision, pay, opportunities for promotion and growth, and organizational involvement. Participation was not related to improvements in satisfaction with co-workers or with greater commitment. Employee participation was associated with higher motivation and performance, fewer intentions to quit, and lower turnover. Participation was not related to fewer physical complaints and less emotional stress.

All of the above reviewers found considerable heterogeneity in their reviews. Studies examining the same outcomes would find totally different results. In addition, Guzzo et al. (1985) and Spector (1986) found very different and much more positive outcomes for employee participation than did Locke and Schweiger (1979). Why do these differences exist?

Contextual Factors Affecting Involvement

Regardless of their views on its efficacy, all of the writers on employee participation agree that contextual factors will influence the impact of that participation. Many have argued that successful participation can occur only when certain factors are present (e.g., Levine, 1990; Margulies & Black, 1987). In the following chapters I discuss many of the variables that will influence each form of employee involvement. Here, however, I discuss those factors that have been examined as generally affecting the impact of employee participation.

Personality

One obvious contextual variable is *personality*. Singer (1974) discussed how most theorists and researchers of employee participation have ignored individual differences. As he stated, "to assume that *all* workers desire [involvement] opportunities is to lack sensitivity to *individual* needs—the antithesis of the humanization that ardent proponents . . . advocate" (p. 359).

Vroom (1959) was the first to attempt to study the effects of personality on reactions to employee participation. He found that individuals with weak desires for independence were unaffected by participation, while those with strong independence needs showed increased satisfaction when involved. Tosi (1970), however, was unable to replicate Vroom's results using the same instruments. The remainder of the studies examining personality have tended to focus on job enrichment, typically studying growth need strength within the Hackman and Oldham (1980) job characteristics model. These studies are reviewed in Chapter 7. The issue of individual differences is still a greatly underresearched topic within job involvement.

Participation Processes

Miller and Monge (1986) conducted a meta-analysis to examine what variables might moderate the relationship between employee participation and the outcomes of satisfaction and productivity. They focused on three general models: cognitive models, affective models, and contingency models. *Cognitive models* suggest that participation is effective because it enhances the flow and use of important information in organizations. *Affective models* argue that participation is effective because it satisfies workers' needs and thereby increases satisfaction and morale. *Contingency models* propose that participation will affect satisfaction and productivity differently for different people and situations.

Miller and Monge found no support for the contingency models; neither job type nor organizational type was a significant moderator of employee participation outcomes. These authors did find some evidence for the cognitive models. The relationship between participation and productivity was stronger than that between participation and satisfaction. However, there was also support for the affective models. Very strong correlations were found between satisfaction and participative climate, suggesting that widespread participation was better (in terms of satisfaction) than participation on a single issue.

Miller and Monge (1986) also found that the research setting (laboratory vs. field) and type of subject (employees vs. students) were significant moderators. The laboratory versus field findings contradict those of Schweiger and Leana (1986). This difference probably is due to employing a meta-analysis, as well as a somewhat different sample of studies.

Methodology

Wagner and Gooding (1987a) examined the impact of time and methodology on research findings concerning employee participation. These authors conducted a meta-analysis of research studies published between 1950 and 1985. They found that a number of aspects of the research changed over time, these changes mirroring changes in societal issues and overall liberalism-conservatism in the American culture.

Wagner and Gooding first examined the impact of time on the methodology the researchers used, contrasting studies that had only perceptual data (questionnaires) of the outcomes versus studies that had objective measures, or different respondents for participation and outcome measures, or a longitudinal break between measures of participation and the outcomes. These authors found that methodology changed over time. Specifically, researchers were more likely to employ only perceptual data during the 1961-1975 period than the 1950-1960 or 1976-1985 periods.

The second (and more interesting) finding from Wagner and Gooding's meta-analysis was that studies employing only perceptual data tended to find stronger effects for employee participation than studies using more objective measures. These authors suggested that the shift in societal interests, the focus of research questions, the use of methodologies, and the presumed success of employee involvement are all intertwined. They argued that growing liberalism during the 1960s led researchers to use a methodology that focused on more popular outcomes (employee attitudes rather than productivity) and also tended to find more favorable results for employee involvement.

Wagner and Gooding's results are disturbing for those who favor employee involvement. It should be pointed out, however, that a number of employee involvement studies were not included in their review. The authors noted that they excluded studies involving sociotechnical interventions (self-directed work groups), Scanlon plans, employee stock ownership, and board representation. As they pointed out, these studies often incorporate more than just employee participation. Although this incorporation allows for a more precise examination of participation, it also excludes many of the more popular (and powerful) forms of employee involvement.

Wagner and Gooding (1987b) performed additional analyses on their original meta-analysis to examine the effects of four situational variables (group size, degree of task interdependence, task complexity, and use of performance standards) on employee participation. As with the first paper, Wagner and Gooding reported significant effects for the methodology in terms of task performance, satisfaction, and acceptance. However, few significant effects were found with the situational variables.

Form

The final contextual variable, the primary one employed in this book, is the *form* that the employee involvement may take. Cotton, Vollrath, Froggatt, Lengnick-Hall, and Jennings (1988) argued that much of the confusion regarding the effectiveness of employee involvement exists because the reviews are counting apples and oranges. In Locke and Schweiger's (1979) review, for example, the authors grouped together in one category studies involving Scanlon plans (Frost, Wakeley, & Ruh, 1974), Lewin's research on group discussions versus lectures (Lewin, 1947), self-directed work teams (Trist & Bamforth, 1951), goal setting (Lawrence & Smith, 1955), and use of a junior board of directors (McCormick, 1938). Given the variety of forms that employee involvement has taken, it is not surprising that the results have been confused.

Cotton et al. (1988) employed the dimensions outlined by Dachler and Wilpert (1978) to distinguish between different forms of employee involvement. They divided their review into six groups: participation in work decisions, consultative participation, short-term participation, informal participation, employee ownership, and representative participation. Their review found positive effects for participation in work decisions, informal participation, and employee ownership on performance/productivity. They found positive effects for informal participation and employee ownership on job satisfaction. Short-term participation and representative participation produced no effects for productivity or satisfaction; consultative participation had inconclusive effects.

Leana, Locke, and Schweiger (1990) argued that the Cotton et al. (1988) classification scheme was inadequate and that the sample was arbitrary. Leana et al. presented a separate classification and sample, with disparate findings. In reply, Cotton, Vollrath, Lengnick-Hall, and Froggatt (1990) argued that differences in definitions and study samples led to the divergence in findings. In short, how one defines the form of participation will, in large part, determine the results one finds.

The debate between Cotton et al. and Leana et al. highlights a basic problem with the research on employee involvement. Those studies examining the most powerful forms of employee involvement (e.g., self-directed work teams, employee ownership) are also the studies that tend to include factors in addition to participation (e.g., changes in incentives) and to have the weakest methodologies (e.g, lack of control groups).

Locke and Schweiger (1979) and Leana et al. (1990) focused on the methodology by which the studies were conducted. Cotton, Vollrath, Froggatt, Lengnick-Hall, and Jennings (1988) and Cotton, Vollrath, Lengnick-Hall, and Froggatt (1990) focused on the form of the employee involvement. Unfortunately methodology and form are correlated. Therefore, Leana et al. (1990) argued that the more positive results are due to a looser methodology. Cotton et al. argued that these results are due to the form of the involvement. Neither side can prove that it is right.

These same issues can be found in the Wagner and Gooding (1987a, 1987b) studies. These authors found that studies using more questionable methodology (perceptions of both participation and outcomes) led to stronger findings for employee participation. Are the stronger findings due to a more direct (perceptual) methodology, or are they simply artifacts? We have no way of determining this. If employee involvement operates through affective reactions to the participation, it seems reasonable that the perception of participation would be a more sensitive measure than more "objective" measures of participation. In addition, greater control and more objective measures are easier in short-term laboratory studies, which also would be less likely to find significant results.

This controversy seems to be an insolvable problem, and I have no solution. As the reader can see, I believe the methodological problems are hiding the truth. The reviews in the chapters to follow demonstrate that several forms of employee involvement are successful—whether because of the participation or other factors is impossible to determine. However, it is clear that involvement or participation per se will not always produce effects. Some forms of employee involvement are effective; others are not.

The preceding sentence reiterates the theme of this book: There is no single (or "correct") form of involvement. There are many diverse forms of involvement, each having its own issues and producing its own results. This plethora is why seven chapters describe employee involvement, not one. Whether or not self-directed work teams are effective is irrelevant when speaking about employee ownership. Although both are forms of employee involvement, they are very different.

Models of Employee Involvement

As I have indicated above, *employee involvement* (or employee participation, or worker democracy, or . . .) is a relatively slippery concept. For example, in Europe, involvement may be defined as workers' councils; in Israel, the kibbutz; in the United States, quality circles, a Scanlon plan, or other programs (Strauss, 1982). As Schregle (1970) commented, "Worker's participation has become a magic word in many countries. Yet almost everyone who employs the term thinks of something different" (p. 117). Given these several forms and myriad definitions, it is not surprising that many models of how employee involvement operates also have been developed. In the following pages I discuss the many models that have been proposed. These models are summarized in Table 2.1.

In one of the earlier models, Lowin (1968) defined *participative decision making* as a situation "in which decisions as to activities are arrived at by the very persons who are to execute those decisions" (p. 69). He went on to hypothesize what factors should lead to successful employee involvement. In his model the effectiveness of involvement depends on the personality and attitudes of

Table 2.1 Summary of Participation Models

Lowin (1968)
- Process — Participative decision making
- Leads to — Satisfaction of subordinate's and manager's motives (dependent on personality and attitudes, the extent, importance, and visibility of the issues, and the clarity of the process)
- Outcomes — Subordinate's and manager's behavior and attitudes toward participation

Sashkin (1976)
- Process — Participation and psychological need (control over own behavior, task closure, positive relationships)
- Leads to — Means of effect (psychological ownership, information flow, development of skills, development of shared norms and values)
- Outcomes — Acceptance and commitment, quality, support, adaptive capacity of organization

Locke & Schweiger (1979)
- Process — Joint decision making
- Leads to — Value attainment
- Leads to — Cognitive effects (increase in knowledge, information, and creativity in solving problems) and
  Motivational effects (greater trust, greater feeling of control)
- Outcomes — Satisfaction and productive efficiency

Schuler (1980)
- Process — Participation
- Leads to — Role clarification (reduced role conflict and role ambiguity) and Enhanced expectancy perceptions (performance-reward)
- Outcomes — Satisfaction with work and supervisor

Strauss (1982)
- Process — Participation on issues (multiple forms and many different possible issues)
- Leads to — Degree of control (from joint consultation to self-management) and Ownership (from none to completely owned)
- Outcomes — Impact on society, survival of organization, productivity, and worker satisfaction

Leana (1987)
- Process — Joint decision making
- Leads to — Sharing of authority, not passing of authority
- Outcomes — Subordinate satisfaction and performance

Tjosvold (1987)
- Process — Opportunity to discuss problems
- Leads to — Constructive interaction (cooperative context and productive controversy)
- Leads to — Effective problem solving (quality solutions, commitment to implementation)
- Outcomes — High productivity and high morale

Conger & Kanungo (1988)
- Process — Participative management
- Leads to — Self-efficacy information (enactive attainment, vicarious experience, verbal persuasion, emotional arousal)
- Leads to — Strengthening belief in personal efficacy (empowerment)
- Outcomes — Initiation/persistence of behavior to accomplish task objectives

---

those involved; the extent, importance, and visibility of the issues addressed; and the quality of the participation process (e.g., clarity of goals, amount of useful information available exclusively to the subordinate, and extent to which subordinates can exert control over productivity).

Sashkin (1976) presented a model that focuses on the psychological target of the employee involvement. He first differentiated between four types of involvement (participation in goal setting, decision making, problem solving, and change) and argued that each can produce such psychological and cognitive effects as psychological "ownership," development of shared norms and values, and information flow. These effects then lead to increased quality, acceptance and commitment, increased support for involvement, and an increased capacity of the organization to adapt. Sashkin argued that congruence between the type of involvement and the aim of the involvement will lead to more effective change.

In their well-known review of the employee participation literature, Locke and Schweiger (1979) presented a model of the participation process. Locke and Schweiger's model differentiates between cognitive effects (more upward communication, better understanding of job) and motivational effects (increased trust, more ego involvement, group pressure) of involvement. These cognitive and motivational effects together produce higher productivity.

As Locke and Schweiger pointed out, many proponents of employee involvement tend to focus on the motivational aspects, assuming that greater morale or commitment is responsible for improved productivity. However, Locke and Schweiger made a cogent argument that the cognitive factors produced by involvement may be more responsible for improvements in productivity.

Schuler (1980) and Lee and Schuler (1982) attempted to incorporate concepts from expectancy theory and role theory with employee participation. In Schuler's model greater employee involvement serves first to reduce role conflict and role ambiguity. The more involvement an employee has with his or her supervisor and fellow workers, the more chances there are for role clarification and role conflict reduction (Schuler, 1980, p. 334). In addition, employee involvement will tend to increase the employee's expectancy between performance and potential rewards. As the employee becomes more involved, he or she will learn more clearly which behaviors are rewarded and which are not. Finally, the reduced role conflict and role ambiguity and the increased performance-reward expectancy should lead to greater satisfaction with the work and with the supervisor. Schuler's (1980) findings, Lee and Schuler's (1982) results, and those of Smith and Brannick (1990) support this model.

In an extensive review of worker participation in management around the world, Strauss (1982) presented a taxonomy of participation employing four dimensions: organizational level, degree of control, issues, and ownership. In terms of *organizational level*, most American experiments in employee involvement have focused at the departmental or individual level, whereas Europeans stress the plant or company levels. *Degree of control* refers to whether employees are consulted, have joint decision making with management, or have complete control. *Issues* can range from production methods and job content to major investment decisions. *Ownership* refers to how much of the company is owned by the workers. Strauss employed this taxonomy to describe how employee involvement varies around the world.

Leana (1987) differentiated between *employee participation,* which she defines as joint decision making between superior and subordinate, and *delegation,* which is a process whereby the manager transfers decision-making autonomy to a subordinate. Her distinction is similar to Strauss's dimension of control; employees can have partial control (participation) or complete control (delegation). In addition, Leana emphasized that delegation focuses on individual autonomy and argued that managers delegate to individuals, not to groups.

Leana (1987) presented data indicating that managers tend to use the importance of the decision and the characteristics of the subordinate in deciding whether to involve employees in participative decision making or to delegate. She argued that these findings indicate participation and delegation are not simply points along a continuum, but rather are distinct and different decisions for managers.

Tjosvold (1987) defined *employee involvement* as a subset of group problem solving. From this perspective, involvement can improve organizational effectiveness because several persons can increase the information and ideas considered and can develop higher quality solutions. For employee involvement to be successful, however, the employees must work together effectively. Tjosvold argued that cooperative goals and productive controversy are necessary for optimum efficiency. Tjosvold (1986, 1987) described methods to achieve these group processes.

Conger and Kanungo (1988) addressed the concept of *empowerment*. These authors developed a 5-stage model of empowerment, in which the use of participative management, job enrichment, and other managerial strategies provide self-efficacy and confidence, leading to the experience of empowerment. In their approach the crux is the *perception* of empowerment by the employee; the use of employee involvement by management simply helps produce this perception. Conger and Kanungo also addressed factors that lead to perceptions of powerlessness. Their model has been developed further by Thomas and Velthouse (1990).

By looking at Table 2.1, which summarizes the models, the reader can see that it is difficult (if not impossible) to integrate the various models above. One problem is that the models focus on different outcomes of the participative process. Lowin (1968) focused on attitudes about the process, Strauss (1982) on the impact on society, Sashkin (1976) on commitment to change, and Conger and Kanungo (1988) on the perception of empowerment. It is unlikely that a common process would lead to so many different outcomes.

A second problem is that all of the models employ different theoretical perspectives. Of those authors explicitly examining the participation process, Sashkin followed a psychological need approach, Schuler employed role and expectancy theories, and Tjosvold examined it from a group problem-solving perspective.

A third problem is that many of the authors differ about how they define *participation*. Leana (1987) narrowly defined it as "joint decision making" (p. 228); Sashkin (1976) described "several different types of participation as well as different methods of participation" (p. 76), and Conger and Kanungo (1988) distinguished between participation and empowerment.

In reading through the models above, my narrative begins to sound like the story of the blind men describing an elephant. One man describes the tail, while another has hold of the trunk, while a third is touching the side of the elephant. All of the men are accurately describing what they feel, but each has only a portion of the elephant. Trying to develop a single model of employee involvement may be as fruitless as the blind men describing the elephant. In physics the term *equifinality* is used to explain how a system may reach the same final result from a number of different beginnings and paths. To say that one of the above models is correct is not to say that the others are wrong. Although some may have greater generalizability, all of them are probably correct to some extent.

To assist the reader, I focus not so much on the many processes by which employee involvement may influence outcomes, but rather on the *form* of the involvement. Below, described in detail, is a relatively complete model that has the most relevance to this volume.

Dachler and Wilpert's Model

Like other theorists (e.g., Russell, 1988), Dachler and Wilpert (1978) focused on describing dimensions that can be used to describe employee involvement. In this way they take the approach followed in this volume: Employee involvement takes very different forms, which often have very little relation to each other.

Dachler and Wilpert identified four general aspects of the involvement process: (a) the values, assumptions, and goals of the implementers; (b) the properties of the employee involvement; (c) the contextual factors within which involvement occurs; and (d) the outcomes (p. 3).

The theories and goals underlying employee involvement refer to the values, ideologies, and orientations of those advocating or implementing employee involvement. These are interesting issues and are addressed briefly in Chapter 6, where I discuss how the motivations behind employee involvement differ across national boundaries. The contextual factors and outcomes are discussed in the chapters to follow as they relate to the various forms of employee involvement.

Our interest here concerns the characteristics that Dachler and Wilpert outlined to describe the properties of employee involvement. They proposed five general dimensions to describe employee involvement: formal-informal, direct-indirect, level of access, the content of the employee involvement issues, and the social range of the involvement.

Formal employee involvement refers to a "system of rules . . . imposed on or granted to the organization" (Dachler & Wilpert, 1978,

p. 10). *Informal involvement,* in contrast, is a consensus that arises in a casual way. For example, a quality circle program or a gain-sharing program would be formal forms of employee involvement. Where a supervisor casually allows his or her workers to make decisions about how their work is done would be an example of informal involvement. A formal program has a paper trail (often a substantial bureaucracy develops), whereas informal involvement has no paper trail, no legal status.

Direct involvement refers to "immediate personal involvement of organizational members" (Dachler & Wilpert, 1978, p. 12). This is typically face-to-face involvement where workers can have an immediate and personal impact. *Indirect involvement* incorporates some type of employee representation in which, rather than the employee interacting, his or her representative is involved. An example of direct involvement is quality circles; indirect involvement includes worker councils or employees on the board of directors.

Level of access refers to the amount of influence that organization members can exert when making a decision. Dachler and Wilpert employed a continuum of access (from Tannenbaum, 1968): (1) no (advance) information is given to employees about a decision, (2) employees are informed in advance, (3) employees can give their opinion about a decision to be made, (4) employees' opinions are taken into account, (5) employees can negatively or positively veto a decision, and (6) the decision is completely in the hands of the employees.

Several of these access distinctions are difficult to make in practice (how do we distinguish between employees giving their opinions versus their opinions being taken into account?). Because of this difficulty, I limit influence to only three levels: (1) no influence, (2) employee is consulted, (3) employee decides. An example of the first category is an employee in a traditional top-down organization; an example of the second category is the quality circle; an example of the third category is self-directed work teams.

It is important to distinguish carefully between the last two categories, as either may be part of employee involvement. However, as the reviews in subsequent chapters show, there is a considerable difference in the impact of giving an opinion (quality circles) versus actually making decisions (self-directed work teams).

The *content of the issues* in which the employees are involved is the fourth dimension Dachler and Wilpert (1978) described. Although most programs of employee involvement focus on issues and decisions directly related to the individual's work, this is not always the case. For example, gainsharing programs can focus on general improvements in productivity. An employee might make suggestions concerning aspects of work outside of his or her usual job. Members of an employee-owned company may be concerned with larger policy issues as much as day-to-day operational decisions concerning their own jobs.

The *social range of involvement* dimension refers to who is involved: Is everyone involved, only certain levels of employees, only certain locations or departments, or what? This dimension also can refer to whether the involvement is on an individual level or group level: Do employees participate as part of a group (e.g., self-directed work teams) or as individuals (work redesign)? The psychological dynamics are obviously different in these two types of involvement.

The dimensions above can be used to describe and categorize the various forms of employee involvement that are described in Chapters 3 through 9. I have attempted to do this in Table 2.2. The reader will notice that although many possible combinations of the dimensions are possible, only a few are outlined in Table 2.2. For example, only one cell is given under the Informal category. This is because it is impossible to assess the other dimensions when the involvement is informal. In addition, the content of participation is not addressed. Differences occur across this dimension (e.g., quality circles have a much more limited range of topics than gainsharing plans), but most forms of involvement will address a variety of different topics. Although the chapters do not completely correspond to Dachler and Wilpert's (1978) dimensions, the reader will, I hope, find these dimensions useful.

Overview of the Following Chapters

The following chapters present the various forms of employee involvement. Each of these chapters has three parts. First, there is a description of the employee involvement, along with a short illustration of a firm taking that approach. These examples are designed to give concrete demonstration of how the involvement operates.

Table 2.2 Examples of Employee Involvement Using Dachler and Wilpert's Dimensions

| | *Formal involvement programs: Direct involvement* | | |
| | | *Social range* | |
	Individual	*Group/Department*	*Entire organization*
Influence/Access:			
Medium	Formal participative decision making	Quality circles (Chapter 4)	Quality of work life (Chapter 3) Gainsharing (Chapter 5)
High	Work redesign (Chapter 7)	Self-directed work teams (Chapter 8)	Employee ownership (Chapter 9)

| | *Formal involvement programs: Indirect involvement* | | |
| | | *Social range* | |
	Individual	*Group/Department*	*Entire organization*
Influence/Access:			
Medium			Representative participation (Chapter 6)

Informal involvement programs
Informal participative decision making

Second, each chapter has a review of the relevant research on that form of involvement, and a summary of what the research has found. Third, issues and concerns with the implementation of involvement are presented. These outline the events that occur and actions that are taken when organizations set in motion that form of employee involvement. Because each form is very different, the chapters are relatively independent.

It could be argued that other techniques, such as management by objectives (MBO), also should be included in this volume because MBO also has a participative component. However, I have chosen to describe approaches in which the *primary* focus is on the participation/involvement of the employees. Although MBO incorporates participation in the setting of objectives, its focus is on employing objectives to guide and motivate individual employees. The participation, although important, is subordinate to the objectives. Therefore, I discuss only those approaches/techniques in which involvement is the fundamental focus. Other perspectives (such as collective bargaining or leadership styles) are not included.

The order of the following chapters is idiosyncratic but not random. They begin with *quality of work life* because this term has been used to describe all forms of employee involvement. After that the chapters are ordered from less to more influence (access, in Dachler & Wilpert's dimensions) and from individually focused, to group, and to organizationwide programs (small to large social range). Although it is tempting to try to organize the chapters from less successful to more effective forms of employee involvement, it becomes clear that such comparisons between the different forms are extremely difficult.

Chapter 3 describes quality of work life programs. *Quality of work life* is a term that has been employed to describe a wide range of involvement programs, most of which are included in the following chapters. I focus only on cooperative projects between companies and unions.

Chapter 4 examines *quality circles*. These are programs involving lower level workers who spend some time discussing production/service issues and make recommendations for management to consider. Quality circle groups are similar to self-directed work teams, but the employee influence is much lower.

Chapter 5 concerns *Scanlon plans* and other gainsharing plans. These programs involve employees by actively soliciting their ideas and suggestions and by rewarding them financially for productive recommendations.

Chapter 6 describes the varieties of *representative participation*. Employing Dachler and Wilpert's (1978) dimensions, this is indirect involvement, where employees are not involved directly but are represented. This representation typically is conducted through a worker council or employee representatives on the board of directors.

Chapter 7 examines work redesign, also known as job enrichment. *Work redesign* consists of attempts to change individual jobs to give employees more input. The focus is on increasing involvement through the individual job, rather than on the work group or organization.

Chapter 8 portrays *self-directed work teams.* Here the employees, working as a group, essentially replace the first-level supervisor. The work group decides everyday operational issues, such as scheduling, quality issues, and so on, and may be involved in hiring and firing employees.

Chapter 9 reports on *employee ownership*. This form of involve-ment can come about in a variety of ways (e.g., ESOPs, buyouts, stock ownership plans). Although they may not be engaged in the daily management of the company, the employees own a signifi-cant portion of the company.

Chapter 10 presents an overall review of the preceding chapters, with conclusions about which forms are most effective and which factors are important in that success. In this chapter I also discuss future directions for research and practice.

Chapter 11 is a postscript, summarizing what I have found in this review of employee involvement. There are a number of implications for both academe and industry.

The alert reader may notice that I do not discuss two forms of employee involvement listed on Table 2.2—informal participation and formal participative decision making. In my original plans for this volume, these chapters were included. However, page restric-tions forced their deletion. The informal participation chapter was not included because this form grows out of the individualistic relationship between a superior and a subordinate. It is therefore impossible to describe or categorize. Formal participative decision making involves *only* participation, with no other factors present. Many of these studies tend to be either laboratory research with little generalizability, or research on participation in goal setting, or organizations where employees participate in only one deci-sion. Their findings may be germane to the narrow concept of *participation* but are not as relevant to employee involvement.

3 Quality of Work Life Programs

What is Quality of Work Life (QWL)? It is not simply a job enrichment program. It is not simply a quality circles program, or gainsharing, or employee representatives, or self-directed work teams. However, all of these or any combination of them may be part of a QWL program. Or a QWL program may have none of the above. What is Quality of Work Life? Of all of the types of employee involvement, quality of work life (QWL) has been the most difficult to define because, as Walton (1973), Nadler and Lawler (1983), and Guest, Williams, and Dewe (1980) have pointed out, QWL has meant so many different things to different people.

Nadler and Lawler (1983) described six different definitions of QWL. The first definition is QWL as a variable. In this sense *quality of work life* is employed as an overall term for outcomes from a job. Walton (1975), for example, gave eight conceptual categories for the concept of *QWL*. Levine (1983) provided an inductive example of this approach. He had employees develop their own measures of QWL, first generating 95 QWL concepts and then eventually reducing these to just six items.

The second definition describes QWL as an approach. In this sense it is defined as a program between management and the union, a program designed to improve cooperation and to help both the worker and the organization. This is the definition used in this chapter. I focus on QWL as cooperative labor-management

programs, generally programs designed to increase the involvement of employees. Lawler (1986) also employed this definition.

The third definition of *QWL* is as a set of methods, generally
encompassing job enrichment, self-directed work teams, and so
on. From this perspective, this book could be retitled *QWL: Methods for Improving Performance and Work Attitudes.* All of the programs and approaches described in this volume would be included in this definition of QWL. Lawler and Ledford (1981/1982)
and Mohrman and Lawler (1984) took this approach somewhat,
discussing a variety of organization change levers such as work
redesign, participation in decision making, gainsharing, and team
building.

Yet a fourth definition is *QWL* as an ideology and movement. In
this perspective the third definition is expanded to include not
only the many methods but also the conviction that such methods
are necessary; that is, QWL methods are desirable, moral, and
obligatory. QWL has moved from the practical to the ethical.

The fifth definition of *QWL* is that it has become everything. Any
type of improvement, organizational development, or change in
effectiveness is labeled QWL. If this seems extreme, consider what
you can find in a search of the literature. In doing a computerized
search with *quality of work life* as the key phrase, I found a variety
of definitions for the term. Some of these definitions can be found
in Table 3.1. In addition, the term *quality of work life* is found to
relate to numerous other variables. Some of these can be found in
Table 3.2. As these tables show, numerous definitions of QWL are
being used, and the term has been related to almost every topic
conceivable. QWL has become almost everything.

The final definition of *QWL* is that it is nothing. Any term used
so widely and associated with so many other variables loses its
meaning. Unfortunately this has become the perspective of many
who have lost interest in QWL.

Because of the problems with multiple definitions, I will stick
with the second definition, focusing on QWL as a joint labor-
management program designed to increase employee involvement and to help both the worker and the organization. Used in
this way, I think the term has some value. Employing Dachler and
Wilpert's (1978) framework, this form of involvement is formal,
there is medium influence, and the involvement can be direct

Table 3.1 Definitions of Quality of Work Life

Reference	*Definition*
Efraty & Sirgy (1990)	Need satisfaction
Karasek (1990)	Job control and health
Boissoneau (1989)	Decentralization and matrix management
Gates (1989)	Employee motivation
Covey (1989)	Acceptance, challenge, purpose, fairness, and balance
Adair-Heeley (1989)	Outcome of just-in-time methods
Giallourakis (1989)	By-product of corporate loyalty
Harders & Wisniewski (1989)	Commitment to human resources systems work
Martin (1988)	Work restructuring
Alexander (1988)	Fully using one's skills, talents, and abilities
Miller (1988)	Technical systems are supported by effective social systems
Cherns (1986)	Concept with many political dimensions
Nirenberg (1986)	Subjective assessment of the relationship between management and labor
Samuel (1987)	Productivity-enhancing programs
Daily (1986)	The work environment, including safety
Trist (1986)	Communitywide effort
Hill (1986)	Working atmosphere, attitudes, and methods

NOTE: Often multiple usages of QWL were employed in the articles, but the above examples indicate the more novel uses.

(being on a team) or indirect (union representatives on a committee). In addition, it encompasses a wide variety of work issues and involves the entire organization.

Many management-union programs are intended to get employees involved but do not belong in the other chapters in this book. This grab bag becomes QWL. In addition, the reader will find some examples in this chapter that involve gainsharing, self-directed work teams, or some form of quality circles. Examples also can be found in other chapters that involve unionized workers. Why are some found in this chapter, while others remain in other chapters? My basic criterion has been whether the focus of the program (or those describing it) has been on the management-union cooperation, the teams, or the compensation program. If the emphasis is on the relationship between the union and management, it is discussed in this chapter.

Table 3.2 Topics Related to QWL

Topic	Reference
Mexican maquiladoras	Sanderson & Hayes (1990)
Coronary heart disease	Karasek (1990)
Alcohol abuse and dependence	Sonnenstuhl (1988)
Just-in-time	Adair-Heeley (1989)
Automation	"Simplify" (1989)
Communications	Stebbins & Shani (1988)
Mission statements	Covey (1989)
Strategic planning	Burack (1988)
Statistical process control	Bushe (1988a)
Ergonomics	Czaja, Cary, Drury, & Cohen (1987)
Material requirements planning	Callerman & Heyl (1986)
Team discipline	Barkman (1987)
Impact of computers	Huff (1986)
Emotional disorders	Jansen (1986)
Safety	Dailey (1986)
Marketing	Coppett & Sullivan (1986)
Video display terminals	Brooks (1986)
Office automation	Kaye & Sutton (1985)
Corporate culture	Stackel (1985)
Military readiness	Freeman (1985)
Employee assistance programs	Masi & Bowler (1988)

Paid Educational Leave (PEL)
at AC-Rochester, Oak Creek

For a week each month, about 18 to 30 employees at General Motors's AC-Rochester plant in Oak Creek, Wisconsin, get to go back to school.[1] Each month a different group takes 5 days with pay to learn more about General Motors, the automotive industry, economics, global competition, and other topics.

The genesis of this project came from the national contract that General Motors (GM) and the United Auto Workers (UAW) signed in 1984. The purpose of this project was to foster "a spirit of cooperation and mutual dedication that will permit the full development of the skills of our people and meaningful involvement in the decision-making process" (from the 1990 contract).

The local paid education leave (PEL) program was spun off from the national PEL program, which involves upper- and middle-level management and union officials. This program lasts 4 weeks, with segments in Ann Arbor, Boston, Washington, DC, and Detroit. The participants meet with industry experts, university analysts, political officials, and government representatives to discuss the issues in detail. The intention of the program is to provide the same background information for both management and union, plus put them in a situation where they can interact without the typical sources of conflict. The participants of the national PEL program felt it was so successful that it should be repeated at the local level with all employees.

Personnel at each General Motors plant are encouraged to start local PEL programs, funded by the national joint training fund. These programs are directed and coordinated by a joint team of UAW leaders and GM managers from the UAW-GM Human Resource Center. In fact, at every level of the program, you have "jointness," with a GM person and a UAW person.

In the local PEL program at AC-Rochester (it varies across locations), a typical week goes like this: On Monday the participants meet each other and learn about the program. Then they learn about strategic management and are given a brief history of the automotive industry in the 20th century. Tuesday morning is spent in extensive discussion of the current situation within the automotive industry; on Tuesday afternoon the global competition from Japan, Mexico, and other international competitors is described. All day Wednesday is spent covering the basics of economics. On Thursday the morning focus is on technology and the work organization (often including employee involvement programs); Thursday afternoon includes a discussion of labor relations with a labor-management bargaining simulation. On Friday the local management and union leaders come to talk and answer questions; a graduation ceremony follows.

Each PEL group has both management and hourly workers deliberately scattered across the room so that each table may have some of each. Because everyone is dressed casually, it is often difficult to determine whether an individual is a manager, an engineer, or an hourly production person.

Why do the company and the union support this program? The purpose is to "provide participants with greater understanding of the issues facing the industry" and to "encourage those who participate to take a more active role in initiating and carrying out joint decision-making activities" (PEL instructor's manual). The program is not intended to make direct changes in local plants, but to prepare workers and managers for the changes that General Motors expects.

Many of the employees come to PEL somewhat cynical, seeing this as simply another program in a long line of programs at GM. However, PEL does not promise to change their jobs or the company; its only goal is to educate. PEL is the foundation necessary for employees to understand why the local, divisional, and companywide changes are occurring. In this way, it is hoped, those changes become easier. Many of the participants leave charged and impressed by what they have learned and experienced. Regardless, they leave better informed than when they arrived.

Research on QWL Outcomes

I review first the better known case studies of QWL programs. These serve to outline the ways in which such programs are begun and structured. Then I summarize those investigations involving comparison across different site or surveys of multiple organizations. The latter studies are typically more valuable in drawing conclusions about the outcomes of QWL programs.

Auto Industry Case Studies

A major impetus for QWL programs has been in the auto industry, as well as other industries with national unions (such as steel and communications). The poor performance of the auto companies in the late 1960s and early 1970s, the oil crisis of 1973, and growing absenteeism and dissatisfaction of employees over working conditions (the "Lordstown syndrome") motivated the auto companies to make national agreements with the United Auto Workers (UAW) to improve the quality of work life. As Kochan and Dyer (1976) hypothesized, such pressures are likely to lead to alternative joint ventures.

In 1973 a letter of understanding was negotiated between General Motors and the UAW. This letter established QWL as a national strategy within General Motors. As part of the 1973 memorandum, local projects were started with guidance and monitoring from the national level (Siegel & Weinberg, 1982). In 1979 Ford and the UAW signed a letter of agreement to cooperate jointly in an effort to increase the involvement of employees. Ford and the UAW agreed to establish a national joint committee that would oversee local programs (Banas, 1988).

The first QWL program within General Motors was begun in the car assembly plant in Tarrytown, New York (Guest, 1979, 1982b; Rubinstein, 1987). In the late 1960s and early 1970s, this plant was known as one of the worst within GM in terms of labor relations and productivity. The Tarrytown program initially involved joint training in team building, understanding problems, problem-solving strategies, and testing, implementing, and evaluating solutions in two departments. After this approach faltered in 1974, voluntary joint problem-solving teams were set up. In 1977 the program was expanded, launched on a plantwide scale. Although workfloor problems were not addressed by the workers, relations between the union and management improved dramatically. Grievances and absenteeism went down sharply, and the overall quality (in comparison with other GM plants) improved (Guest, 1982b; Rubinstein, 1987).

One of the earliest and best-known QWL projects was implemented at a plant of Harman International Industries in Bolivar, Tennessee (Macy, 1979). Launched in 1972, this program involved a network of more than 30 shopfloor committees by which employees could influence decisions in the plant (Zwerdling, 1984). The researchers found that employees were treated in a more personal way and that the jobs involved higher skills and greater job security. However, they also found greater physical and psychological stress and less satisfaction with pay and pay equity. Overall, the program was assessed as successful (Macy, 1982). Macy argued that the majority of the effects were generated directly by the program, but effects also were produced indirectly through other factors (improved managerial effectiveness and capital investment, and the 1974-1975 recession).

General Motors has been using its new Saturn division as a laboratory to further develop QWL methods (Fisher, A. B., 1985; Gwynne, 1990; Taylor, 1988; Whiteside, Brad, Schiller, & Gabor, 1985). As an independent entity, Saturn has its own contract with the UAW, policy is set by a council that includes a UAW representative, and workers are paid on a salary plus performance basis. The distinctions between workers and management are minimized in every way possible

(Ephlin, 1986). The plant began production in mid-1990, and, despite several delays and embarrassing recalls (White, 1991; White & Guiles, 1990), General Motors and the UAW are generally happy with its progress (Hegland, 1991; Treece, 1991). Labor-management relations appear to be very positive, and quality is high; however, productivity is lower than expected (White, 1991: Woodruff, 1991).

The Ford plant in Sharonville, Ohio, began a QWL program in employee involvement in 1980 (Copenhaver & Guest, 1982/1983). The plant established a joint coordinating committee, which, after establishing guidelines and communicating with management and the workers, set up problem-solving committees composed primarily of hourly workers plus a few management personnel. Later, salaried employees also formed problem-solving groups. Although no formal evaluation of Sharonville's QWL program was made, in 1982 the overall plant performance in terms of quality reached its highest level in years. Reports of improvements in efficiency and productivity from the groups were also positive (Guest, 1982a).

Summary

The case studies from the automobile industry are the best-known examples of QWL. Overall, the results generally have been positive. However, they typically do not provide hard data for productivity, and it is very possible that other factors may be responsible for at least some of the positive effects ascribed to the QWL programs. For example, employees in the Saturn division volunteered to join that plant. Therefore, it would not be surprising if these employees produced high quality.

Other Private Sector Case Studies

Although the auto industry is the best-known source of QWL programs, such programs also can be found in other industries. For example, the steel industry and the United Steelworkers' Union began to push for participative QWL programs in the 1980s (Bernstein & Rothman, 1987; Hoerr & Collingwood, 1987; Kochan, Katz, & Mower, 1984). One example of QWL in the steel industry is given by McKenna (1985).

A classic example of labor-management cooperation in the airline industry can be found at Eastern Air Lines (Walton & Lodge,

1985). Struggling to avoid bankruptcy in 1983, Eastern agreed to work with its unions to involve employees in improving productivity. The unions granted wage and productivity concessions; the company traded stock, access to the company books, and representation on the board of directors. This agreement proved to be very successful, especially with the International Association of Machinists (IAM). Employee attitudes seemed higher, and estimates were that the machinists' union committees were responsible for productivity gains of $30 million in the first year (Kuttner, 1985). However, expensive commitments for new planes and cutthroat competition were battering Eastern. Unable to keep the fragile union-management cooperation intact, Eastern was sold to Frank Lorenzo in 1986. Lorenzo repeatedly clashed with the unions, suffered a strike in 1989, and plunged Eastern into Chapter 11 bankruptcy proceedings before leaving the company in 1990. Eastern stopped flying in January of 1991. Here is an excellent example of how even a successful program cannot overcome other problems that an organization may face.

An example of QWL in the food-manufacturing industry was described by Moch and Bartunek (1990). These authors used the concept of *schemata* to explain how a QWL program could change the way participants view the world. A joint management-union QWL committee was formed to identify problems and address concerns. A number of concerns and problems were addressed, leaving the impression that the QWL program was effective. However, Moch and Bartunek pointed out that although outcomes were influenced, the basic process by which decisions were made at the plant was unaffected. In fact, the program may have reinforced this process.

QWL has been applied in many other types of organizations. Reports have described positive QWL programs at Xerox (Pace & Argona, 1989), General Foods (Olkewicz, 1981), the *Minneapolis Star* and *Tribune* (Kochan et al., 1984), and many others. Like the case studies in the auto industry, these examples have tended to be success stories, although the outcomes often have been qualitative in nature.

Public-Sector Case Studies

In contrast to many of the other forms of employee involvement, QWL programs have been prominent in the public sector. Although the programs have not been discussed as widely as those in the auto or steel industries, they have been growing, especially in the late 1970s and 1980s. Accordino (1989) reported that, in 1985, over 25% of 2,603 cities surveyed claimed to have some form of employee involvement program in place. Although many of these programs could be discussed in other chapters (e.g., Chapter 4 on quality circles), they tended to focus on union relations, and so are labeled QWL programs.

Public-sector QWL programs often vary from private-sector programs in terms of their impetus. Accordino (1989) described and reviewed five long-term QWL programs involving large cities. Most of these programs started through what Accordino labeled an "ideological stimulus." Rather than addressing some specific need or problem, the programs were initiated because city management and/or labor thought it was a good thing to do. Although the programs all survived at least 10 years, they tended to be housed in the personnel departments and had little broad impact on labor-management relations or day-to-day workplace activities.

A number of public-sector programs have not been successful (e.g., Brower, 1983; Ronchi & Morgan, 1983). Krim and Arthur (1989) described the difficulty of QWL program survival. They reported that, of some 30 public-sector QWL programs initiated between 1975 and 1985, only 10 remained active in 1986. In Massachusetts the first six attempts at municipal QWL failed either before the programs were implemented or in the first year of operation (Krim & Arthur, 1989, p. 15). After reviewing one program in detail, Krim and Arthur presented a model of how the organizational and political spheres interact in public-sector QWL programs. Their major point is that the QWL practitioner in the public sector has to work in both the organizational and political spheres. To ignore the political aspects is to ensure failure.

A number of public-sector QWL programs are described in a volume edited by Herrick (1983a). These programs include examples from Canada (e.g., Mears & Brunet, 1983) and the United States, focusing primarily on city governments (e.g., Columbus and San Francisco). Like the other case studies, they presented few outcome results for the QWL programs. As Herrick (1983b) pointed out, measuring economic results in the public sector is extremely difficult.

Even programs that were considered to be successes were not uniformly effective. Nurick (1982, 1985) described a number of successes with the QWL program in the Tennessee Valley Authority (TVA). Employees perceived a greater voice in decision making, a number of important problems were solved, long-term issues were explored, and management was seen as more open by employees. However, expectations were initially too high, power struggles became a part of the program, and communications were often inadequate. In large part the QWL program was successful, but shortcomings were also apparent. In his analysis Nurick argued that these problems occurred because there were no strong problems forcing change, no strong leader to guide the change, and a tendency to avoid conflict among groups in the program. His first two points agree with those made above by Accordino (1989) and Krim and Arthur (1989).

Summary

It appears that public-sector QWL programs have at least two characteristics that differ from private-sector programs. First, these programs seldom are motivated by real need, but rather tend to be implemented because government or union officials feel that "it is the right thing to do." Second, because of the bureaucratic nature of public-sector organizations, power relationships become even more important. This is not to say that power relationships are unimportant in private-sector organizations, but it seems to be more common in the public sector.

Findings Across Multiple Sites

Although the reports concerning QWL are often extremely positive (e.g., Moskal, 1989), case studies have limited generalizability, and the issue of positive bias in the research exists (Golembiewski & Sun, 1989, 1990a, 1990b). Research across several sites, however, allows us to generalize more easily, as well as to focus on what factors may facilitate or inhibit the effectiveness of QWL programs. The studies to follow vary from examinations of two divisions in a single company (Macy, Peterson, & Norton, 1989), to dozens of plants in a single company (Katz, Kochan, & Gobeille, 1983), to hundreds of facilities in an industry (Kelley & Harrison, 1992).

A quasi-experiment comparing one division of a company having a QWL program to another not having such a program was described by Macy et al. (1989). The QWL program involved a joint management-union committee that worked with consultants to identify problems within the division. The committee then set up 13 cross-functional task forces with approximately equal numbers of management and union members. These groups were to address the identified issues and, if possible, to improve the situation.

Three groups of employees were surveyed over time on a variety of job perceptions and attitudes. The groups included those directly involved in the QWL program (on the committee or a task force), those indirectly involved (at the site but not directly involved), and the control group (those in a similar division at another site without a QWL program). The results indicated that individuals at the experimental site (both directly involved and indirectly involved) reported greater increases in a variety of perceptions and job attitudes than respondents at the control site. In addition, those participants who were directly involved demonstrated greater increases than those who were indirectly involved. This latter finding is discussed in more detail in Chapter 6, concerning representative participation.

Bushe (1988b) described the impact of QWL programs in five manufacturing plants of one corporation. Although the impetus for all of the programs came from discussions between the company and the national union, three of the plants used quality circles, while the other two used problem-solving groups as part of parallel organizations. After 2 years, two of the plants (those with parallel organizations) were judged to have successful programs in terms of increased productivity, decreased grievances, and greater trust between the union and management. Interestingly Bushe found that many of the prescriptions from the QWL literature to assist these programs were not useful. An intergroup theory perspective (Alderfer, 1987) appeared to be more useful in explaining the effects.

Katz, Kochan, and Gobeille (1983) examined the impact of QWL on product quality and productivity in 18 plants within one division of General Motors. Katz et al. first assessed the intensity of QWL efforts between 1977 and 1979 by analyzing reports of the plants to division headquarters. They then related this measure of QWL activity to the dependent measures of product quality and direct-labor efficiency from the years 1970 to 1979. Their analyses indicated that greater QWL effort was significantly related to higher product quality but not to efficiency. Although efficiency was not directly related to the QWL effort, it was related to the number of grievances at the plant, and the QWL effort was related to fewer grievances, suggesting a possible indirect effect. A follow-up study by Katz, Kochan, and Weber (1985) expanded the sample to 25 manufacturing facilities and found similar results.

A survey of 20 QWL programs in federal settings was reported by Sulzner (1982). He surveyed management and union respondents about joint cooperation committees established in their locations. Sulzner found that larger units were more likely to have cooperation committees, that the success of the committees depended on the relationship between management and the union, and that these committees tended to be most effective as conduits for communication between both sides.

Cooke (1989) presented a study examining the impact of QWL programs on productivity and product quality in 109 unionized manufacturing companies. The results indicate that changes in (self-reported) productivity were positively influenced by having more union leaders on the steering committee. They were negatively affected, however, by having fewer active meetings (less often than every 2 weeks). Finally, no difference was found between team forms of QWL (e.g., quality circles) versus committee forms (e.g., labor-management or productivity committees). Perceived changes in product quality also demonstrated these influences, and quality was higher with multiple programs and with programs of about 8 years in length.

A related analysis was presented by Cooke (1990a). Specifically he tested the impact of a number of variables describing the QWL program on the relationship between supervisors and the work force. Cooke found that the supervisory relationship was significantly improved when the QWL program involved work area teams composed of employees and supervisors who meet regularly. No effects were found, however, when the QWL program involved the committee approach, in which union and management representatives would meet regularly. In addition, improvements in relations were *negatively* related to seniority and whether the plant was small (fewer than 500) or large (more than 3,500).

Voos (1987) surveyed 379 unionized Wisconsin firms concerning a variety of QWL programs (gainsharing, profit sharing, employee

participation, and joint union-management committees). She found
that 28% of her respondents had joint union-management committees and that the respondents reported improvements in product
quality, productivity, unit labor cost, and profits with the committees. However, almost all of the various types of programs were
evaluated as having a positive effect by the respondents, providing an extremely enthusiastic (and probably overly positive) perspective of such programs.

In the largest survey of QWL programs, Kelley and Harrison
(1992) surveyed a nationally representative, size-stratified sample
of machining companies in the United States. A total of 1,015 plant
managers were surveyed, of which 40% had formal joint labor-
management problem-solving committees. Employing production efficiency, employment security, and worker control over
technology, the authors found unimpressive effects for joint committees. Overall, the presence of committees tended to have negative effects. For example, plants with no unions and joint problem-solving committees were less efficient and had lower security
than unionized plants. However, unionized plants with joint committees were more likely to have worker control than unionized
plants without committees.

Overall Findings

A fundamental question throughout this volume is whether or
not employee involvement programs exhibit beneficial effects. Do
QWL programs generate positive outcomes? Table 3.3 presents a
summary of the outcomes from the case studies and studies across
multiple sites. Overall, the case studies indicate that QWL programs tend to improve labor-management relations, product or
service quality, and productivity. The studies across multiple sites,
however, suggest caution. It appears that QWL programs typically
improve labor-management relations. There is also some evidence
for improvements in quality. However, there is less evidence of
increased productivity or any direct impact on firm competitiveness. In fact, several studies (Kelley & Harrison, 1992; Moch &
Bartunek, 1990) found decreases in productivity with a QWL
program. An additional note of caution is that the results for
quality and productivity are typically self-appraisals by management and therefore are subject to inflation.

Table 3.3 Research Findings on QWL

	Management/union relations	Product/ service quality	Productivity
Case studies:			
GM Tarrytown plant	+	+	+
Guest (1982b)			
Harman Industries	+	+	+
Macy (1979, 1982)			
GM Saturn division	+	+	−
Hegland (1991)			
White (1991)			
Ford Sharonville plant	+	+	+
Guest (1982a)			
Copenhaver & Guest (1982/1983)			
5 city programs			+ 0
Accordino (1989)			
TVA Utility	+		
Nurick (1982, 1985)			
Eastern Air Lines	+ 0	+	+
Walton & Lodge (1985)			
Kuttner (1985)			
Food-manufacturing plant	0		−
Moch & Bartunek (1990)			
Multiple site studies:			
25 manufacturing plants	+	0	0
Katz, Kochan, & Weber (1985)			
5 manufacturing plants	+		
Bushe (1988b)			
109 manufacturing companies		+	+
Cooke (1989)			
2 divisions of company	+		
Macy, Peterson, & Norton (1989)			
20 federal QWL programs	+ −		
Sulzner (1982)			
379 unionized firms		+	+
Voos (1987)			
1,015 machining firms			−
Kelley & Harrison (1992)			

NOTE: + indicates the outcome was improved; O indicates no change in the outcome; − indicates the outcome worsened; multiple signs indicate multiple effects.
In the Macy, Peterson, and Norton (1989) and Nurick (1985) studies, employee attitudes were assessed, but labor/management relations were not directly measured; however, these were qualitatively appraised.

A second concern is whether those outcomes that have been found persist and diffuse into the rest of the organization. Seashore (1981), Kochan and Cutcher-Gershenfeld (1988), and others pointed out that QWL programs do not tend to spread additional change throughout the organization. Goodman and Dean (1983) referred to this phenomenon as "institutionalization" of the QWL. A number of programs show positive effects but nevertheless die or are thrown out (e.g., Eastern Air Lines). In addition, many programs are criticized because they may address specific outcomes but have not influenced the process within the organization (Moch & Bartunek, 1990). Why has QWL been unsuccessful at this second level?

Most of the examples of QWL have been where a national union and a large corporation have decided to implement such programs within individual plants. The plants then are encouraged and given resources to conduct such a QWL program. The program typically is drafted at the national level and involves external consultants and an outside evaluation. It is interesting, for example, how many of the cases described above were instigated by the national union and top management, with the assistance of the Institute for Social Research at the University of Michigan and/or the American Center for the Quality of Work Life (Lawler, 1986). It seems that this mechanical, top-down process is most successful when it keeps a relatively narrow focus and acts to maintain the status quo.

A third issue, not widely discussed, focuses on the form of the QWL program. The studies above are testimony to the wide variety of forms that QWL has taken, from training, to quality circles, to joint committees, and so on. Is there any common element? It seems that most QWL programs have in common the use of a parallel organization (Stein & Kanter, 1980). Every program has some type of joint union-management steering committee or some other type of joint bureaucracy that is attached to the current organization. The parallel organization is not intended to replace the current organization but to supplement it.

Although parallel organizations have been recognized and acknowledged as part of many employee involvement programs (Lawler & Mohrman, 1985), they have not been studied widely (Herrick, 1985). A simple question (but difficult to answer) might be whether the positive impact of QWL programs is due to the teams, the quality circles, or whatever. Or is a portion of the positive outcomes due to the parallel organization, the joint union-management group that is part of the package? Is the parallel organization necessary for these positive outcomes, or is it simply an additional price of working with a union?

Role of the Union in QWL

When discussing QWL programs, a common concern is how the union fits into the picture. Is the QWL program to the union's advantage, or is it a threat? Although there have been successes with QWL programs, there has often been strong resistance—from unions, academics, and workers.

Several legal arguments have been used by unions against QWL programs. Sockell (1984) argued, for example, that if a union did not control the QWL program, it could file a grievance against the National Labor Relations Board (NLRB), and the grievance probably would be upheld. The logic is that, through such a program, substantial issues concerning work conditions might be decided by QWL groups without the official negotiating committee. This ruling would be tantamount to a refusal to bargain with the certified representative and thus would be an unfair labor practice (Employment Policy Foundation, 1991; Staff, 1991b, 1991c).

In 1989, at a DuPont plant in New Jersey, an NLRB suit was brought and won by the union. A design team originally established in 1987 involved supervisors and workers in discussions about work conditions. The local union filed a charge of unfair labor practices and won a judgment from the NLRB (Koenig, 1990). Rather than fight the charge, DuPont disbanded the team. In early 1990 additional teams or committees at the same plant were challenged by the union. Another similar suit has been filed against Electromation, Inc., in Indiana ("Are Work Teams," 1992; Bernstein, 1992; Gunderson, 1991).[2]

As long as the union agrees to endorse the QWL program, there is no legal issue. If, however, the union changes its mind or multiple unions are involved, some having endorsed the program and others not, this can be a problem for QWL programs.

A number of criticisms have been made of QWL programs (and employee involvement programs in general) by academics and others who believe strongly in the need for unions to protect employees from management. Wells (1987) argued that QWL programs actually increase the control that managers have over employees by undermining worker solidarity. Heckscher (1988) raised the issue that joint labor-management programs and employee involvement programs in general will transform traditional labor-management relations, possibly in negative ways.

Grenier (1988) gave an excellent example of how an employee involvement program (quality circles) can be used by management as a tool to fight unionization. Grenier studied a new plant in the Southwest with a program designed to increase employee involvement through quality circles. Through his investigation, the author discovered that the quality circles were being used by management to avoid being organized by the Amalgamated Clothing and Textile Workers Union. Grenier made a number of good arguments about how involvement programs can be used to reduce the power of unions.

The growth of QWL programs in the auto industry has produced considerable dissent concerning teams and union-management cooperation among members of the United Auto Workers (Hoerr, 1989; Zellner, 1989). In a scathing indictment of the use of teams in the auto industry, Parker and Slaughter (1988) cited the GM-Toyota, NUMMI plant as a perfect model of what they term "management-by-stress." These authors described the pressures on employees for punctuality and work attendance, for keeping productivity high, sometimes at the expense of quality, and for complying with heavy work demands. They argued that stress serves as the force that drives and regulates the production system and that work teams operate to monitor employees and to provide stress. QWL programs also have been attacked by Canadian Auto Workers (Blount, 1990).

The ambivalent response of union leaders to QWL programs is outlined in an interesting case study by Hammer and Stern (1986). These authors argued that union leaders in cooperative programs alternate between cooperative and adversarial behavior, a "yo-yo" model of behavior. An analysis of relations between the union and Rath Packing Company found such a pattern, with the union taking both adversarial and cooperative positions three times between 1978 and 1985.

Perceptions About Union Participation

A number of studies have tried to estimate the impact of QWL programs on the union. Typically they have focused on how the union's participation influences perceptions about the union, differences in perceptions about the QWL process, or differences in how labor issues should be resolved.

Thacker and Fields (1987) examined the impact of a QWL program on perceptions about the union. Studying a program in a public utility, these authors found that workers wanted the union to become involved both before and after the program started. In addition, the participants generally perceived greater union influence from the program. Finally, when the QWL program was seen as successful, credit was given to both the union and management; when it was seen as unsuccessful, blame was assigned to management. In a later study on the same organization, Fields and Thacker (1992) discovered that employees' commitment to the company increased only when the QWL program was perceived as successful. Commitment to the union, however, increased regardless of whether or not the program was seen as successful. If these findings were generalized to other organizations, they would suggest that union leaders have little to lose and much to gain by supporting QWL programs.

On the other hand, Ellinger and Nissen (1987) pointed out some of the dangers in a case study of a failed QWL program. These authors found that the failure of the program led to criticisms and eventually to the removal of all but one of the local union leaders. Ellinger and Nissen used the case study as a warning for labor educators to be cautious about promoting QWL programs.

Hanlon and Nadler (1986) compared the attitudes toward quality of work life of union officials, managers, and rank-and-file employees of organizations with QWL programs. These authors found that the groups significantly disagreed about what problems they perceived in the QWL program. Rank-and-file employees cited authority and control problems, while the union brought up problems in getting involvement, and management cited problems in getting started and keeping the program moving. In terms of evaluating the overall QWL program success, union leaders were the most positive group, while the rank-and-file employee were the least positive, with management in between.

In another study examining the attitudes of rank-and-file union members, Holley, Field, and Crowley (1981) asked railroad workers about which vehicle would be most appropriate for different employee issues. These workers felt that traditional issues (e.g., pay, job security) should be addressed through collective bargaining, and QWL issues (e.g., job duties and responsibilities, flexibility to choose work methods) through joint union-management efforts.

Union Involvement and QWL Outcomes

In a study of five organizations with QWL programs, Verma (1989) examined the hypothesis that if the union is a cosponsor of the program, favorable union outcomes will occur. The results demonstrated that QWL participants had greater satisfaction with the union and involvement in union offices than nonparticipants. These effects were not simply due to subject self-selection, as one of the comparison groups included nonparticipants who had volunteered.

Eaton (1990) explored the factors that influence how much control unions have in QWL programs. Two types of control were examined in the study: guarantees against layoffs, and proactive involvement by the union. Eaton tested a variety of predictors of control in 86 organizations. She found that the degree of control by the union was predicted by local union resources (but not bargaining power), by the attitudes of the international union toward QWL programs, and by how much of a threat the program appeared to be to the union.

Verma and McKersie (1989) reported on outcomes when the union is *not* involved in the QWL program. They surveyed employees of a large manufacturing plant that introduced quality circles without the union. Union leaders did not actively support or oppose the program. The authors found that the employees who volunteered for the quality circles had greater desires for involvement in decision making and lower involvement with the union than those who did not volunteer. In addition, the experience of being in a quality circle increased identification with the company but did not influence attitudes toward the union. Verma and McKersie interpreted their findings as encouragement for unions to get involved in QWL programs.

An interesting outcome of a QWL program was reported by Bocialetti (1987). He found that the QWL program in a metals-processing plant produced overall positive effects. However, the workers of relatively low seniority benefitted more than those of high seniority. In fact, the benefits to the low-seniority workers sometimes came at the expense of those to the high-seniority workers. The reason for these differences was that the younger, lower seniority workers were more willing to become involved. Because seniority is a cornerstone of union practices, these types of findings might tend to make union leaders hesitate to advocate QWL programs.

Summary

Although there has been considerable distrust and fear of QWL programs by unions and many academics, this has been changing in the 1980s (Hoerr, 1990). Rather than opposing programs as a new means of manipulating workers, recent writers have advocated that unions get involved in these programs and take control if possible. The research reviewed above suggests this is the most effective strategy. Experiences with QWL programs generally improve the perceptions of the union by the workers. Not becoming involved leaves the union in a reactive situation and allows the company the opportunity to increase employees' involvement with the company and not the union.

Implementation Issues
With QWL Programs

The case studies described earlier outline in detail the failures and successes of many QWL programs. From these and other discussions, a number of issues can be identified that influence the effectiveness of QWL programs. I first summarize some of the conditions often described as necessary for successful programs and then discuss the changes that occur in the supervisor and labor leader roles.

Conditions for Successful QWL Programs

A number of authors have discussed the conditions necessary for a successful QWL program. One condition outlined by Sharp (1985) and others is the shared recognition of a need for change. In other words, both labor and management have to recognize that serious problems exist. Drexler and Lawler (1977), like Sharp, pointed out that pressures for change are necessary to begin the process. However, considerable inertia exists from the traditional labor-management relationships. This inertia consists of (a) the different goals of management and labor, (b) the lack of a model or experience with QWL, (c) the desire on both sides to maintain the contract, (d) the risks in making changes, and (e) the time and cost necessary to change. Interestingly one factor that has pulled the union and management together is a concern about the rebelliousness of younger workers.

The second condition for QWL success is strong leader commitment (Cooke, 1990b; Peterson & Tracy, 1988; St. George, 1984), again from both the union and management. This leadership needs to be at the local level, although national leadership (in the case of a national union and/or company) is also useful.

A third condition concerns planning for change. This planning needs to be a collaborative process involving a shared vision and custom-designed format. Part of this format needs to be a structure and model for problem solving. If anything important is to be attempted, the participants will face problems. They need the tools and a structure to address these problems.

A fourth condition suggested by Drexler and Lawler (1977) and others is an external and neutral third party for most large QWL projects. The third party can introduce new ideas, serve as a communications link, and help eliminate stereotypes and distrust (Cooke, 1990b). Thacker and Kulick (1986) even suggested the use of two consultants—one taking the union's position, the other taking management's position.

The final condition focuses on the need for adequate resources to manage the change. These resources include financial, human, and time assets. Considerable education typically is necessary for success.

Building on the points by Lawler and Drexler (1978), a model of QWL success was presented by Nadler, Hanlon, and Lawler (1980). They argued that QWL project effectiveness is determined through ownership of the project by key groups, goal clarity and agreement, consultant effectiveness, functioning of labor-management committee, and organizational context (p. 57). These authors went on to test this model by employing a sample of 16 projects.

Their results indicated that the functioning of the labor-management committee, the organizational context, and the effectiveness of the consultant were related most strongly to success, followed by goal clarity and agreement. Surprisingly ownership of the project by key groups was not significantly related to project success.

Mohrman, Ledford, Lawler, and Mohrman (1986) outlined the human resource systems that will need to change when implementing a QWL approach. These authors described potential changes in job design, job evaluation, selection processes, training and development, performance appraisal, compensation, and labor relations. Although not all systems will need to be altered for all programs, changes should at least be considered.

Middle-Level Managers and Supervisors

Like the other forms of employee involvement described in this volume, QWL requires considerable adjustments for middle managers and supervisors. As Klein (1988) pointed out, they are "the least protected (and least involved in the innovations) but the most affected employee group" (p. 3).

For example, surveys of supervisors' attitudes toward a wide variety of employee involvement programs have found that they perceive it as good for the company, good for the employees, but bad for themselves (Klein, 1984). There are several reasons why supervisors feel this way: They fear losing prestige, they do not trust upper level management, they feel that they are being bypassed and that these programs interfere with how they work with the employees, or they simply do not believe involvement will work (Klein, 1984). Bushe (1987) argued that the negative attitudes of managers are not due to giving others power, but rather to the experience of powerlessness the managers feel as part of a QWL project.

Schlesinger and Oshry (1984) described how QWL programs can produce some factors that disrupt middle-level managers. For example, these managers receive little recognition or support, even though they are directly implementing the QWL. They have to continue to meet the short-term demands of upper level management while trying to promote the long-term demands of QWL. These programs typically lead to less influence and often do not promote integration across departments for the managers. Schlesinger (1982) and Walton and Schlesinger (1979) presented several case studies, describing the difficulties for middle-level managers in QWL programs.

Resistance at the lower and middle levels of management should be expected (Klein, 1988) and addressed. Schlesinger (1982), Schlesinger and Oshry (1984), and Walton and Schlesinger (1979) offered numerous recommendations to improve the plight of middle-level managers. Schlesinger and Oshry focused primarily on encouraging greater integration of middle-level managers. They suggested developing a cross-departmental team of middle managers operating without superiors. In this way the managers can share information, consult with each other, engage in joint planning and strategy sessions, or even develop their own power bloc.

Schlesinger (1982) and Walton and Schlesinger (1979) suggested that organizations not underestimate the difficulties in new programs and make plans to give increased supervision when necessary. In addition, supervisors are often an island of stability in an often unstable QWL program; organizations should be careful about removing this security. Finally, the recruitment, selection, training, evaluation, and reward systems of the supervisors must change in an employee involvement program.

Klein (1988) also made several suggestions. First, QWL programs should be voluntary for managers if they are voluntary for the workers. Second, care should be taken to ensure that not only workers but also low-level and middle-level managers understand the QWL program. Third, training is necessary for supervisors and managers, as well as for workers. Interestingly it appears that the skills that identify good supervisors in a traditional setting are also those necessary in a QWL setting (Klein, 1988; Klein & Posey, 1986). Attempts to improve supervisory skills through training (e.g., Clark et al., 1986) could employ similar training whether or not QWL is involved.

Roles that managers *can* play in a QWL program (or any other participative program) were described by Fisher (1986). Fisher first outlined a model of how the participation program evolves and then described the new roles of leader, facilitator, enabler, and coach that a manager can take. Elucidating these roles can serve to give managers a sense of where they are going, and the successful use of the roles will improve the participation process.

Union Leaders

In addition to those of lower level management, Cutcher-Gershenfeld, McKersie, and Wever (1988) pointed out that the roles of union leaders also change dramatically within QWL programs. One way in which this happens is the union is put in the role of reacting to the initiatives of others, rather than creating its own. Second, a number of new issues occur in the collective bargaining, such as seats on the board of directors, no layoffs, and others. Finally, there is greater likelihood of divergent perspectives between local and national leaders. With greater trust at one level than the other, one set of leaders may be willing to experiment with QWL, while the other is reluctant.

At the workplace level, QWL requires a great simplification of work rules and job classifications. Seniority rules may be changed or even eliminated. Grievance procedures may be altered. In addition, QWL programs likely will require local joint labor-management activities. Local union leaders probably will find themselves working more closely with their management counterparts than before. Finally, as with any type of change, the QWL program possibly will alter the power relationships between the local and national unions, between the local union and management, and perhaps between the local union and the workers.

It is often difficult for union leaders to adapt to these new roles. Strauss (1977) gave several reasons why this may be. First, unions are typically suspicious of management's motives for the program. This suspicion often includes external consultants working on such programs (and paid by management). Second, unions often find it difficult to break out of their traditional adversarial relationship with management. Third, unions may fear that their traditional economic objectives will be ignored. Although most workers desire involvement, earnings and fringe benefits are typically their primary concerns.

All of the aforementioned points indicate the changing roles of union officials because of QWL programs. Like low- and middle-level managers, the union officials may find the adjustment difficult.

Overall Conclusions

In going through what is presented in this chapter, several themes become apparent. The first concerns the outcomes of QWL programs. Although there have been many QWL successes, the demonstrated outcomes have not been exceptional except in terms

of improving labor-management relations. It seems that cooperative labor-management QWL programs are successful in promoting better labor relations. There are also indications of improved
product quality and productivity. However, these latter effects,
found primarily in case studies, are much less certain.

Second, where outcomes have been successful in terms of employee attitudes, quality, or productivity, it seems likely that the
quality circles or teams employed were responsible, rather than
the joint union-management cooperation. As such, the QWL approach seems to be useful primarily as a vehicle for arranging
some type of effective employee involvement. In other words, it
is not the QWL program that is responsible, it is the specific
procedures *within* the QWL framework (e.g., the teams, groups,
whatever). The QWL program may be a necessary condition for
employee involvement in a unionized setting, but it is not a
sufficient condition. Another way of viewing this is that QWL is a
first stage, or a stepping stone, to more advanced forms of cooperation and employee involvement (Lawler, 1986).

Third, the approach in developing QWL programs has been
very top-down and mechanistic, and those programs have tended
to be made up of parallel organizations that have not influenced
the remainder of the organization. However, the specific form of
the program (which may be responsible for positive effects) is left
up to local leaders and varies tremendously from location to
location. In this chapter I focused, as have many other authors, on
the external facets of QWL programs, the contract language, the
joint committees, the use of external consultants, and so on. Perhaps we should focus on the specific methods and ignore the QWL
framework. We may have been concentrating on the wrapping
and ignored the present inside.

4 Quality Circles

Probably the most widely discussed and undertaken formal style of employee involvement is the quality circle. In researching this chapter, I found almost 500 articles published in the last 5 years dealing with quality circles, an average of 100 articles per year. There is even a journal devoted almost exclusively to quality circles: *The Quality Circles Journal,* since replaced by the *Journal for Quality and Participation.*

Over the years a number of changes have occurred in how quality circles are defined (Van Fleet & Griffin, 1989). I describe them as they are generally specified in American companies. A *quality circle* is essentially a small group of employees (anywhere from 5 to 15) meeting on a regular basis (usually once a week) on company time to discuss issues of quality and related problems. These groups are voluntary and typically do not offer financial rewards for ideas (although other programs, such as gainsharing, might be incorporated to provide bonuses). From their discussions the groups make recommendations, which they then present to management for judgment.

Although quality circles usually are thought of in terms of manufacturing (e.g., Japanese auto industry), they can be applied to almost any industry, any job, and any group of employees. Table 4.1 lists some of the jobs and occupations in which quality circles have been attempted. In addition, although they were begun by the Japanese to improve quality, quality circles have not always

Table 4.1 Quality Circles in Different Settings and Jobs

Job or setting	*Reference*
Improving creativity	DeToro (1987)
Marketing	MacStravic (1986)
Blood plasma products	Blake (1991)
Information systems	Maletz (1990)
Auditing	Pasewark (1991)
Safety	Menefee & Owens (1988)
Software	Rahman (1987)
Credit unions	Donovan (1987)
Zoos	Glines (1987)
White-collar jobs	Temple & Dale (1987)
Upper level management	Pipkin (1989)
Hospitals	Burda (1990)
Schools	Wilson (1990)
Construction	Isaac (1989)
Utilities	Copp & Nielsen (1989)
Hotels	Comen (1989)
Banks	Sheridan (1990)
Financial institutions	Hopkins (1989)
Insurance	Lansing (1989)
Nursing	Helmer & McKnight (1989)
Service industries	Lee & Dale (1988)
Postal Service	Tymoski (1987)
Hospitality industry	Bozman & Gibson (1986)
Newspaper	Halcrow (1988)

been confined to just that issue. In some organizations they also may discuss a variety of job issues and concerns, so they frequently go by other names. In one survey, for example, it was found that 92% of the companies employed some label other than quality circles (Nale, 1989).

Although worker problem-solving teams can be traced back to World War I, quality circles were developed by Japanese manufacturers in the early 1960s. The Japanese had suffered with terrible (and deserved) reputations for poor quality throughout the 1940s and 1950s. To change this perception, the Japanese government made quality a national priority. The development of quality circles came out of this overall strategy (Cole, 1979; Munchus, 1983).

The concept of *quality circles* then spread to the United States, where it was tried first by Lockheed and Honeywell in the mid-

Table 4.2 Quality Circles Around the World

Country	Reference
South Africa	Heath (1990)
Israel	Elizur (1990)
Saudi Arabia	Elmuti (1989)
Singapore	Putti & Cheong (1990)
Brazil	Gaetan (1988)
Denmark	Lund (1987)
Australia	Dunford & McGraw (1986)
India	Khan (1986)
Italy	Ferrari (1986)
China	Bank (1987)
Malaysia	Jain (1990)
Philippines	Tolentino (1984)
Norway	Aune (1984)
West Germany	Deppe (1990)
Southeast Asia	Sohal, Tay, & Wirth (1989)
Sweden	Norrgren (1990)
Canada	Jain (1990)
United Kingdom	Isaac (1989)
Scotland	Ram (1989)
France	Orly (1988)
Spain	Luzon (1988)
Ireland	Hill (1989)

1970s. With the success of the Japanese and the futility of American manufacturing in the 1970s, quality circles became emblematic of the "secret" of the Japanese advantage and overwhelmed America in the 1980s. The gospel of quality circles now has been spread throughout the world. Table 4.2 lists some of the countries where quality circles have been undertaken.

In terms of Dachler and Wilpert's (1978) typology, quality circles and employee teams are a formal program of direct, face-to-face involvement with a medium level of influence. These groups can generate ideas, but they can only suggest them to their superiors, who decide whether or not to follow the group's recommendations. The social range is typically a work group or department. Not all departments have quality circles.

Quality circles are similar to self-directed work teams (Chapter 8), except for the dimension of influence. Quality circles make suggestions for someone else to decide; self-directed work teams make decisions and then act on those decisions. In addition, self-directed work teams can address almost any aspect of the daily work, while quality circles often focus primarily on quality issues.

Quality Circles at Design House

Design House, formed from a merger of Benson Manufacturing and the Butter Company, has grown rapidly, from 50 people in Benson Manufacturing to about 200 employees at Design House. But the quality circles have not met at Design House since 1989. They are currently on sabbatical and are due to return in a few months. Setting up and training the quality circles is just too much work. In addition, the quality circles were getting bogged down by the same old problems and were not generating new ideas.

Quality circles started at Benson Manufacturing in 1981, when the president, Marvin Pinter, learned about them and became intrigued with the notion of employee participation. When the concept was explained to the employees, 100% volunteered to participate. All of the members were given 20 to 30 hours of training that focused primarily on identifying problems, collecting data, how to act as a group, and how to present proposals to management. The circles started by meeting for 1 hour per week, with the foremen as circle leaders. As the groups matured, they met more or less often, with other members taking over as leaders.

The only air-conditioned room in the Benson plant is the quality circle room. On the walls are the rules that the groups live by. Certain topics are off-limits: wages, benefits, discipline, personalities, and personnel policies. There are also rules for brainstorming and newsprint with ideas from previous meetings. There is a sense of history, a sense that much has happened in this room.

Over the years a number of issues have been tackled by the quality circles. For example, the circles justified going from two plastic extruders to four machines, requiring an investment by management of $40,000 per machine. The payback was achieved in 4 months. Many of the projects eventually were abandoned when the groups realized that their ideas would not work or that the problem was not worth the time and effort. However, when the quality circles made a proposal, management listened.

Every recommendation made by the quality circles was accepted by management within a week. The managers kept track of where the circles were going (from minutes of the meetings or by dropping in to observe). If an idea had no chance (e.g., improving the manufacture of a product that was about to be discontinued), things were explained to the circle, and they would go on to another issue. Management let the circles go with issues to see what could be done. Said one manager, "It's worth it if they work for 6 months and *they* decide it won't work."

Both management and employees have been happy with the quality circles at Design House. Some of the proposals have led directly to savings for the company. But the company has not kept formal records of the successes made by the quality circles. Although the suggestions were always good ones, they did not always register on the bottom line; sometimes it just made the work safer or easier. The biggest gain, according to Kevin O'Neill, manufacturing manager and facilitator of the program, has been in terms of attitudes. The employees feel that management listens, and this perception reinforces the family attitude of the firm. More important, quality circles influence the attitudes of supervisors, demonstrating that the workers can think, come up with good ideas, and should be consulted about the work.

In addition to the positive attitudes, the employees can see other rewards from the quality circles. The company has an excellent profit-sharing and bonus program, so the workers can see a payoff in that sense. At another level, the continued profitability of the company, growing numbers of jobs, and plentiful overtime are additional payoffs.

When the number of employees stabilizes, the quality circles will be started up again. The quiet room will get smoky and noisy again, the paper on the walls covered with scribbles and notes. With the new employees and the extended break, there should be plenty of new ideas.

Research on Quality Circles

Although other terms are occasionally employed by organizations, I stick with *quality circles* in this chapter. Because almost all of the research has employed this term, it makes sense to continue that tradition.

Many of the findings concerning quality circles (as with most forms of employee involvement) come from anecdotal case studies (e.g., Barra, 1983; Bradley & Hill, 1987; Dillon, 1985; Kelly, 1985; Thompson, 1982; Trump, 1985). As Ledford, Lawler, and Mohrman (1988) pointed out, anecdotal case studies have a number of problems. First, the costs and benefits are calculated casually, with many of the benefits estimated prior to their implementation. Subsequent, hidden costs are not taken into account. Second, success stories about a single circle may overwhelm the failures and frustrations of other teams within the same program. Finally, quality circle success stories are probably overreported. Although failures have been reported, these are probably only a small percentage of the total failures. Because of these concerns, my review focuses on quasi-experimental studies in which the impact of quality circles is compared to some form of control group. This type of study provides a more reliable test of quality circle outcomes.

Quasi-Experimental Studies

Rafaeli (1985) explored whether participation influences employee attitudes. He surveyed 760 employees of a large electronics manufacturer about their perceived influence, job satisfaction, job characteristics, and experience with quality circles. Rafaeli found that quality circle members reported significantly greater influence, less desire to quit, and higher perceptions of task variety than nonmembers. However, no differences were found in terms of job satisfaction or other aspects of job design (job autonomy, interaction with others). As the author pointed out, the quality circle members were volunteers, so any differences between these groups also could be due to self-selection.

Steel, Mento, Dilla, Ovalle, and Lloyd (1985) examined the responses of quality circle participants and nonparticipants in samples of maintenance personnel and hospital personnel on a U.S. Army installation. The participants were members of departments whose supervisors had volunteered, and the nonparticipants were chosen by management from functionally equivalent work centers. Employing a pretest, posttest, nonequivalent control group design, Steel et al. found significant differences between the groups at the posttest on 7 of the 20 measures. Significant effects were found for job satisfaction, group cohesiveness, participation in decision making, work group support, egalitarianism, and impersonality of the institutions.

Mohrman and Novelli (1985) compared attitudes and productivity in two similar departments of a warehousing operation for retail supermarkets. One department implemented a quality circles program with four teams, while the other department (selected to match on size, nature of jobs, and structure) did not. Attitude data were collected 5 months prior to the start of the program, 3 months after the start, and 10 months after the start of the program. In addition, data on costs, overtime costs, absenteeism, and two productivity measures were obtained from archival records. In general, their results indicated that the department without quality circles had decreases in employee attitudes, while the employee attitudes in the department with quality circles remained constant. Productivity measures indicated a slight improvement for the quality circle department, with little improvement for the control department.

Marks, Mirvis, Hackett, and Grady (1986) examined the impact of a quality circle program on a variety of outcomes. They compared quality circle participants and nonparticipants in the manufacturing department of a large corporation shortly before and 20 months after implementation of the quality circle program. Employing the pretest scores as a covariate, the authors found that participants in the quality circle program reported making more suggestions, significantly greater satisfaction with their participation in decision making, better work group communication, greater job opportunities for accomplishment, and better opportunities for advancement. However, no differences were found for organizational communication, meaning and challenge of the job, or personal responsibility of the job. Company records indicated that quality circle participants spent more hours on production and demonstrated greater efficiency and productivity. No differences were found in absenteeism. One caution raised by the authors was that quality circle participants did not improve on the measures of quality of work life. Rather, they remained constant, while the nonparticipants became more negative. In this case the quality circles may have operated as a buffering mechanism against more difficult times.

The impact of quality circles on perceived job characteristics was studied by Head, Molleston, Sorensen, and Gargano (1986). They predicted that participation should influence the five job characteristics from Hackman and Oldham's (1980) model, as well as job satisfaction and internal work motivation. The authors surveyed employees from four separate plants of a large manufacturing organization at the beginning of a quality circle program, and then again 4 to 5 months later. Two of the plants implemented quality circles, while the other two did not. The results demonstrated no significant differences between participants and nonparticipants on any of the variables. No differences were found over time; however, there was a trend for several of the variables to become more negative for the quality circle participants.

Drago (1986) presented a class conflict perspective on the outcomes of quality circles. In a survey of 42 firms, he found that workers perceived little autonomy concerning their work. However, the level of autonomy was positively related to cost savings by the firm, increased job satisfaction and commitment to quality circles, and quality circle program survival.

Griffin (1988) examined the impact of quality circles in a longitudinal, quasi-experimental design. He compared responses from participants in quality circles at one manufacturing plant with responses from another plant that produced the same set of products. Griffin collected data at both plants before the implementation of quality circles and then 6 months, 18 months, and 36 months after the first assessment. He assessed job satisfaction, organizational commitment, intentions to leave, supervisory ratings of performance, and managerial assessments of the quality circle program. Griffin found that the quality circles members indicated higher organizational commitment at the 6-month assessment and greater job satisfaction, organizational commitment, and higher supervisor performance ratings at the 18-month appraisal. However, no significant differences were found at the 36-month period. The reports from the managers mirrored these results; the greatest benefits from the quality circles came during the second and third years, with minimal benefits during the last year. Griffin concluded that the quality circle programs were successful for about 2 years but then began to decline.

Ledford and Mohrman (1988) examined the attitudes of employees who were current members of quality circles, former members, or never members. The authors surveyed 823 employees from nine sites of a large corporation. Their results indicated that current members of quality circles have more positive attitudes about the program than those who never participated. Former members of quality circles, however, have essentially the same attitudes as those who never participated. In addition, the attitudes of current members toward their jobs and the organization were not different from those who had never participated or those who were former members. As the authors pointed out, the positive attitudinal effects of quality circles were limited to the program itself and seemed to disappear when the employee left the program.

Steel and Lloyd (1988) investigated cognitive, affective, and behavioral outcomes from quality circles on a U.S. Air Force base. The authors surveyed 225 employees on a wide range of outcomes, including job satisfaction, organizational commitment, sense of control over the job, and perceptions of the work setting. In addition, they obtained intentions to quit and supervisors' evaluations and self-evaluations of job performance. The variables were assessed at two times, about 14 months apart. In the four groups observed, two implemented quality circles immediately after the first observation, one group implemented them 3 months after the first observation, and one group did not implement quality circles. The results indicated that experience with quality circles influenced perceptions of the congruence of personal and organizational goals, interpersonal trust, influence competence, and intentions to quit. As the authors pointed out, these results indicate, at best, marginal support for quality circles.

Bushe (1988b) compared five manufacturing plants within one company that implemented quality circles or parallel organizations as part of a general quality of work life program. The parallel organizations involved problem-solving groups integrating managers and labor representatives. Employing interviews with managers and supervisors, as well as company records, Bushe concluded that the two plants implementing parallel organizations were more successful than the three implementing quality circles. The two plants initiated six to eight times more employee involvement groups, improved union-management relations, increased productivity, and reduced grievances. Bushe discussed these findings as exemplars of how well-accepted prescriptions for employee involvement were not followed by the successful plants.

Freiman and Saxberg (1989) compared two plants, one with and one without quality circles, within a multiplant food-manufacturing firm. Employing time-series analysis, they examined productivity and quality data over a 23-month period. Differences in the measurement of productivity and quality made interplant comparisons impossible, but comparisons over time were possible. Although differences occurred, no significant changes over time were found.

The impact of quality circles on perceptions of participating supervisors was investigated by Berman and Hellweg (1989). These authors compared the perceptions of members in newly formed quality circles and members of existing quality circles concerning their supervisors. They found that members of quality circles that had been in existence for 6 months reported greater satisfaction with their supervisors and perceived their supervisors as having greater communication competence than members of new quality circles. Interestingly, the supervisors themselves did not perceive any differences in their competence.

Elmuti and Kathawala (1990) examined the impact of quality circles on productivity and satisfaction during the introduction of a computer system. They compared the productivity and job satisfaction of 42 employees who volunteered for the quality circles to 42 nonvolunteers. Productivity and satisfaction were measured before the program began and then again 12 months later. Quality circle employees showed significant increases in job satisfaction and productivity over the 12-month period, while the nonparticipants demonstrated no change. In addition, the entire firm was able to reduce operating expenses by 20% over this period.

A variety of attitudinal and behavioral outcomes was examined by Steel, Jennings, and Lindsey (1990). These authors studied both quality circle members and nonmembers in a United States mint. The attitudinal outcomes included job satisfaction, job involvement, organizational commitment, participation, perceived job performance, and several other measures. The behavioral outcomes consisted of job performance, number of suggestions and employee grievances, and several other measures. The data were collected in three waves, over a period of 14 months. The analyses indicated that perceptions concerning participation, group cohesion, and work group support improved with quality circle involvement. In addition, the number of suggestions was higher for groups with quality circles. No other outcomes, including job satisfaction, job involvement, and job performance, were significantly influenced.

Adam (1991) examined both performance and attitudinal effects of quality circles in two industrial firms. Members of quality circles were compared to nonmembers in terms of job design, general satisfaction, attitudes about quality, supervision, rewards, and the general environment. Although there were differences across the companies and over time, Adam found almost no attitudinal differences between those employees in quality circles and those not in circles. However, two of the four quality circles generated cost savings.

In the only true experiment examining quality circle outcomes, Eden and Japhet-Michaeli (1991) conducted a field study in which teams of employees were assigned randomly to a quality circle condition, a quality circle plus increased expectations condition, and a control condition. A total of 72 Israeli workers who soldered and assembled electronic components completed both a pretest and a posttest concerning perceived influence, organizational commitment, and job satisfaction. The pretest was administered before introduction of the quality circles and increased expectations manipulation, and the posttest was conducted 7 months after the introduction. The results indicated that workers in both quality circle conditions had increased perceptions of influence. However, organizational commitment and job satisfaction increased significantly only in the condition with both quality circles and increased expectations. Quality circles alone showed no difference in comparison to the control condition. In contrast, measures of performance found that teams with quality circles only significantly increased their performance, while control teams and quality circle plus expectations teams showed no effects.

Focusing only on perceptions of participation, Liverpool (1990) surveyed 294 nonsupervisory employees from three manufacturing firms. He predicted that quality circle members would report higher levels of participation than nonmembers and would desire more participation than nonmembers. The results indicated that quality circle members reported greater participation than nonmembers on 6 of 15 decision areas. In terms of desired participation, the quality circle members indicated greater desire for participation on 14 of the 15 decision areas.

Attacking a somewhat different set of outcomes, Buch and Spangler (1990) tested whether a quality circle program affected the job performance and promotions of participants. These authors surveyed 236 employees of a large utility, half of whom were members of quality circles, and the other half matched in terms of department, race, gender, job classification, tenure, and preparticipation performance level. They then examined the annual performance appraisals and promotion records of these two groups. Their results indicated that the performance evaluations of quality circle participants increased more than nonparticipants' evaluations. In addition, of 11 promotions awarded during the 1-year duration, 7 went to quality circle participants. This latter effect, however, was not significant. The authors used these results to argue for the developmental value of quality circles.

Summary of Quality Circle Outcomes

The studies above are summarized in Table 4.3. Quality circles varied considerably in their effectiveness. However, some conclusions are possible.

First, we must distinguish between program-specific attitudes (perceptions of influence, satisfaction with quality circles) and general employee attitudes (job satisfaction, organizational commitment). The empirical evidence suggests that quality circles have a positive effect on the program-specific attitudes. The findings concerning general attitudes, however, are almost totally negative.

In terms of performance or productivity, almost half of the studies found significant improvements, while the rest found no effects. It seems safe only to conclude that positive effects can occur but that they are by no means guaranteed.

Ironically, only one study (Freiman & Saxberg, 1989) of quality circles examined quality itself as an outcome. These authors found no change in quality after a quality circle intervention. Two other studies (Griffin, 1988; Steel & Lloyd, 1988) incorporated quality as part of the performance measure, and it is impossible to differentiate the impact of quality alone. Therefore, no conclusion can be made concerning this outcome.

Literature Reviews

Because of the large number of case studies and the evident popularity of quality circles, several reviews have attempted to determine the effectiveness of quality circles.

Table 4.3 Summary of Findings on Quality Circles

Study	Program-specific attitude*	General job attitude	Productivity or performance
Rafaeli (1985)	+	0**	
Steel, Mento, Dilla, Ovalle, & Lloyd (1985)	+	+ 0	
Mohrman & Novelli (1985)		+	+
Marks, Mirvis, Hackett, & Grady (1986)	+	0	0
Head, Molleston, Sorensen, & Gargano (1986)		0	
Drago (1986)		0	
Griffin (1988)		+ 0	
Ledford & Mohrman (1988)	+	0	
Steel & Lloyd (1988)	+	0	0
Bushe (1988b)	0		0
Freiman & Saxberg (1989)			0
Berman & Hellweg (1989)	+		
Elmuti & Kathawala (1990)		+	+
Steel, Jennings, & Lindsey (1990)	+	0	0
Adam (1991)		0	+
Eden & Japhet-Michaeli (1991)		0	+
Liverpool (1990)	+		
Buch & Spangler (1990)			+

NOTE: *These include perceptions of influence, satisfaction with participation, and satisfaction with the quality circle program.
**Zeros indicate no change or no effect.

Steel and Shane (1986) examined both the outcomes and the methodological rigor of research on quality circles up to that point. They concluded that "the majority of studies constituting the quality circle evaluation literature are, at best, seriously flawed and, at worst, potentially misleading" (p. 450). In focusing on the more rigorous studies, the authors reviewed 14 papers. In addition to summarizing the findings, they critiqued the studies described in these papers. Their review found "no clear trend in support of or against the effectiveness of quality circles" (p. 458). The authors ended their review with a call not for more research, but for better research concerning quality circles.

Barrick and Alexander (1987) reviewed 33 studies of quality circles, including all 14 studies reviewed by Steel and Shane (1986). In addition to their review, Barrick and Alexander examined the issue of potential positive bias in these studies. All but two of the studies reported results on individual outcomes (employee attitudes), and 12 of the 33 studies reported organizational outcomes (quality or productivity). In their review the authors found that 48% of the studies reported uniformly positive results, 27% reported mixed or nonsignificant results, and 24% reported uniformly negative results. Overall, the circles were effective. In addition, there was no indication of a positive-findings bias; the outcomes were not related to the level of methodological rigor.

Greenbaum, Kaplan, and Metlay (1988) presented a framework for evaluating problem-solving groups and then reviewed and evaluated 16 studies of quality circles in terms of their model. They found that most of the studies focused on output variables (e.g., task results, changes in individuals, changes in group relations), while some included input, process, and feedback variables. However, no single study examined all of the variables in their model.

In the most recent review of quality circles, Van Fleet and Griffin (1989) described the history of quality circles and carefully described how they are defined. They then went on to raise a variety of questions about quality circles. The first question is, Where are quality circles most effective? They reviewed a variety of anecdotal successes and several studies of quality circles and concluded that they are effective over short periods of time. However, the few data that exist indicate that the positive effects disappear over time. The authors called for more and better research on what factors are necessary for quality circles to be effective.

Factors Influencing Quality Circles

A number of authors (e.g., Brockner & Hess, 1986; Van Fleet & Griffin, 1989) have argued that rather than trying to assess the overall impact of quality circles, it would be more effective to examine what factors influence their productivity. For example, in their review of 33 quality circle studies, Barrick and Alexander (1987) found that the duration was positively related to circle success. In contrast, Griffin (1988) found that the effects dissipated over time. Barrick and Alexander found that volunteers for quality circles are different from nonparticipants, a finding that requires further investigations of these differences.

One study of individual differences was conducted by Brockner and Hess (1986), who examined the impact of personality. These authors hypothesized that the self-esteem of members of a quality circle is related (positively) to the group's effectiveness. They assessed the self-esteem of 66 members of nine quality circles in one organization. Effectiveness was assessed as successfully proposing at least two suggestions that were accepted by management. Brockner and Hess found that the self-esteem of the effective groups was significantly higher than that of the ineffective groups. Unfortunately it is not possible to determine whether the self-esteem produced effective circles or whether success within the quality circle influenced self-esteem.

A number of studies have examined how quality circle volunteers may be different from nonvolunteers. The reasons behind volunteering for quality circles were examined by Dean (1985). He interviewed and surveyed 74 blue-collar workers, 72% belonging to quality circles, and 28% not. Dean used a Logit analysis to examine a variety of reasons that might predict joining a quality circle. His analysis indicated that "individuals who desire greater organizational involvement and individuals who think that QCs will succeed in accomplishing their goals" (p. 323) are more likely to join. Open-ended responses tended to reinforce these findings. Social variables, such as whether your friends had joined, were not related to quality circle participation. It appears that the perspective of quality circle participants is very similar to that of management.

The decision to volunteer for quality circles was examined also by Stohl and Jennings (1988). Employing Hirschman's (1970) exit, voice, and loyalty model, they predicted that quality circle volunteers are committed to the organization but experience greater job dissatisfaction, poorer communication, and less participation than nonvolunteers. The authors surveyed 250 employees in a maintenance department, of whom 80 had volunteered to begin quality circles (but had not actually started). Their results indicated that volunteers did not differ from nonvolunteers in organizational commitment and job satisfaction but did differ in satisfaction with the amount of influence they had, the communication climate, and job satisfaction intrinsic to the job. In addition, volunteers tended to be younger, to have less tenure in the organization, and to have more education.

In another study on volunteers for quality circles, Tang, Tollison, and Whiteside (1987) examined motivation to attend and motivation to work hard in quality circles. The authors argued that these outcomes are influenced by whether management or the employees initiated the circle. They found that self-initiated quality circles had significantly more members but no difference on attendance rate. Management-initiated circles solved more problems and solved them faster than employee-initiated circles. The authors used these results to suggest that how circles are initiated should depend on the organization's overall concerns.

Another area of research has been the impact of management commitment on quality circles. The influence of management commitment on quality circle productivity was examined by Tang, Tollison, and Whiteside (1989). These authors surveyed 47 quality circles in a fabrication and assembly plant in terms of the number of problems they solved and the amount of time required for problem solving. The results indicated that quality circles with high attendance by management solved more problems and solved them faster. Whether management or the employees initiated the quality circles had no direct effect, but there was an interaction with management attendance. Those circles that were initiated by the employees and that had low management attendance solved significantly fewer problems and took significantly longer than all other quality circles. Finally, whether the participants were white-collar or blue-collar employees had no impact on quality circle productivity. The authors pointed out that with the correlational nature of the data, it is not possible to determine whether upper management attendance at the meetings influenced quality circle productivity or whether more productive circles were visited more often by management.

An interesting distinction was made by Abbott (1987), who described three types of circles: management-dominated circles, stable circles, and circles in crisis. *Management-dominated quality circles* included a majority of the groups that Abbott examined. In these groups the manager took over and became the focus of the groups. *Stable circles* were not dominated by management; they met regularly, made progress, and generally were the most successful. *Circles in crisis* were those that appeared largely ineffective, showed little progress, and were plagued by poor attendance, high turnover, and low morale. Abbott went on to recommend interventions at the group level, tailored for the specific group situation.

Finally, some research has examined the group processes within quality circles to see how these affect quality circle outcomes. Factors that influence the effectiveness of quality circles were examined by Griffin and Wayne (1984) and Wayne, Griffin, and Bateman (1986). They surveyed 457 employees organized into 44 quality circles and investigated differences between more and less effective groups. The results indicated that effective and ineffective quality circles did not differ in terms of average member age, age range, tenure, satisfaction with leader, or extrinsic satisfaction. However, significant differences were found between effective and ineffective groups in terms of cohesion, performance norms, job satisfaction, intrinsic satisfaction, co-worker satisfaction, self-esteem, self-monitoring, and the organizations's commitment to quality circles. Although all of the differences can be readily explained through a small group theoretical perspective, it is impossible to determine from this design whether the differences between the groups led to differential effectiveness or the variations in effectiveness led to the differences between the groups.

Nykodym, Rudd, and Liverpool (1986) examined the impact of communication training—specifically, transactional analysis—on quality circle outcomes. The authors employed a pre- and posttest design with a quasi-control group. They gave transactional analysis training to one work group from the home office of a large corporation and compared them to another work group that did not receive the training. The training consisted of six half-day sessions describing the concepts behind transactional analysis (Coleman, 1974) and employing video presentations, exercises, role plays, and reading assignments. The results indicated no change over time for the control group but a significant improvement in group communication for the employees who had received transactional analysis training. These results suggest that transactional analysis training (or some other type of communication training) may be valuable for increasing quality circle effectiveness and survival.

Drago (1988) explored the factors that influence quality circle survival. Examining 34 organizations, he found that 80.4% of the circles initiated during the programs' first year still existed at the time of the survey. Drago's analyses indicated about 10% to 13%

of the quality circles initiated the first year will fail each year thereafter. A number of factors were found to be related to quality circle survival. A quality circle was more likely to survive if the program was relatively young, if employees had considerable input in doing their jobs, if there had been recent layoffs, if the union was strong, and if the employees tended to be unskilled.

Interestingly there has been little focus on why quality circles should work and what processes are responsible for the outcomes associated with the circles. Wood, Hull, and Azumi (1983) presented several theoretical models that can be incorporated into quality circles. They suggested that job enrichment may be responsible for more positive attitudes. However, participants' jobs are enriched for only a maximum of 1 hour per week. Another potential approach is goal setting, that quality circles assist employees in focusing on specific problems, setting goals and providing clear feedback. These processes operate directly on the problems that the quality circle addresses and could spill over to the members' jobs. Another model is that the group can serve to satisfy self-esteem and affiliation needs of the members.

Overall Summary of Quality Circle Research

To say that the research findings concerning quality circles are mixed is an understatement. Although a simple, overall conclusion may not be possible, several inferences can be drawn from the data.

First, the findings from the quasi-experiments indicate that quality circles improve attitudes concerning participation and the quality circle program but have little impact on general job attitudes. The findings concerning performance are evenly split, and there are too few findings concerning quality to make a conclusion. Although the anecdotal evidence is relatively positive, the more careful research is much less optimistic.

Second, it seems clear that quality circle success varies over time. A large number of circles probably fail early, and many fail after 1 or 2 years. Most studies have focused on relatively short-term outcomes. When positive outcomes were followed up later (Griffin, 1988), they disappeared. The anecdotal evidence on failures suggests that most of these occur in the first 9 months or so (Shea, 1986). Therefore, the greatest period of quality circle success is probably between 6 and 18 months.

The findings above have additional complications. Many of the studies reviewed are confounded by sampling problems with their respondents. Because American quality circles are typically voluntary, any differences between quality circle members and other employees could be due to the quality circles or to personal differences that also led the quality circle members to volunteer. Although some studies have avoided this problem (e.g., Ledford & Mohrman, 1988), it is a common difficulty in the literature.

Another concern with the research is the question of biased selection. If the empirical studies I reviewed above centered only on successful quality circle programs, any positive findings may mask a more general failure. There are two reasons that this masking should be especially problematic in the quality circle literature. First, quality circles have been implemented in literally thousands of organizations, yet only a tiny percentage have been studied in any formal way. The number of missing cases vastly outnumbers those we have, making it possible that our sample is radically biased. Second, there are large numbers of anecdotal failures to match the many positive case studies.

The research on factors related to quality circle success is fragmented and incomplete. However, two tentative conclusions can be made. First, quality circle volunteers are probably different from the typical employee. They tend to be more committed to the organization and desire greater participation. Second, although it is difficult to operationalize management commitment empirically, such commitment is linked to quality circle success.

Criticisms of Quality Circles

Following the rapid growth and spread of quality circles in the early 1980s, problems and concerns began to rise (Bank & Wilpert, 1983; Geber, 1986; Metz, 1981a; Ramsing & Blair, 1982). The long-term experience with quality circles has not been positive. For example, Lockheed, the first company to try quality circles, has abandoned them. In addition, many anecdotal reports indicate that failures are frequent.

One survey examined 29 firms with quality circles and found that 21 of them were unsuccessful (Staff, 1982). Another study by the same consultants assessed 41 programs and found that 28 failed to produce measurable benefits that exceeded their costs (Wood, 1982). Marks (1986) reported one consultant estimating that quality circle programs had failed in more than 60% of the organizations in which they had been attempted. Another consultant estimated that nearly one-third of all quality circles in the United States fail (Cook, 1982). Metz (1981a) mentioned that only one-third of the quality circles initiated in Japan were successful and predicted that United States firms will have even less success. From these reports it appears that quality circles, the management fad of the 1980s, have become a flop.

Part of the criticism of quality circles comes from the fact that they have been changed considerably from what they were in Japan (Wood et al., 1983). Quality control circles (as they are known in Japan) are not intended to motivate employees or to democratize the workplace (Marsh, 1992). They are simply a tool, a methodology for identifying and solving quality control problems and for decentralizing quality control (Shea, 1986). We have taken this practical methodology and have attempted to use it for improving quality, productivity, employee attitudes, and employee motivation and for solving almost every problem but ozone depletion in the upper atmosphere. Wood et al. (1983) argued that the major cause for the failure of quality circle programs is unrealistic expectations. As Shea (1986) pointed out, the confusion in the purpose behind quality circles is a sure formula for failure.

A number of authors have begun to question the basic assumptions on which quality circles are based. For example, Ferris and Wagner (1985) addressed three basic assumptions: Is a group of workers more effective in identifying and solving problems? Does greater participation lead to more positive job attitudes and higher productivity? and Do workers desire greater participation? The answer to all three questions is, sometimes. Ferris and Wagner used the fragility of these assumptions to explain why quality circles often fail and to make suggestions for quality circle implementation.

Krigsman and O'Brien (1987) commented that the fault may not be in the quality circles themselves but in the criteria for evaluating the circles. Many critics of quality circles may have expected too much. As the authors pointed out, quality circles were not introduced in Japan (and originally in the United States) as quality of work life programs but as a quality control technique.

Among the most influential criticisms of quality circles are the papers by Lawler and Mohrman (1985, 1987; Lawler, 1986). Their 1985 paper described the typical phases of a quality circle's life, characterizing the variety of factors in each phase that can lead to the destruction of a circle. Their conclusion was that quality circles are an unstable organizational structure ready to self-destruct. They suggested that circles be used as a group suggestion system, for special tasks or problems, or as an interim structure as the organization moves to other forms of participation, such as self-directed work teams.

Meyer and Stott (1985) reviewed two case studies of organizations that experienced problems with implementing quality circles. The authors then analyzed these problems in terms of three different perspectives. The first perspective, the marketing-and-training perspective, focused on the creation of quality circles as the goal and end point. The program was successful if quality circles began and flourished. The second perspective, the interest-group perspective, centered on how quality circles influenced the relationships between groups. For example, quality circles could be seen as a quality of work life program whose purpose was to improve the relationship between employees and management (see Chapter 3). In the third perspective, a systems perspective, the quality circle program was simply part of a larger system, often an auxiliary part. If employee participation was not compatible with the organizational culture, a quality circle program was almost certain to fail. Meyer and Stott (1985) encouraged the use of multiple perspectives to examine quality circles and their problems. Taking these different perspectives would give a richer and more productive view of quality circles.

A different type of criticism is presented by Grenier (1988). He described the creation of a new plant in the Southwest where quality circles were to be the primary tool in an extensive labor-management cooperative program. However, the quality circles were also intended to keep out unions. The company employed the circles and a variety of other tactics to fight the Amalgamated Clothing and Textile Workers Union, which was trying to organize the plant. Grenier is obviously biased against employee involvement; however, he effectively argued how this type of program can be used as an antiunion tool.

Implementation of Quality Circles

In their *Harvard Business Review* article on quality circles, Lawler and Mohrman (1985) described the various phases a circle can go through and the typical forces for destruction in each phase. Although their intention was to demonstrate the inherent instability of quality circles, their points also can be used to make recommendations for how to maintain quality circles.

In the first phase, the start-up, Lawler and Mohrman mentioned potential problems with a low volunteer rate, inadequate funding, and the inability of group members to learn group-process and problem-solving skills. In the second phase, initial problem solving, the difficulties include disagreement about what problems to address and a lack of knowledge of operations by the circle members. The third phase, approval of initial suggestions, raises resistance by staff groups and middle management and poor presentations by quality circle groups. The fourth phase, implementation, can produce problems in terms of prohibitive cost of suggestions and resistance by the groups that have to implement the suggestions. Expansion of the problem solving, the fifth phase, brings member-nonmember conflict, raised aspirations, savings not realized by the company, rewards wanted by members, expense of the program, and potential lack of problems. The final phase, decline, can bring cynicism and burnout (Lawler & Mohrman, 1985, p. 67). These problems can be avoided or reduced, but it requires training, considerable work with those people *not* in the circles, and careful coordination of the program. Most of the recommendations to follow can be seen as attempts to avoid the destruction inherent in these phases of quality circles.

Starting a Quality Circle Program

A number of publications give recommendations for starting successful quality circle programs. Baloff and Doherty (1989) discussed some of the potential problems for employees during the start-up of a participation program. Although these points can be applied to most of the approaches discussed in this volume, I discuss it in this chapter because it is one of the earlier chapters and quality circles have been implemented so widely. Baloff and Doherty foresaw problems in three general areas: peer group pressure, management coercion or retribution, and readaptation after leaving the program (p. 53). As these authors pointed out, participants in quality circles probably will be under some peer group pressure not to become involved. This will be especially true in the early stages of such a program. On the other side, participants also are subject to the pressure of their supervisor or other members of management. To the extent that circles examine the "wrong" problems or make "bad" recommendations (from management's point of view), the members of the quality circles can be coerced or punished by management. Finally, when the program ends, the participant is forced to return to his or her old job. If the quality circle provided interesting tasks, ego involvement, a sense of purpose, and so on, these are now lost to the employee. The old job may seem very drab after the interesting experiences in the quality circle.

A common suggestion when beginning a quality circle program (e.g., Hill, 1989) is to establish clear objectives. In this way, confusion and unrealistic expectations can be avoided. Quality circles cannot be all things to all people. In addition, authors suggest that the objectives be significant to the organization. Castorina and Wood (1988), for example, argued that quality circles can survive in a bureaucracy but must be able to demonstrate positive outcomes that are of value to the bureaucracy.

Many writers (e.g., Bagwell, 1987) focus on the organizational culture and training as the keys when beginning a quality circle program. The organization's management must be prepared for this type of program, and the employees involved require considerable training. The amount of training involved can often be a plus for employees, as they appreciate this investment by the organization in their development. However, there is a built-in failure with the training: It typically is used only in the circle meetings or during presentations to management (Lawler, 1986). A common source of frustration is the fact that employees are taught problem-solving skills but typically are not allowed to use these skills during their 39 hours per week of normal work.

Like all of the employee involvement approaches described in this book, an effective quality circle program requires management commitment. Many consultants recommend a thorough diagnosis before beginning a quality circles program (Meyer & Stott, 1985) and that organizations not implement quality circles until management and the organizational environment are ready for employee participation (Pati, Salitore, & Brady, 1987).

It is useful, although not necessary, to form quality circles where the members work together and share common work problems and issues. It is much more difficult to develop a cohesive group and generate useful suggestions when the members of the group have very different work environments or essentially work alone. As Vogt and Hunt (1988) pointed out, this is a common problem with public-sector quality circles.

A number of articles give relatively detailed information on starting a quality circle program. An article in *Small Business Report* ("Quality control circles," 1986), for example, goes through a variety of issues to consider when planning and starting such a program. Some of the points involve calculating costs in terms of both funds and management and employee time, returning savings to the employees, thoroughly preparing employees for the program, gaining visible management support, and carefully introducing the circles into the organization.

One of the advantages and, ironically, one of the disadvantages of quality circles is that they are not integrated into the organizational hierarchy (Vogt & Hunt, 1988). This separation makes it easier to start up a quality circle program, but it also makes the program more likely to fail. It is much simpler to give up and eliminate a parallel structure than to change the basic hierarchy.

Training

Training is a part of almost every quality circle program. One survey of quality circle programs found that about 89% provided 4 or more hours of training for circle members (Seelye & Sween, 1982). The median amount of training was between 9 and 12 hours.

A number of authors (e.g., Pascarella, 1982) have argued that inadequate training is the main cause of quality circle failure. There is some empirical evidence that training is the most important single factor for predicting quality circle effectiveness. Honeycutt (1989, 1990) examined the effectiveness of member training, volunteering, and perceived management support in predicting participants' perceptions of quality circle effectiveness. Although management support was a significant predictor, the best predictor of perceived effectiveness was training.

The skills necessary for an effective quality circle can be divided into two groups: individual technical skills and group process skills. The former are necessary for employees to recognize and correct problems. The latter are responsible for effective group functioning. Individual technical skills include the ability to (a) understand statistical techniques, (b) analyze and evaluate data and information, (c) contribute relevant and timely information, and (d) make decisions. Group process skills include the ability to (a) accept criticisms or questions about viewpoints, (b) give other members an equal opportunity to contribute, (c) be tactful with group members, and (d) listen to others' points of view.

Surveys of quality circle members have shown that they perceive the group process skills as being more important than the individual technical skills. In fact, the ability to listen to others' points of view was rated as significantly more important than all of the technical skills in one study (Smeltzer & Kedia, 1987).

The Japanese training typically focuses on statistical analysis and problem-solving ability (e.g., Ishikawa, 1985). It is felt that the members of the group need to learn the technical skills to identify important problems and solutions. The Japanese as a culture are effective at working in groups, so group process training is not emphasized. However, American quality circles typically need training on group processes, decision making, and so forth, often in addition to the statistical and problem-solving skills.

Ingle (1987) presented an interesting perspective on quality circle training, comparing the typical training in the 1970s with that in the 1980s. Training in the 1970s tended to follow the Japanese and focused more on technical skills, such as Pareto analysis, cause-and-effect analysis, control charts, and so on. The major change in the 1980s was a greater emphasis on team building, including communication skills, listening skills, and leadership training. Ingle suggested further changes for second-generation quality circles, including more sophisticated statistical techniques (like those in Japanese groups), as well as nonstatistical techniques (such as force-field analysis and cost/benefit analysis) and other types of training to improve team building.

Maintaining a Quality Circle Program

As significant as the implementation of quality circles may be, maintaining the program can be even more difficult. It has been estimated that quality circles fail in more than 60% of the American organizations in which they have been tried (Marks, 1986). Hill (1989) surveyed 28 companies in 1981 that had instituted quality circle programs. He resurveyed the companies again in 1985. Of the 27 companies on which Hill obtained information, 13 still had quality circles, while 14 had abandoned the programs. However, Hill pointed out that even the organizations that had terminated quality circles responded that many of the objectives that led them to start quality circles had been achieved.

A common problem with maintaining quality circles, related to the lack of managerial commitment, is a lack of feedback and/or recognition for quality circle activities. Quick feedback and recognition are critical for teams (Penzer, 1990). Quality circles devote considerable time and effort in identifying problems. When their recommendations are not followed through or are ignored, or if they receive no feedback on their ideas, motivation will drop. Meetings, rallies, recognition awards, and other celebrations of the teams can help reward the quality circles. Many authors feel that, eventually, incentives for the groups may be necessary (Lawler, 1986).

To maintain an existing program, Geber (1986) recommended developing what she calls "second generation groups." These are not called quality circles; they go by other terms, such as employee involvement teams, and their objectives are broader than finding quality problems. They also tend to be more deeply imbedded in the organization and, it is hoped, become part of the corporate culture.

A different type of recommendation comes from Cheal (1987), who envisioned electronic quality circles. In this approach, employees may be geographically apart but communicate through some type of electronic mail. In addition, a data base of employees can be established, organized around specific skills, experiences, and talents of individual employees. When a specific need is established, employees fulfilling that need are identified, and they are formed into a group. After the problem is solved, the group may move on to other problems, adding or subtracting members as needed, or the group may dissolve and its members join other groups. Although this is an interesting combination of electronic hardware and group process, Cheal presented only theoretical notions; there is no information on actual organizations that have attempted this technique.

Letize and Donovan (1986) suggested that the employee involvement in quality circles can be expanded through the use of focused task forces. *Task forces* are similar to quality circles in that they are groups of employees meeting on company time to address problems. However, task forces are temporary, typically are made up of employees chosen for specific skills, are apt to be from a cross section of positions, and membership in them may not be voluntary. Task forces can address problems unavailable for quality circles, can continue the development of employee involvement, and can increase cross-sectional communication. Gabor (1986) examined the factors necessary for quality circles to move to task forces and also recommended some steps in moving to these groups.

Lawler and Mohrman (1987) suggested that quality circles can be a good first step in the employee involvement process, leading to other, more participative programs. The authors examined three ways that organizations can move beyond quality circles. The first way includes expanding the kinds of decisions made by circles, similar to Geber's (1986) notion of second-generation quality circles. The second way is to allow employees greater authority in making the decisions. This might involve having the quality circles eventually transform into another form, such as self-directing work teams (Chapter 8). A third way is to alter the context in which the quality circle program exists, making the program more durable. Suggestions that Lawler and Mohrman gave include (a) creating management development programs for supervisors and other managers, (b) helping them transform their jobs, (c) giving the groups more training and information so that they can function more effectively, and (d) perhaps adding a bonus system such as gainsharing (Chapter 5).

Overall Steps When Implementing Quality Circles

Although a number of different models exist, the following is one that blends the suggestions of several authors (Claire & Wexler, 1985; Ingle & Ingle, 1983).

1. *Get management commitment.* This is a problem with any employee involvement program. There needs to be an informational overview for those in senior management so that they understand what type of commitment is necessary.

2. *Assess the organization.* Most consultants (e.g., Metz, 1981b) agree that some organizations are not ready for quality circles.

3. *Select objectives.* What is expected of the quality circles? Are they to improve quality, productivity, employee attitudes, all of the above?

4. *Prepare and train middle-level managers and supervisors.* The support of these individuals is necessary for program survival. They will feel the greatest threat.

5. *Select and train facilitators.* The facilitator acts as the link between the circles and management. This is a difficult role and is critical to quality circle success (Patchin, 1981). In addition, the facilitator often will act to train the circles.

6. *Inform employees and ask for volunteers.* Almost all quality circles in the United States are voluntary. Employees do not have to be in the quality circle, and, typically, not everyone is. This guideline eliminates the problem of those employees who do not want greater involvement in their work; they do not volunteer.

7. *Train circle leaders.* This is not a normal supervisory position. This probably will be a new role, requiring new skills.

8. *Train participants.* This should include both decision-making and group process training.

9. *Set goals and boundaries.* Ideally quality circles should have a clear notion of what they are trying to do and why.

10. *Give circles time to establish roles.* Groups are not effective immediately. Give them time to establish roles, to thrash out conflicts, and so on. It is hoped they will develop a climate of trust, mutual respect, and innovation.

11. *Recognize and implement.* Try to recognize the group and what it is doing.

12. *Evaluate quality circles.* Ideally you should focus on the goals that are determined above. These may be measured in terms of economic value (Barrick & Alexander, 1992). The organization also can measure the "health" of the quality circles by assessing the participants' willingness to create and maintain circles. Evaluation typically is seen as necessary to keep quality circles going (Bowman, 1989; Tortorich et al., 1981).

Overall Conclusions

The research on quality circles has its positive aspects, but overall the findings are not optimistic. First, the evidence is considerable that quality circles have a high rate of failure. I think the fact that so many quality circle authors discuss why circles fail is significant. In the other areas of employee involvement, authors suggest ways to improve involvement or factors favoring involvement. In the quality circles arena, however, they discuss why circles have failed. This discussion reinforces the perception of many failures and the need for consultants to focus on avoiding these failures.

Second, where quality circles have survived and have been examined, the research is not very positive. In general the findings indicate that attitudes toward employee involvement and quality circles are improved; general work attitudes are not. Productivity or quality effects are unpredictable; some find these improvements, and others do not.

It should not be surprising that quality circles have so little impact on employee attitudes and perceptions. At most, these programs operate for 1 hour per week, with the remaining 39 hours unchanged. Why should changes in 2.5% of a person's job have a major impact?

The major problem with quality circles is that they are seen as an "encapsulated addition to the organization" (Thompson, 1982, quoted by Shea, 1986, p. 36); that is, quality circles have been so popular because they are seen as simple, off-the-shelf programs that can be added on to an organization with few changes outside of the program itself. This ease of implementation has made quality circles the most popular employee participation program in the world. However, it also tends to imply to management that its implementation should be easy, that there should be few adaptations, and that the only significant involvement by management is funding the program. W. Edwards Deming, the eminent quality guru, has been quoted fearing that "most QCs in America are . . . management's hope for a lazy way out, management in desperation" (Deming, 1982, p. 109 quoted in Bowman, 1989, p. 378). These low expectations make it easy to start a quality circle program but also make it less likely to be effective. The reason for their success is also the cause of their failure.

A final problem with quality circles is the lack of theory on which to explain effects (Van Fleet & Griffin, 1989). Because quality circles are a technique rather than a concept or theory, there is often disagreement over their definition, their intended focus, and how they are to operate. Given these difficulties, it is not surprising that they tend to be less effective than other approaches to employee involvement. Perhaps, as Van Fleet and Griffin (1989) and others have proposed, a new operationalization of quality circles is needed. Although some argue against moving beyond quality circles (e.g., Beardsley, 1986), such a shift may prove necessary.

5 Scanlon Plans and Other Gainsharing Plans

This chapter examines compensation plans that directly reward employees for being involved by giving bonuses for improved productivity. The plans may operate by offering bonuses for effective suggestions (e.g., Scanlon plans) or for increases in productivity (Improshare). Although the oldest and best known system is the Scanlon plan, other approaches have become as, or perhaps even more, popular in recent years. This chapter describes the plans, reviews the empirical evidence as to their effectiveness, and discusses issues in their implementation.

All gainsharing programs have in common three factors: (a) They are formal supplemental compensation systems aimed at individual departments, plants, or companies; (b) they focus on improvements in labor productivity or cost reduction, not sales or profits; and (c) they offer financial bonuses to employees for these improvements in productivity. In Dachler and Wilpert's (1978) framework, this would be formal and direct employee participation, with an intermediate level of influence (where employees make suggestions that management can accept or reject). Generally the plans include all nonmanagement employees, although some plans may cover only a single department or group of employees. The suggestions typically focus on work processes, but they can encompass almost any issue within the organization.

The Scanlon Plan at Eaton in Watertown

In late 1985 and early 1986, management at the Watertown, Wisconsin, plant of Eaton Corporation decided to make some changes to become more competitive.[4] This plant, part of the Logics Controls Division, manufactures timers, counters, and controllers. Management changed the job classifications at the plant, reduced 88 job classes to 19, reduced the pay of the employees about $1 per hour, got rid of their piece-rate bonus system, put everyone on salary, and, oh yes, they instituted a Scanlon plan. Any consultant will tell you that you do not implement a gainsharing plan when you are reducing pay and eliminating other bonuses. However, it has worked and has become one of the longer lasting gainsharing plans within the far-flung Eaton organization.

Like most Scanlon plans, the Watertown plant has two levels of committees. Fifteen action teams of elected employees generate and evaluate ideas. They can approve any suggestion costing up to $500. The screening committee is made up of the chairs of the 15 action teams, plus the business unit manager, the controller, and the HR manager. This group oversees the plan and evaluates larger, more expensive suggestions. Each month they determine how the plant has done in sales, materials, and labor costs and how much they will have for a monthly bonus.

Some months are good, others are not so good. Overall, the gainsharing plan has paid out an average of $1,330 per employee per year in bonuses. During January, February, and March of 1991, there were no bonuses. In April, there was a $0.20 per hour bonus, giving employees an average bonus of $34.67. Unlike most Scanlon plans, productivity in the plan is compared against the yearly business plan, which changes every year. To maintain the bonuses, productivity must go up.

The bonuses are paid to all employees. Those individuals who actually make suggestions have their names put in a lottery for Milwaukee Brewers baseball tickets. Names of frequent contributors are put on a plaque.

Some of the improvements in productivity come from suggestions to improve operations. A machine shop operator suggested that they not polish the shafts on their counters. This idea produced yearly savings of $8,300. Other improvements come from reducing costs. One assembly operator suggested that instead of using corrugated board in their product packaging, they use the cheaper chipboard. This idea produced yearly savings of $1,500. Finally increases in productivity can come without suggestions, simply by working harder.

In addition to the financial savings (half of which go to the company), management likes the fact that the Scanlon plan requires that employees pay attention to how the plant is doing. As Steve Sheppard, the HR manager said, "Gainsharing is the greatest educational tool we have. It forces us to keep people abreast as to what is going on in the business." In addition, it forces management to be realistic in its business plan and accurate enough on a month-to-month basis in predicting sales and costs. A sloppy business plan can lead to overly large or small bonuses.

The greatest cost to management is the time spent in meetings, explaining what is going on in the business. They hate to take the time, but it is necessary. They also find that it keeps them well acquainted with the business plan and their current performance. Surprisingly little effort is needed to monitor the numbers part of the plan. Each month the current data are punched into a spreadsheet, the analyses are conducted automatically, and the monthly numbers pop out.

Doyle (1983) perceived gainsharing as a step along a continuum of participation. First-degree participation is the suggestion box. Second-degree participation is the suggestion committee, typically found in Scanlon plans and Rucker plans. Third-degree participation involves work teams and represents the widest degree of participation. Gainsharing was the first step in employee involvement at Watertown. The plant has moved on to establish self-directed work teams and is beginning merit pay for all employees, with peer evaluations often determining merit increases. The first step was the Scanlon plan.

Types of Gainsharing Plans

In the following sections I describe the various types of gainsharing plans. However, most plans today are custom tailored to an organization's objectives and human resource strategies (Beck, 1992; Markham, Scott, & Little, 1992). Although a particular plan may be labeled a Scanlon or Improshare plan, it could be very different from the description below.

Scanlon Plans

Scanlon plans are named after their originator, Joseph N. Scanlon, a labor union leader in the steel industry during the 1930s. Scanlon found that productivity improved when the company and the union worked together to solicit ideas from workers to eliminate waste, improve efficiency, reduce costs, and improve quality. With these improvements, management was able to avoid bankruptcy and to increase wages and improve working conditions. In 1946, after being a steelworker, a local union president, and Director of Research and Engineering for the United Steelworkers of America, Joe Scanlon began teaching in the Industrial Relations Section at MIT. He continued to teach there and to spread his gospel of participation, until his death in 1956.

A Scanlon plan has two basic facets: (a) establishing a productivity norm and devising a bonus formula for improvements in productivity and (b) initiating the actual participation process (Lesieur, 1958). The *productivity norm* originally involved comparing the sales value of production to payroll costs for a typical production facility. It has, over the years, become increasingly more complicated. The formula typically employed is labor costs divided by the value of goods produced (Lawler, 1988b).

The *participation process* involves setting up production committees and a screening committee. Each major department in a facility has a production committee. These committees have representation from both management and labor and meet at least once a month to discuss ways and means of eliminating waste, improving jobs, increasing productivity, and so on. The committees also review ideas that are submitted by other employees of the departments who are not on the committees. These ideas may be accepted and implemented, may be rejected, or may be studied for a later decision. The screening committee meets about once a month to evaluate progress on the plan, to determine whether a bonus is appropriate, and to evaluate the ideas already scrutinized by the production committees.

When a gain in productivity occurs, the savings are divided between the company and the employees. This division can be 50-50 or any other agreed-upon split. The payments to employees come in the form of (typically) monthly cash bonuses, the individual bonus determined by the monthly wages. Employee bonuses of 10% to 15% are common (Doyle, 1983).

Table 5.1 Comparison of Three Gainsharing Plans

	Scanlon	Rucker	Improshare
Background perspective	Organizational development	Economic	Industrial engineering
Measure of productivity	Labor costs divided by value of goods	Percentage of value added	Labor hours
Type of participation	Production committees and screening committees	No set procedure	No set procedure
Suggestion making	Formal system	None	None
Coverage	Plantwide	Plantwide	At any level
Participants	Ideally, all employees	Hourly plus management sometimes	Hourly employees only
Bonus frequency	Monthly to quarterly	Monthly to quarterly	Weekly
Philosophy	Participative	Economic	Economic
Expected focus of management on participation	Heavy	Slight	None

NOTE: These points are taken from a variety of sources.

One significant point about the Scanlon plan is that it expects managers to take a participative, or Theory Y, approach (McGregor, 1957) to management. It is assumed that managers will encourage their employees to learn, grow, and develop as individuals. This assumption is built into the committee structure of the plan, but it is also a part of the philosophy behind the plan and all literature connected with the Scanlon plan. For example, it commonly is recommended that all employees (including managers) participate in the same bonus program. Comparisons of the Scanlon plan with the other two main types of gainsharing are presented in Table 5.1. These points come from a variety of sources.

It has been estimated that as many as 500 companies have implemented Scanlon plans. These have tended to be established in small- to medium-sized manufacturing companies in the Midwest and Northeast (near Michigan State University and MIT), but larger companies, service organizations, and companies in other locations also have tried these plans.

Rucker Plans

The Rucker plan was developed by Allan W. Rucker, an economist, in the late 1940s. It is based on Rucker's finding that, over time, labor costs are typically a stable percentage of value added; that is, when one examines a company (or an industry) over time, the relationship of labor costs to value added is relatively constant. If this ratio can be determined for an individual company, it then can be used as a baseline with which to measure future productivity improvements.

In addition to the difference in measuring productivity improvements, Rucker plans differ from Scanlon plans in how participation is structured. Rucker plans have no set procedure for employees to be involved. Early plans employed suggestion boxes, some companies have used suggestion committees, and some larger firms have used multilevel committees similar to Scanlon plans (Doyle, 1983). Participation is acknowledged in Rucker plans as being important, but managers can shape this participation in any way they wish.

Although the Rucker plan has been around almost as long as the Scanlon plan, it has not been implemented as widely, nor has it been as widely described. Doyle (1983) estimated that between 200 and 300 Rucker plans were in operation in the early 1980s.

Improshare

Improshare (*Improved Productivity Sharing*) is the work of Mitchell Fein, an industrial engineer, writer, and consultant. In addition to cultivating gainsharing programs with many organizations, Fein has written about Improshare (Fein, 1981, 1982b), as well as financial motivation in general (Fein, 1982a).

Improshare is a gainsharing plan, but it varies considerably from the Scanlon plan and the Rucker plan. First, unlike the Scanlon plan, it has no explicit participation process. Although Fein (1982b) acknowledged that worker involvement and participation is a necessary ingredient, this idea is downplayed in his plan, in contrast to the Scanlon approach. Second, unlike the other two plans, Improshare does not have to be implemented at a plant level; it can be aimed at a particular department or class of workers. In practice, however, Improshare generally has been applied at the plant or company level. Third, productivity measurements in the bonus formula are converted into time standards. Productivity is assessed in terms of the labor hours, both direct and indirect, necessary to produce one unit of product. Productivity improvements are recorded as hours saved.

The Improshare plan has been extremely successful in recent years. Fein (1982b) reviewed the results of 72 companies that implemented Improshare between 1974 and 1981. Graham-Moore (1983) called it "the fastest growing productivity gainsharing plan in the 1980s" (p. 89). Much of its appeal is probably due to not having to accept the assumptions and managerial changes required in the Scanlon plan. In addition, Fein presented it as an alternative to traditional engineering techniques, not as "psychobabble," which many industrial engineers and manufacturing managers tend to avoid.

Other Gainsharing Plans

Doherty, Nord, and McAdams (1989) reported on two types of gainsharing programs: performance improvement programs and team suggestion programs. The former program rewards employees for improvements in actual performance, the latter program rewards employees for cost-saving suggestions. Both are gainsharing programs, but they both focus at the team level rather than at the plant level. In addition, they are designed to be short term, with team suggestion programs lasting several months and performance improvement programs for fewer than 2 years. Finally, both programs award points toward merchandise, rather than cash bonuses.

Additional gainsharing plans occasionally have been discussed. For example, Miller and Schuster (1987b) discussed the Darcom plan, which calculates the bonus according to work centers and individual performance, not at the plant level as the other types of plans do. In this sense it is applying the principles of gainsharing at the department or group level (e.g., Nickel & O'Neal, 1990).

Geare (1976) mentioned the Hunter plan, which he described as similar to the Scanlon plan but designed independently in New Zealand at about the same time. The major difference between the Hunter plan and the Scanlon plan is that the Hunter plan distributes the bonus to workers on an equal share basis rather than as a percentage of a worker's wage.

I do not review profit sharing in this chapter, even though it is a compensation system designed to reward improvements in productivity. I do this for two reasons. First, profit sharing does not focus on employee productivity, but on overall efficiency (profit) of the organization. It therefore incorporates many factors besides the employees. Second, profit sharing is not a technique to increase employee involvement. Some could argue that Improshare also is not focused on employee involvement, but it is included in this chapter because Improshare is a popular alternative to the Scanlon plan.

Research on Gainsharing Plans

As previous authors (Lawler, 1988b; Schuster, 1983; White, 1979) have noted, reviewing the Scanlon plan literature (or the gainsharing literature in general) is difficult. Unlike other approaches to employee involvement reviewed in this book, the Scanlon plan was derived in practice and is virtually void of theory. In addition, most of the research studies can be described as "magazine reports" (Lawler, 1988b, p. 326). Case histories ("Case history," 1987; Davenport, 1950; Geber, 1987; Lesieur & Puckett, 1969; Masternak & Ross, 1992) offer encouraging results, but it is unclear whether the positive findings are actually due to the programs. There are virtually no control groups for comparison, little standardization in implementation, and a paucity of statistical tests. In spite of these problems, a review (certainly not exhaustive) is presented below.

An initial question in a review of gainsharing outcomes is whether one type of plan (e.g., Scanlon plan) is better than another type (e.g., Improshare). However, for several reasons this question is impossible to answer. First, these terms are labels for different approaches, with a number of different alternatives within each approach (Ost, 1989). For example, with a Scanlon plan, a set percentage of the increased profits goes to the workers, with the rest remaining with the company; this percentage differs across companies. Second, few companies implement a "pure" Scanlon plan or Rucker plan; most are customized to some extent (Miller & Schuster, 1987b). Third, most authors have focused on gainsharing in general, so reviews of case studies often do not differentiate among the different formats. For these reasons I summarize the findings for gainsharing as a whole.

Organizational Outcomes

The various forms of gainsharing are expected primarily to improve productivity and perhaps quality and/or service (Geare, 1976). The evidence on organizational outcomes comes from three sources: reviews of case studies, surveys of companies, and more carefully controlled longitudinal studies. The following discussion first summarizes the reviews of the many individual case studies and then describes three longitudinal studies.

One of the first reviews of Scanlon plan cases can be found in a chapter by Puckett (1958). In reviewing 10 applications of the Scanlon plan, Puckett found impressive improvements. In the first year under the Scanlon plan, the companies averaged a 22.5% increase in productivity, ranging from 6.8% to a high of 38.7%. Productivity improvements in the second year averaged 23.7%. The employees earned in bonus approximately 17.4% of their gross pay during the 2-year period.

The second major review of gainsharing was performed by Frost, Wakeley, and Ruh (1974). These authors first reviewed the classic research on participative decision making and gainsharing and concluded that Scanlon plans can improve organizational effectiveness and employee attitudes (p. 150). However, the lack of quantitative data made any conclusions speculative. Frost et al. went on to review the findings coming out of their research program and concluded that perceptions of participation were consistently related to positive employee attitudes. However, the Scanlon plans were not always effective methods of promoting participation.

In their volume examining quality of work life programs, Cummings and Molloy (1977) reviewed eight Scanlon plan studies. Their summary (incorporating many studies reviewed earlier) stated that all of the studies found improved productivity and reduced costs. In addition, six of the eight studies reported unqualified improvements in quality of work life, while two reported mixed results.

After an exhaustive search of the literature, Bullock and Lawler (1984) found only 33 case studies of gainsharing with enough evidence to review. In all, two thirds of their sample of plans were successful. About three quarters reported improvements in employee attitudes, over three-quarters reported more ideas and innovations, and over half reported improved labor-management relations.

Schuster (1983) also presented an exhaustive review of research on Scanlon plans, relating the descriptive literature, as well as the more empirical studies. Schuster found only seven empirical articles. He concluded (as have many others) that for such an important concept, the empirical evidence is very meager. The limited evidence that exists, however, suggests that Scanlon plans can serve to increase organizational effectiveness and productivity and can stabilize employment.

In another review, Schuster (1984b) described four case studies involving Scanlon plans at six sites. Five of the six sites found significant increases in productivity; the sixth had a nonsignificant increase and later dropped the plan.

Fein (1982b) reviewed changes in productivity of 72 companies after Improshare plans were established. Of the 72 companies, 57 still had plans operating at the time of the paper. Across all companies, Fein found an average 9.4% increase in productivity after 12 weeks and an average 22.2% increase after 1 year. Including only those companies still having plans, the average productivity increases were 10.3% after 12 weeks and 24.4% after 1 year.

In another review of Improshare plan effectiveness, Kaufman (1992) surveyed 112 companies, all of which implemented Improshare from 1981 to 1988. Employing actual productivity data for 44 companies, the author found that the median productivity improvement was 8% in the first year and nearly 18% by the third year. Productivity improvements generally leveled off after 3 years.

In his review of the existing literature, Lawler (1988b) concluded, "Perhaps the most important thing known about gainsharing plans is that they work" (p. 326). Lawler reported that the evidence suggests that gainsharing plans are successful in about 50% to 80% of the reported cases. Typically the focus has been on improved labor productivity, but other benefits (better acceptance of change, improved attitudes, better union position) often are cited as well.

Several surveys of gainsharing effectiveness have been conducted by agencies of the United States government. The first, a review conducted by the National Commission on Productivity and Work Quality (1975), surveyed a total of 44 Scanlon and related plans. In this review the commission found 30 successes and 14 failures, for a success rate of better than 2 to 1.

A second government study was conducted by the General Accounting Office (GAO) (1981; Preiwisch, 1981), investigating 38 firms with some form of gainsharing plan. The results were very positive: Of 24 firms providing financial information, work force savings averaged about 16% to 17%. In addition, 80% of the firms reported improved labor-management relations. Finally, many companies reported improvements in employee attitudes, absenteeism, and turnover.

The New York Stock Exchange (1982), in a study on people and productivity, surveyed 1,158 companies with 100 or more employees. The survey found that approximately 15% of United States companies with 500 or more employees have some type of gainsharing plan. (They defined *gainsharing plan* as a piecework, group productivity, profit sharing, or stock purchase plan.) Of the companies reporting group productivity plans, 74% reported those plans as successful, and only 2% reported them as unsuccessful.

The most recent and the most extensive survey was conducted by Markham, Scott, and Little (1992). These authors sampled 10,000 human resource professionals, obtaining responses from 1,639. They found that 13.4% had gainsharing plans, of which the most popular were customized plans, followed by profit sharing, Scanlon plans, employee ownership plans, Improshare, and Rucker plans. In general, the plans tended to be successful, paying out bonuses 69% of the time, paying an average of 7.6% of the total payroll, and generating medium to high levels of satisfaction from both managers and employees. Although gainsharing plans were successful overall, large differences were found across industries, with some industries exhibiting much more success.

In one of the few longitudinal studies, Schuster (1984a; Miller & Schuster, 1987a) examined the Scanlon plan in a large manufacturing plant over a 9-year period. He found that productivity improved after beginning the plan and continued to improve modestly over time. Employment and turnover remained stable, while union-management relations were enhanced.

Employing an inductive approach, Doherty, Nord, and McAdams (1989) examined four performance improvement and team suggestion programs in four locations. The samples were chosen to provide a manufacturing and a service example for each type of gainsharing program. These authors found significant short-term improvements on a variety of productivity measures. Quantitative long-term measures were not available.

Hanlon and Taylor (1991) tested a communication model of gainsharing, arguing that gainsharing improves organizational communication, which leads to higher performance. They tested this model by using a quasi-experimental design, comparing an experimental site (with a gainsharing plan) to another site in the same company without a plan. Both groups were surveyed before implementation of the plan and again 6 months later. Because the two groups demonstrated differences on the pretest, pretest responses were included in the analyses as covariates. The analyses indicated that the gainsharing site had significantly improved communication across a variety of measures. In addition, the gainsharing plan was economically successful, improving productivity and providing bonuses.

Individual Outcomes

In addition to organizational outcomes, a number of studies have examined the impact of gainsharing plans on individual outcomes, typically employee attitudes. Examining the impact of Scanlon plans on employee attitudes, Ruh, Johnson, and Scontrino (1973) surveyed employees from 15 Scanlon plan sites of six organizations. These authors found that self-reported participation in the Scanlon plan varied significantly across both locations and individuals. In addition, participation was highly related to job involvement, motivation, and identification with the company.

White and Ruh (1973) surveyed 19 plants of six manufacturers with Scanlon plans. They found that job involvement, motivation, and identification were all highly and positively related to perceived participation in decision making. Unfortunately, as the authors pointed out, it is not possible to determine whether the Scanlon plans are producing these positive job attitudes or employees with these attitudes are more likely to perceive the Scanlon plan as a means of participation.

In another survey of employee attitudes and Scanlon plans, Goodman, Wakeley, and Ruh (1972) surveyed employees at 21 sites of six companies. They found a positive correlation between the respondent's level in the organization and the favorableness of their attitudes about the plan; supervisors and managers tended to be more positive than workers. Forty percent of the employees indicated they would like to be on a production committee, evidence that many felt it was a worthwhile venture. However, it also seemed that participation in these plans generally was perceived as producing increased information, not greater influence.

To examine how the greater participation from gainsharing plans might interact with individual characteristics, Ruh, White, and Wood (1975) examined how involvement might moderate the relationship between participation and job attitudes. These authors found that job involvement was highly related to perceived participation but that job involvement did not moderate the relationship between participation and job attitudes.

Goodman and Moore (1976) conducted one of the few longitudinal studies of gainsharing by assessing beliefs about (a) whether suggestions would affect bonuses and (b) the likelihood of being able to make a suggestion. These beliefs were assessed before the Scanlon plan was announced, before the first bonus was paid, and 6 months after introduction of the plan. Considerable differences were found among individuals in terms of their beliefs. Surprisingly the beliefs did not change for a majority of the employees. In fact, despite the success of the plan over the 6 months, some participants remained skeptical about future bonuses and the plan.

Bullock and Perlow (1986) examined the impact of gainsharing on a variety of job attitudes within one company over 5 years. The authors found significant increases in job involvement, personal impact, perceived influence, and intrinsic satisfaction following the gainsharing plan. In addition, greater involvement in the gainsharing committees was significantly related to improvements in job satisfaction, organizational involvement, personal impact, influence, intrinsic satisfaction, and trust.

In a narrower study, Hauck and Ross (1988) examined the impact of a performance gainsharing plan at Volvo's Kalmar plant on employee attitudes about pay. After developing and implementing a gainsharing plan, the employees were asked about their preferences for pay plans. Overall, 65% of the employees preferred the gainsharing plan, as opposed to team-based wages, individual piecework, or fixed wages. However, those employees most directly concerned with production (assembly workers) were the least satisfied with the gainsharing plan.

In a study of prosocial behavior, Hatcher, Ross, and Collins (1989) found that the number of suggestions that employees made in gainsharing programs was related to perceptions of job complexity. The number of suggestions also was related to prosocial behavior, but only for employees who perceived their jobs as being relatively complex.

Focusing on the management perspective, Hatcher and Ross (1986) surveyed more than 100 managers in eight firms with gainsharing plans. The survey was intended to examine how managers' jobs were affected by the plans. Contrary to their expectations, Hatcher and Ross found that managers felt they had *more* influence and a greater ability to get work done after the implementation of a gainsharing program. In addition, the managers indicated they felt that their subordinates' concern for costs, productivity, and quality and that their involvement and commitment had increased with the gainsharing program. Unfortunately the authors did not present any tests indicating that the increases are statistically significant.

Summary

Overall, the success rate of the Scanlon plan appears to be fairly good, about the 65% estimated by Ross (1983) or the 50% to 80% suggested by Lawler (1988b). The research has focused primarily on improvements in productivity, but there are also indications of improvements in employee attitudes, ideas, and innovation, and better union-management relations. The findings concerning individual reactions are interesting but too fragmented to allow drawing overall conclusions.

**Factors Related to
Gainsharing Plan Success**

Among the studies to examine factors influencing the implementation of Scanlon plans are those of White and Ruh (1973) and Ruh, Wallace, and Frost (1973). These authors hypothesized that managerial attitudes toward participative practices were significantly correlated with whether or not the Scanlon plans were maintained. Ruh, Wallace, and Frost (1973) found, for example, that managers in organizations that abandoned a Scanlon plan were less favorable toward participative decision making than managers in organizations that retained the plan. In addition, managers of abandoned plans held less favorable attitudes toward the traits and abilities of rank-and-file employees. Of course, it is not possible to determine whether the negative attitudes led to abandonment of the Scanlon plan or an unsuccessful plan led to the more negative attitudes.

On the other hand, White and Ruh (1973) found that individual values did not moderate the relationship between participation and job attitudes. Greater participation was linked to greater job involvement, motivation, and company identification, regardless of the individual's values.

White (1979) examined the impact of a variety of variables on success of Scanlon plans in 23 companies. He found that the perception of participation by employees was highly related to the Scanlon plan success. In addition, managerial attitudes were related to success. Finally the number of years a company had a Scanlon plan was related to its success. Other variables, such as company size and technology, seemed unrelated to the success of the Scanlon plan.

In a summary of earlier reviews, Welbourne and Gomez-Mejia (1988) concluded that small firms have more successful gainsharing programs than large firms. In addition, they reported that old plans continued to be successful, although alternative explanations are possible for this finding. The presence of a union and financial difficulties were often present when gainsharing was implemented, but there was no indication that these were required for gainsharing to be successful.

In their study of short-term gainsharing programs, Doherty et al. (1989) found the programs to be successful in both manufacturing and service organizations. These authors also identified a variety of implementation factors affecting the success of the plans. These factors included participants' distrust of the plan, problems in the plan's procedures, and the implementation process.

Bullock and Tubbs (1990) conducted a meta-analysis of 33 case studies of gainsharing spread over 50 years. These authors tested a variety of hypotheses concerning several structural, implementation, and situational factors that might be related to gainsharing success. Their results indicated that having a formal employee involvement structure, shorter (monthly) payouts, employee involvement in the design, an outside consultant, positive employee attitudes, and a participative management culture were related to success. In general, the implementation factors were most likely to influence success, while situational factors (size, union, technology, environment) were least likely to affect success. Success was assessed in terms of program survival, organizational effectiveness, employee attitudes, innovation, and labor-management relations.

Why Do Gainsharing Plans Work?

Like most of the approaches described in this book, gainsharing works by getting workers involved, thinking more, and working smarter. However, little attention has been paid to how this happens or why it works.

Gainsharing might operate in two ways to improve involvement and lead to greater productivity. The first way, coming from the viewpoints of Joe Scanlon and Douglas McGregor, is that workers desire greater participation and become more motivated under this type of management (Lesieur, 1958). "All principles of management that encourage people to identify with their work group, that encourage people to participate as much as they can . . . are seen as ways of applying the Scanlon Plan philosophy" (Frost et al., 1974, p. 1). A related version of this approach is presented by Hanlon and Taylor (1991), who argued that gainsharing increases organizational communication. The improved communication then increases the level of job-related knowledge and attitudes, and this increase leads to higher performance.

A second way is presented by Geare (1976), who argued that the impact of gainsharing plans is strictly economic. In short, these plans improve productivity because they reward such improvements. The greater participation by workers may be part of how this happens but is probably unnecessary and irrelevant to produce a successful plan.

The latter approach is typified by Improshare (Fein, 1982b). Fein argued that financial incentives are a more powerful means of motivating workers than increased job enrichment, participation, or job satisfaction (Fein, 1982a). The concern is not with employee attitudes and involvement, but with employee productivity. Fein (1982a) reported that some form of worker involvement (e.g., productivity teams) is useful for creating and spreading receptive employee attitudes. The major motivation, however, comes through the financial rewards.

One attempt to disentangle the participation from the rewards in gainsharing plans was made by Rosenberg and Rosenstein (1980). These authors analyzed detailed records of productivity meetings from one company by measuring the frequency of meetings, the relevance of subjects discussed, the number of interchanges, and meeting attendance and representation. They found that the frequency of the meetings and the number of interchanges (discussion quantity) significantly predicted productivity. Monetary rewards also predicted productivity but added little beyond the participation measures. Rosenberg and Rosenstein concluded that the results strongly support the hypothesis that participative activities are related to productivity, but the authors did not support a major emphasis on monetary rewards (p. 367).

The issue of what process (or processes) is (are) responsible for effective gainsharing is more than a theoretical concern. If we could better understand why gainsharing plans work, we could design more successful plans.

Future Research Agendas

A number of writers have bemoaned the state of research on gainsharing and have made suggestions for improvements. Schuster (1983) recommended that future research include performance measures, control groups, and longitudinal designs. Too much of the research depends on testimonials in terms of productivity, focuses only on gainsharing successes, and is post hoc in nature, totally obscuring causal effects. In addition, few studies have been conducted in non-union environments.

Lawler (1988b) suggested that more research focus on why gainsharing plans work, the processes by which they operate, and the factors that may influence these processes. He also recommended research comparing the different plans and different types of formulas. Which formula works best with which organization? Is the formula that important? Are custom plans better than off-the-shelf approaches? Finally, Lawler suggested that the congruence, or fit, between the plan and the organization be studied. It seems likely that some organizations (and their cultures) would work best with a highly participative Scanlon plan, while others would operate better with the less philosophical Improshare.

Doherty et al. (1989) argued that gainsharing proponents have focused too much on bonus formulas and not enough on the process of implementing these types of programs. They suggested that gainsharing could learn much from traditional organizational development professionals, who have developed numerous ideas and techniques to improve the implementation of organizational interventions. On the flip side, the authors argued that organizational development specialists could learn much from the gainsharing literature in terms of presenting the value of their contributions to managers.

Issues in Implementing Gainsharing Plans

There are a number of implementation issues, some of them common to the different forms of gainsharing, and others specific to a particular plan.

Bonus Formulas

One of the major differences among gainsharing plans is the formula by which productivity is measured and bonuses are paid out. Despite this obvious basis of comparison across different types of plans, virtually no research compares the various measures or different formulas.

In an interesting study, Florkowski (1990) compiled, over a 5-year period, data from a manufacturing firm with a profit sharing plan and then compared the payouts from this plan to what workers would have received if they had adopted a Scanlon plan or a Rucker plan. In general, both gainsharing plans would have provided employees with larger earnings. However, the gainsharing plans were also more variable than the profit sharing plan, with the Scanlon plan having the greatest variability. Of course, comparisons among the plans depend on the precise formulas being used, but the differences in stability are useful for those deciding between motivation and stability.

When implementing a gainsharing program, considerable focus typically is placed on the bonus formula. Two characteristics are necessary for the plan's success. First, the formula needs to be fair and appropriate to the organization and the product/service involved. Second, the formula must be understandable to the employees. As expectancy theory (Porter & Lawler, 1968) would predict, an incomprehensible formula cannot motivate workers to improve productivity. A final issue is whether the payout varies as the performance level changes. Beck (1992) described three types of payout curves showing how incentive bonuses can vary across different levels of performance.

Gainsharing With a Union

The presence of a union is not a prerequisite for an effective Scanlon plan or other gainsharing plan. However, some adherents, including Scanlon himself, feared that where a union was not present, the production committees could become forums for grievances and bargaining problems (Puckett, 1958). In fact, in one experience with a union and a Scanlon plan failure (Gilson & Lefcowitz, 1957), the production committee meetings became a forum for complaints. Nevertheless most modern proponents (e.g., Doyle, 1983) believe that gainsharing can work with or without a union.

Some unions, suspicious of participation programs as attempts to turn workers against other workers, have opposed gainsharing programs. Ross, Hatcher, and Adams (1985) surveyed members of the larger American trade unions to determine the reasons that union leaders would give for favoring or opposing gainsharing programs. The most highly cited reasons that unions gave for opposing gainsharing were "management might try to substitute it for wages," "management cannot be trusted," "peer pressure to perform may increase," and "bonus calculations are not understood or trusted." The most commonly rated reasons that unions gave for favoring gainsharing included "increased recognition of employees," "better job security," "increased involvement by employees in jobs," and "more money." Unfortunately the validity of the responses in this survey are suspect. More than 50% of the respondents rated eight of the nine reasons given as "important" or "very important," a finding that suggests a strong response bias.

Doyle (1983) made the point that management is generally the first to consider gainsharing and that union leaders are unlikely to have any prior experience with gainsharing. Therefore, union leaders will need time and assistance to become familiar and comfortable with the ideas and their role. In addition, each local union will react according to its own situation and perspective. It seems that there is no "union" position, but there is a need for helping union leaders with these notions.

Schuster (1985) found in his study of 33 sites that management respondents were twice as likely as union respondents to state that they believed the cooperative program (often gainsharing) would be effective. Almost one third of the union representatives felt that the program would not be useful, whereas only 9% of the managers felt this way. This finding suggests that managers will need to "sell" gainsharing programs to the union.

Service and Public-Sector Organizations

The vast majority of gainsharing plans discussed have been in manufacturing, with only an occasional service example (Ost, 1990). In fact, Hauck and Ross (1983) asked the question, Is productivity gainsharing applicable to service sector firms? Their answer to this question is a definite yes.

The major concern with service organizations is developing accurate (and acceptable) measures of productivity on which to base a plan. Hauck and Ross (1983) discussed some of the factors for measuring productivity in banking and hospitals. Graham-Moore and Ross (1990) discussed gainsharing examples in both the service and the public sectors. Haskew (1985) described an Improshare plan being used at a medical center. He pointed out that the move to a diagnosis-related groups (DRG) system of reimbursement has simplified the measurement process.

Although the process for establishing a gainsharing plan is probably more difficult in a service organization, it should be just as effective. Like a plan in a manufacturing setting, if the productivity measurement and formula are precise, understandable, and appropriate, the gainsharing plan should be successful.

Factors in Successful Gainsharing Plans

Owens (1988) listed a variety of conditions that are necessary for an effective gainsharing plan: supportive corporate culture, easily available productivity measures, and a potential for productivity growth without layoffs. In addition, he suggested training for management, education for employees, and the monitoring and revision of the plan as necessary.

Lawler (1981, p. 144) listed 21 conditions favoring a successful gainsharing program. These conditions tend to focus on organizational factors (size, age, union status, communication), business factors (seasonal nature, work interdependence, capital investment, product stability), and personnel factors (comptroller and plant manager, management and corporate, work force and support services). Lawler (1988b) also made the point that it is important that the gainsharing plan be congruent with the practices, structures, policies, and managerial behaviors of the organization. It is possible (even likely) that the individual factors are not as important for success as this overall congruence.

Nickel and O'Neal (1990) argued that group incentives (such as gainsharing) are most appropriate where a strong interdependence exists among jobs; that is, when members of a work group must work together and coordination is important, group incentives are useful.

Schuster (1987) gave four keys to the success of a gainsharing program: defining the plan's strategic objectives, devoting sufficient resources to feasibility assessment and plan design, commitment to the concept at all managerial levels, and effective implementation (p. 17). Schuster emphasized the need to conduct a feasibility study to determine how the program should be designed.

Although gainsharing failures are seldom reported, several authors have attempted to describe some of the factors that lead to problems in these plans (Graham-Moore & Ross, 1983, 1990). Doyle (1983) attributed failures to mergers with companies whose management was philosophically opposed to gainsharing, the loss of a strong leader who championed the plan, implementation of gainsharing as a fad and without real commitment by management, poor preparation of supervisors, dishonesty in productivity measurement, and the perception of gainsharing simply as another incentive. Several of these problems were found in a Scanlon plan failure described by Gilson and Lefcowitz (1957). The common theme in these reasons is a lack of management commitment and/or management values opposed to employee participation.

Ross (1983) presented organizational, cultural, and financial variables to explain failures in gainsharing. The *organizational variables* incorporate the levels of trust, confidence and communication, and lack of control over sales and employment. The *cultural variables* include poor industrial relations and a lack of democratic principles. The *financial variables* encompass poor information system, lack of reliability in the financial system, and severe external constraints and competition. In short, when employees and management do not communicate, trust, or have confidence in each other, when there is little knowledge or control over costs, sales, and employment, and when the organizational culture is autocratic, a gainsharing plan probably will fail.

Overall, many factors have been advanced that may assist or hamper a gainsharing plan. Unfortunately, as pointed out earlier, there is little empirical evidence regarding which ones are truly consequential. At the present it seems that those interested in implementing gainsharing can choose whichever list of factors they prefer.

The many conditions above can be summarized into a few general categories:

Commitment of all parties. Like other employee involvement programs, a gainsharing plan must have commitment from both employees and management (Ewing, 1989). A Scanlon plan typically begins with a companywide vote on whether the plan should be instituted. This process demonstrates (and helps solidify) the commitment of the employees.

Management must be supportive of the plan, willing to stick with it through tough times as well as successful periods. In fact, Ross, Ross, and Hatcher (1986) argued that gainsharing will not be successful if it is viewed as a program, such a view implying a temporary focus. Successful gainsharing plans become a way of life, sometimes providing a significant shift in the corporate culture.

Participative culture. The Scanlon plan explicitly requires management to share decision-making power with employees in the committee structure. The other forms of gainsharing do not have explicit arrangements for participation, but the assumption generally is made that employee involvement is necessary for gainsharing to be effective. Without a participative culture, the gainsharing plan will fail in two (or more) ways. Either the plan will be seen by employees as another attempt by management to squeeze more out of the workers, or middle- and low-level management will stifle any attempts by employees to improve productivity.

A common concern within management is the perception that they have lost authority or are being undermined (Hatcher & Ross, 1986). Often supervisors are concerned if too many suggestions come out of their department, the implication being that the department has not been well run in the past (Lesieur, 1958). Ross and Collins (1987) listed six concerns that many managers have about gainsharing and provide a case example that demonstrates how these concerns are inaccurate. Management has to build teamwork between workers and supervisors and has to convince the supervisors that they are being evaluated with criteria different from those used in the past. The best supervisor should be the one whose department has the most suggestions.

Open communication. The plan itself should be clear and unambiguous, with the performance measure and formula understood by all. If employees do not understand the plan, they cannot be involved or be motivated by it. In addition, the managers in charge of the plan must be trusted and be able to explain the financial measures; the company must be willing to share financial results with the employees. Without feedback about the company and the plan, the employees cannot be involved or motivated.

Potential for improvement. Expectancy theory (Porter & Lawler, 1968) proposes that an individual will not be motivated to perform an action if the probability of success (expectancy) is too low. If employees perceive that their input will have no impact or that the likelihood of suggestions being accepted is low, they will not be motivated to participate.

Lesieur (1958) recommended that the production committees in Scanlon plans take more care with rejected suggestions than with those that have been accepted (p. 48). Employees whose suggestions are accepted can see their contribution to the process and are reinforced by having their ideas approved. Those whose ideas are rejected do not know the reason unless they are contacted personally and the reason(s) explained.

A plan also will not be effective if useful suggestions do not influence productivity or if labor costs are dominated by factors outside of the employees' control. If market share is shrinking or financial performance is poor, gainsharing will not work (Rollins, 1989). Gainsharing often is recommended for small companies or plants (fewer than 500 employees) because these are seen as being more easily influenced. Very large plants or companies will have too many extraneous factors influencing productivity, factors a plan cannot control.

Overall Conclusions

With the exception of Lawler (1986, 1988b), most writers of employee participation and involvement have not concentrated on gainsharing. This neglect is unfortunate, because the research indicates that gainsharing is an effective form of employee involvement. Although the processes may not be clear, it is apparent that gainsharing improves productivity in a majority of cases and often has a positive impact on employee attitudes.

Gainsharing has been sold primarily as an incentive technique for improving productivity. However, most proponents of gainsharing have hypothesized that the improvements in productivity come about through increased employee involvement, better communication and cooperation within the organization, improved understanding by employees, and greater acceptance of change. As Hatcher and Ross (1985) pointed out, these are classic organizational development goals, yet for the most part there are few instances in the organizational development literature where gainsharing was used as an agent of change.

Over the years, gainsharing has tended to be atheoretical, the province of traditional personnel specialists and industrial engineers. It has not been a "sexy"area, with theory, counterintuitive predictions, and humanistic ideals to inspire more researchers and authors. However, it has been relatively effective.

Gainsharing is a compensation program, but it is also an employee involvement program. I think the recommendations of Doherty et al. (1989) are extremely valuable. Gainsharing proponents need to think more like organizational development specialists and focus on process, as well as measurement and formulas. Lawler (1981, 1986) recommended using a cross section of employees to help design a gainsharing program. This type of focus on *how* the plan is implemented is as important as the *form* of the plan.

In addition, organizational development professionals should adopt gainsharing as an important tool in changing organizational culture and in promoting employee participation. Too often organizational development has focused only on process and has ignored powerful structures such as compensation systems. A new form of compensation, such as gainsharing, can act as a powerful level for organizational change.

6 Representative Participation

This chapter focuses on indirect employee involvement: when workers do not participate directly, but participate through some type of representative. These representatives can come in the form of a works council, worker representatives on the board of directors, or some other format. The examples of employee involvement that make up this chapter are much more common in Europe than in the United States. The establishment of works councils or the placing of employee representatives on a company's board of directors typically has been accomplished through national legislation. By the early 1980s, almost every country in Western Europe had some type of legislation requiring works councils, board representatives, or both. In the United States, however, having workers on the board of directors or other worker representatives (except union leaders) is a strange concept.

Representative participation is the most widely legislated form of employee involvement around the world. As Table 6.1 shows, laws requiring either board representatives or works councils have been popular in Europe for decades. In addition, legislation has been passed or proposed in Latin America, South America, Africa, and Southeast Asia (Cordova, 1982; Poole, 1979). The European legislation was most popular in the 1970s, when countries were making changes almost yearly.

The intention of this legislation has not been to improve employee attitudes or to enhance organizational productivity. The

Table 6.1 Legally Mandated Forms of Representative Participation

Country	Form of representative participation	Date(s) of legislation
Germany	Board representatives	1951, 1972, 1976
Germany	Works councils	1951, 1972
France	Works councils	1982
France	Health, safety, and working conditions committee	1982
Netherlands	Works councils	1950, 1971, 1979
Netherlands	Board representatives	1971, 1982
Sweden	Board representatives	1973, 1976
Sweden	Works councils	1946, 1973
Ireland	Board representatives	1977 (state-owned firms only)
Norway	Board representatives	1972
Denmark	Board representatives	1974, 1980
Denmark	Works councils	1980, 1986
Austria	Board representatives	1974
Austria	Works councils	1974
Luxembourg	Board representatives	1974
India	Board representatives	1971
Spain	Board representatives	1962
Yugoslavia	Self-management	1950, 1974, 1976

goal is a redistribution of power within firms, putting labor on a more equal footing with the interests of management and stockholders. Because the intended outcomes are different from the focus of this book, it will not be surprising that this type of employee involvement is not very successful in terms of my criteria.

Works councils and board representatives are examples of what Dachler and Wilpert (1978) categorized as indirect participation. In this approach to involvement, most employees do not participate, at least not directly. They elect, or nominate, or are represented by a small group of employees who actually participate. In terms of social range, this form of involvement typically covers an entire organization. In terms of access or influence, this form tends to be medium; employee representatives seldom make decisions, but they often can vote (with management) or are consulted on decisions. The focus of the involvement can be wide ranging, extending from specific daily work issues to general organizational policy issues.

On the Board at the *Milwaukee Journal*

The *Milwaukee Journal* is proud of being the first employee-owned company in Wisconsin. Since the 1940s, it also has been one of the few to have employee representatives on its board of directors. Currently 7 of the 24 seats are designated for workers. Actually employees at the *Milwaukee Journal* (and its sister paper the *Milwaukee Sentinel*, several radio and TV stations, a printing company, and other ventures) are represented by two groups: the unit council and the board of directors.

The *Journal's* unit council consists of 37 employees who are elected by the employee owners of the company. Each employee owner has one vote. The purpose of the council is similar to that of works councils in Europe: to act as a conduit between the employees and management. The unit council raises issues and concerns of the employees and transmits these to management. For example, it has instituted changes in the *Milwaukee Journal* cafeteria, has prodded the company to subsidize mass transit passes, and is trying to convince management to add dental insurance. In addition, the council informs the employees about what management is thinking and doing. Employees can ask questions of their council representatives (by filling out an Ask Your Rep card) that they would not ask their boss.

Seven seats on the board of directors are held by members of the unit council. Another election is conducted, with employees eligible to vote as much stock (units) as they own. The rest of the seats on the board are taken by management, with the exception of one seat, held by the original founding family (which still owns 10% of the company). The role of the board of directors is similar to that of most public companies: to acquire other companies, hire top management, make major policy decisions, and review the financial progress of the company.

In talking with employees and management, it becomes clear that the real action is with the unit council. The board of directors is known for listening to reports and voting on proposals without a great deal of argument. The unit council, however, is known as a place where ideas are generated, and spirited debate can take place.

For those employees who are members of the unit council, the experience is valuable. As part of their participation, they learn much more about how the company operates, what is happening in other parts of the company, and what management is thinking. The representatives typically enjoy the experience and better appreciate their company.

For the rest of the employees, the impact of the unit council is much smaller. Not all employees know what the council is doing, and not all care a great deal about it. But council members are confident that the impact exists. "If nothing else, the whole process reminds employees that they are also owners. . . . If you just offered the stock and didn't have representation, there would be a very different feel for employees."

The employees at the *Milwaukee Journal* are represented by several unions. It is not unusual to have union members participating in the unit council or even sitting on the board of directors. Surprisingly there appears to be little conflict between the roles. The employee representatives see one role for the unions (fighting for better benefits) and a different role for the unit council and board (pushing the company on other issues, communicating to management and the employees). Even when both the union and the council are driving for a common goal (dental benefits), they operate independently, at different levels.

Overall, the impact of the unit council and employees on the board of directors has been modest at the *Milwaukee Journal*. In this sense they are comparable to similar institutions in Europe. Despite the lack of major consequences, however, the individuals involved feel that the unit councils and board are valuable institutions. If nothing else, they serve to keep the lines of communication open between top management and the employees and to remind the employees that they do in fact own the company.

Research on Representative Participation

The variety of forms of representative participation typically varies across national boundaries. The two most common institutions are works councils and worker representatives on the board. Countries may have one of these, both, or neither. Germany and the Netherlands, for example, have both employee directors and works councils. Other countries, such as France and Spain, have works councils, but these tend to be relatively weak. Great Britain has no laws governing these issues at all. The European Commission, attempting to form a united economic Europe, has proposed both worker-directors and works councils for all European countries (Hallett, 1990). The most recent recommendation has been for worker representatives on only large, multinational firms (Bureau of National Affairs [BNA], 1991). It remains to be seen whether this will happen.

The following review is organized by country. As the discussion indicates, many differences can be found across national boundaries. A useful description of these practices organized by country can be found in IDE (1981a). This volume outlines the relevant history of each country, the major legislation, and the rules under which works councils and worker representation operate.

Germany

Codetermination has been defined in several ways (IDE, 1981a). One meaning of this term is the entire network of programs designed to bring workers into organizational decision making (T. H. Hammer, personal communication, March 26, 1992). On the other hand, Kuhne (1976) defined it as "where employees' participation takes the form of admitting employees' representatives as full members on the . . . board of directors, together with representatives of the owners" (p. 18). I generally use the first definition, but I recognize that many authors are applying it more narrowly.

Much of the focus on codetermination has involved worker representatives on the board of directors. It should be pointed out that in some countries (e.g., the United States) only a single board exists. However, a number of Western European countries mandate two boards—a supervisory board that appoints the executive (management) board, and the executive board, which actually operates the firm. Typically worker representatives are part of the supervisory board. This dual board system operates in Germany, Austria, Denmark, Luxembourg, Norway, and the Netherlands (Harrison, 1977).

Since the codetermination law of 1951, the Federal Republic of Germany (West Germany) has legally required that companies with more than 1,000 employees in certain industries have an equal number of employee and stockholder representatives on their boards of directors (Adams & Rummel, 1977). The codetermination law was amended in 1972 and again in 1976. These later laws required a minority of employee representatives for most firms and equal numbers for the large firms in all industries. It has been estimated that codetermination is now required of about 650 corporations, covering over one quarter of the labor force (Benelli, Loderer, & Lys, 1987).

Mazzolini (1978) examined the impact of codetermination in Germany and several other European countries through interviews with top executives. His findings indicated that most executives were extremely apprehensive prior to accepting worker representatives on their boards (viewing it as the downfall of free enterprise). However, their general experience was that the worker representatives did not hamper the functioning of the firms. In fact, worker representatives often were seen as useful, either as spokespersons for board decisions or information conduits for identifying worker concerns.

The experiences of codetermination in Germany have been studied at length by economists interested in whether this sharing of power improves organizational efficiency or reduces it. A number of theorists (Furubotn, 1985, 1988; Jensen & Meckling, 1979) have argued that employers and employees have conflicting goals (e.g., profits vs. jobs). Codetermination requires additional bargaining between the firm and the employees, which should be inherently inefficient. Other theorists (Hodgson & Jones, 1989; Jones & Svejnar, 1982a) have argued that cooperative groups can produce outcomes of greater mutual benefit than would be achieved through competition.

Svejnar (1982) analyzed data on German firms from 1950 to 1976, examining the impact of codetermination laws in 1951, 1953, and 1973. Because different sized firms and different industries were affected by these changes, the impact of codetermination can be inferred from changes after the laws were inaugurated. Svejnar's results showed that the introduction of codetermination in 1951 and 1952 had no significant impact on productivity (as measured by an index of value of net product, or value added). The impact of the 1973 codetermination act was inconclusive, being either insignificant in some analyses or mildly negative.

Benelli et al. (1987) examined the impact of the 1951, 1972, and 1976 laws on firm outcomes. They compared the profitability, size of dividends, and investment policy of 42 affected firms to 42 unaffected firms in the same industries. No significant differences were found between the firms. In a further analysis, the authors compared the stock returns of 40 firms with worker board representatives and 18 similar firms without representatives. Again, few differences were found between the two groups of companies. Benelli et al. concluded that any effects of codetermination were very weak and statistically nonsignificant.

Gurdon and Rai (1990) examined three outcome variables—capital-labor ratio, productivity (revenues per unit of labor), and profitability (profits per unit of capital)—of various groups of German firms. The authors examined these variables for 6 years before and 7 years after the passage of the 1976 codetermination law. Because the law has different requirements for different types of firms, the authors were able to compare groups of firms that had complete parity between stockholders and employees on the board, one-third employee representation on the board, and no employee representation on the board. The results indicated that the capital-labor ratio did not appreciably change with greater codetermination. The second outcome, productivity, was negatively related to worker representation. Those firms with the highest percentage of worker representatives showed a decline in productivity. Finally, profitability increased for those firms with the greatest level of representation. These findings provide both positive and negative results for supporters of codetermination.

A number of opponents of codetermination have argued that where equal numbers of worker representatives are found on boards, key decisions will be postponed and the ability to act will be harmed. Scholl (1987) investigated this issue by surveying 100 firms with more than 500 employees in seven industries. The results indicated that "codetermination does not hamper the ability to act. . . . On the contrary, there is a tendency toward facilitation" (p. 31). It appears that this fear is overstated.

Works councils are groups of employees in a facility who must be consulted when management makes decisions involving personnel. German law mandates that employees in any company with five or more employees can form a works council (Kassalow, 1989). This council must be informed in advance of any major personnel decisions by the firm. In general, each facility has a works council, while representatives on the supervisory board represent employees' interests for the firm as a whole (Schnabel, 1991). Councils complement the national nature of trade unions in Germany. While the unions focus on the national issues, the works councils focus on local concerns (T. H. Hammer, personal communication, March 26, 1992). In this sense, the works councils take a role similar to that of the local union in the United States.

Fitzroy and Kraft (1987) examined the economic impact of works councils in West Germany. They found that works councils had a significant negative effect on productivity. The authors used these findings to argue that the existence of "voice" in Hirschman's (1970) framework does *not* improve organizational efficiency.

Another study examining the impact of works councils was conducted by Bartolke, Eschweiler, Flechsenberger, and Tannenbaum (1982). These authors tested two hypotheses: that increased participation (assessed in terms of more or less powerful works councils) would decrease the influence differential between management and workers and that as participation increased, so would total influence within the organization. The authors examined the degree of influence within 10 German companies, 5 highly participative and 5 not very participative. Employees from all levels in the companies were asked to assess the influence of plant management, other management, and the workers. Respondents indicated that plant management had the greatest influence, followed by other management, and then the workers. In addition, those plants with more powerful works councils tended to have smaller influence differences between management and the workers. Finally, the overall influence of all members (management and nonmanagement) was higher in the participative plants. The influence of the workers was higher in the participative plants, but the influence of management did not decrease.

Kissler (1989) reviewed 53 studies of codetermination in Germany, covering the period from 1952 to 1985. He discussed a variety of issues, but, regarding works councils, he concluded that they are effective in terms of social matters but not in terms of personnel affairs. In addition, large differences were found in the effectiveness of works councils, often dependent on the size of the company and the ability of the work force to mobilize. Kissler concluded that worker representatives on the boards generally were able to work well with the board, especially in terms of social matters.

The Netherlands

Although the Netherlands mandates both board representatives and works councils, most of the emphasis and research has focused on the role of the works councils. In part this focus predominates because works councils in the Netherlands have much stronger legislated powers than those of other European countries (Looise, 1989). For example, in the takeover of a Dutch firm, the works council must be informed at an early stage, and if the council objects, it has 30 days to seek a court injunction to stop the takeover (Kleyn & Perrick, 1990). Dutch works councils are not presided over by management, they have the right to all economic and financial data, and they can take conflicts with the company to arbitration (Kunst & Soeters, 1991).

The experiences of three companies with their works councils in the Netherlands were examined by Koopman, Drenth, Bus, Kruyswijk, and Wierdsma (1981). The authors used a multimethod approach, employing interviews, questionnaires, group feedback analysis, observation, and the analysis of council minutes. Their findings indicated that most of the issues discussed by the councils (50%-60%) dealt with the work itself, followed by personnel policy (20%-30%) and physical work conditions (10%-20%). General company policies were the least popular issues (5%-10%).

Analysis of the process indicated that seldom (5%-11%) were decisions made during the meetings. Most of the time (60%-75%) was spent presenting information, often after a decision had been made. When questioned about the effects of the work consultation, most council members felt that the greatest benefit was that management was better informed about what the workers thought and that people knew better what was going on. Few thought that the council led to increased influence or improved job attitudes. As other authors have noted (e.g., Teulings, 1987) there is a major distinction between the legal powers given to works councils and the actual power demonstrated by the councils.

Kunst and Soeters (1991) addressed an interesting issue with works councils: What are the consequences for those who serve on these councils? Surveys in the Netherlands (and other countries) have found that it is often difficult to find employees willing to participate on the works council. A common perception is that employees fear that this participation might harm their careers in the organization. Kunst and Soeters attempted to determine whether this is the case by surveying present and past members of works councils in 54 firms and comparing the careers described by these respondents with the findings of a large-scale study of Dutch careers. The findings indicated that membership on a works council does not appear to harm a career, but those who volunteer for a council tend to be older and less likely to advance further in the organization.

Self-Management in Yugoslavia

Since 1950, Yugoslavia has had a unique form of employee representation, labeled as self-management (Adizes, & Borgese, 1975). This approach was reinforced in 1974 with a new constitution and in 1976 with the Associated Labour Act, which attempted to give complete decision-making power to the employees (Zwerdling, 1984). The Yugoslavian model has several aspects. First, employee participation is emphasized as a basic aspect of the socialist society. Second, the work organizations are owned by society, not by stockholders or employees. Third, workers' councils and workers' assemblies are mandated as part of the employee self-management of all work organizations (Witt & Brkovic, 1989). Another review of the Yugoslav model, focusing on the economic perspective, is provided by Estrin and Bartlett (1982).

Rus (1970) examined the perceived influence of different occupational groups in Yugoslavian enterprises by employing the control graph, developed by Tannenbaum (1968). In this format, respondents indicate the perceived control they have and the degree of influence they desire. Rus compared the responses of top management, the workers' council, the managing board, staff, middle management, supervisors, skilled workers, and unskilled workers. The data, drawn from seven studies covering thousands of respondents in hundreds of firms, indicated that influence in Yugoslavia is not greatly different from that in other countries. In every study, top management had the greatest amount of influence, and unskilled workers had the least. In general, professional staff followed top management, followed by middle management, the workers' councils, managing board, and supervisors. Interestingly workers' councils varied the most in terms of influence, from being second (behind top management) in one study to sixth (just ahead of skilled and unskilled workers) in another.

The impact of self-management on worker influence was examined over a 5-year period by Kavcic and Tannenbaum (1981). These authors measured the distribution of influence in 100 Yugoslavian firms by using Tannenbaum's control graph procedure. They found that the influence of workers did not change but that the influence of the plant director did increase over the 5 years.

Investigations of the group process in Yugoslavian workers' councils were described by Obradovic (1975) and Bertsch and Obradovic (1979). In these papers the authors described how they gathered observational data collected from workers' councils meetings, as well as survey data from top management. The observational data demonstrated that top management was highly active, dominating the meetings. Central management and central staff had longer interactions, more presentations, more proposals presented, and more proposals accepted in these meetings than any other groups. Shopfloor workers, constituting 67% of all employees, had more interactions, but these were shorter and were lower on all of the other dimensions.

Even prior to the recent political strife and warfare in Yugoslavia, the self-management process was in trouble. In 1988 the economic problems of Yugoslavia included "the disintegration of economic enterprise, declining productivity and production, and, most significant of all, the growing social dissension as proof of government failure" (Stanic, 1988, p. 65). Witt and Brkovic (1989) commented that for years Yugoslavian firms voted to turn profits into wage increases rather than investing them into the organization. Newman (1987) argued that self-management led to low investment, fat raises for workers, inflation, and strikes by the workers against themselves. He reported that workers were tired of self-management and that the worker movement had begun to hand some of the power back to management. Warner (1990) argued that a variety of problems (poor macroeconomic management, ineffective microeconomic administration, ethnic tensions) were responsible for the poor economic performance in the 1980s. In his opinion, self-management probably deserved less credit for the economic successes and less blame for the economic failures.

Legislated Participation in Other Countries

Codetermination in Norway was studied by Thorsrud and Emery (1970), who examined the impact of employee representatives on the boards of five companies. Because they were partially or totally state owned, the companies had experience with worker board directors for over a decade. Interviews with employee representatives elicited that they tended to be under a variety of pressures. Because of these pressures, the employees ended up acting very much like ordinary board members and had little impact. The authors argued that it is more effective to involve employees in other ways.

Englestad and Qvale (1977, reported in Gustavsen & Hunnius, 1981; Brett & Hammer, 1982; Hammer, Currall, & Stern, 1991) also examined the impact of codetermination in Norway. The 1973 Norwegian Codetermination Act required that firms give one third of all board seats to worker representatives. Englestad and Qvale interviewed about 200 members of company boards and assemblies. These authors found that board members (both employee and stockholder representatives) were satisfied with codetermination. In addition, they found that employee representatives felt that they influenced how board decisions were made in small firms. However, few effects were found with larger firms. Similar effects also were found in Sweden (Brett & Hammer, 1982).

Gustavsen and Hunnius (1981) discussed in a broader sense the impact of the industrial democracy program in Norway. This program, launched in the 1960s, incorporated both codetermination (representative participation), as well as sociotechnical job redesign (see Chapter 8). Gustavsen and Hunnius argued that negative evaluations (such as those of Thorsrud & Emery, 1970) are due to unrealistic expectations. If one uses a long time span (decades) and employs as a criterion the use of social science in changing organizations, the industrial democracy program was successful. However, to the extent that major changes occurred, the impact was much more limited.

French law requires that any enterprise employing 50 or more employees must establish a works council and a health, safety, and working conditions committee (CHSCT). Many countries (such as Germany) do not allow representatives of the employer on the council; however, the French include worker representatives and a representative of the employer as chair. Although numerous studies have been conducted to examine the impact of the French legislation, few conclusions have been made. This scarcity is probably because the participative groups were relatively unsuccessful and have tended to disappear (Goetschy, 1991). Delamotte (1988) pointed out that many firms have not formed a works council and that the ones that do exist often do not perform all of their legislated functions.

Great Britain

Although Great Britain has no requirements for either works councils or board representatives, groups such as the Bullock Committee (Bullock, 1977) have proposed requiring worker representatives. Currently, however, representative forms of employee involvement can be found only in a few cooperatives and publicly owned companies.

Positive findings come from a study of British retail cooperatives by Jones (1987). Jones examined the impact of both employee representatives and employee financial participation in 50 cooperatives. His findings indicated that the presence of employee representatives was positively related to productivity. These significant findings (when so many others have found nothing) might be due to the fact that he was concentrating on just one industry or that the organizations were cooperatives.

In the late 1970s, seven union-nominated individuals were appointed to the board of directors for the British Post Office. These worker representatives joined seven executive members plus five part-time outside directors. A careful investigation of these changes (Batstone, Ferner, & Terry, 1983) found that the introduction of the worker representatives had a limited impact on the post office board. The worker representatives tended to focus on employee issues, and conflict tended to grow between them and the management board members. Although they had little impact on board policy, Batstone et al. argued that the worker representatives did influence which issues were examined and which were ignored. Interestingly the worker representative experiment ended after only 2 years, when the new, conservative government, post office management, and unions allowed it to expire.

The experiences of employee directors at the British Steel Corporation from 1968 to 1976 were described by Bank and Jones (1977). As an experiment this nationalized company had three employees join the 13-member board. These numbers eventually were expanded, and union officials were allowed to participate on the board. Although the experiment often was criticized, it was generally perceived favorably by the directors. Surprisingly, although many of the employee directors also held elected trade union offices, only 4 of 17 surveyed reported role conflict in this dual capacity.

Wilson and Peel (1991) examined the impact of employee participation on absenteeism and turnover among British firms. Their participation variables included the presence or absence of a works council. They found that the presence of a works council was negatively related to absenteeism, as they had predicted. However, the presence of a works council was positively related to the rate of turnover, contrary to their predictions, and to other measures of employee participation. The authors offered no explanation for this pattern of effects.

United States

Although codetermination is not mandated in the United States, in a number of situations employees or employee representatives sit on the board of directors (Stern, 1988). Several firms (Chrysler, Eastern Airlines, Pan American Airlines) have swapped seats on the board of directors for union concessions (Backhaus, 1987). In addition, Dilts and Paul (1990) made the point that employee ownership (see Chapter 9) may "constitute a 'hybrid' form of codetermination" (p. 20). As such, their experiences with codetermination are likely to be considerably different from the European experience.

A comparison of German and United States experiences with employees on the boards of directors was presented by Kassalow (1989). The most obvious difference is that, in Germany, some employee representation is mandated by law. In the United States, employee representation has occurred through concession bargaining with a union or with the advent of employee ownership. A second difference is that German boards have, at a minimum, employee representatives as a third of their board members. In almost all American corporations, employee representatives are a small minority (one to three members). Finally, in German firms the major operating officers of the corporation are not members of the board of directors. In American firms, however, the chief executive officer (CEO) is often the chair of the board of directors, with other officers as members of the board.

One difference noted by Kassalow (1989) as well as others (Hoerr, 1987; Stern, 1988) is that American workers on the board of directors often are put in situations with considerable role conflict. As a member of the board, these individuals are responsible for the interests of company stockholders, not employees. When the firm is unionized, this condition presents additional legal issues (Dilts & Paul, 1990; Stern, 1988). In fact, some (Hass & Philbrick, 1988) have argued that current law makes these arrangements illegal. Finally any evidence of employee representatives sharing information with a union or other employee group could produce ostracism from the remainder of the board. German workers, however, do not have the same degree of conflict.

Wever (1989) described the institution of four employee representatives given seats on the board of directors for Western Airlines. Management traded these seats for concessions from four unions in 1984. Wever described how the different dynamics within each of the unions and between the unions and the company influenced their reactions to a merger between Western Airlines and Delta Airlines. The author argued that the success of such programs depends on the security of the union, its strategic vision, and its power in regard to the company.

A personal account of being a worker representative on the board of directors of Hyatt-Clark is presented by Woodworth (1984). He described a series of stages that he and the other worker representatives went through, from quiet participation, to protest, and finally to growing strain and conflict with the rest of the board. Hyatt-Clark later declared Chapter 11 bankruptcy, and creditors (including the union) lost millions (Woodworth, 1988).

Hammer et al. (1991; Hammer & Stern, 1983) examined worker representatives on a variety of company boards in American firms. They first presented a model showing how management and labor will influence the roles of worker representatives. The authors then developed several hypotheses from their model and tested them with a sample of 38 employee directors from 14 firms. Their results indicated that worker-directors preferred greater labor advocacy than the traditional directors, that labor advocacy was correlated with role conflict among worker-directors, and that worker constituents tended to evaluate worker-directors in terms of their labor advocacy. However, there was no indication that management attempted to train (and socialize) worker-directors to take less of an advocacy role or that labor advocacy would lead to pressure from the rest of the board.

A number of authors have argued that the participative programs in Europe could be adopted with success in the United States (McIsaac, 1977; Mroczkowski, 1983; Weiler, 1990), while others have argued that such attempts would not be very effective (Alkhafaji, 1987; Soutar, 1973). Kovach, Sands, and Brooks (1980) pointed out that labor groups are uncertain about issues like codetermination, while management tends to be uniformly opposed. Levitan and Werneke (1984) made the point that worker participation in Europe is based on political ideals, not on economic or labor-management models. On the one hand, both management and labor leaders have been reluctant to push this approach. On the other hand, some authors (e.g., Ackoff, 1981, 1989) have pushed for this type of (non-legislated) board structure. Overall, there is little to indicate that employee representatives on boards of directors in the United States are likely to become common.

Summary

The research on the various forms of representative participation has not demonstrated many effects. Although worker representatives on the board of directors would seem, on the face of it, to be a powerful form of employee involvement, there are few indications that it has any type of impact. Works councils have been mandated with relatively strong powers. However, the available evidence suggests that they are dominated by management and have little impact on employees or the organization. Yugoslavia's self-management was clearly the most ambitious, the most radical attempt to give power to the employees. Yet even this experiment has shown few effects. As one writer put it, "There has invariably been a gulf between the theoretical and actual functioning of works councils in Europe" (Davies, 1978, p. 133).

Overall, there seems to be little impact from these approaches to representative participation on the organizations involved. Unfortunately most of the research focuses on economic outcomes, often summarizing across a variety of industries or across several years. It is unclear whether a single factor, such as the presence of codetermination or a works council, would have an effect powerful enough to be noticed through the noise of other factors. Despite this caveat, the preponderance of research, both economic and behavioral, suggests small or insignificant effects.

Representative Participation
Versus Direct Involvement

In addition to research on the variety of indirect participation programs described above, a small literature directly compares direct and indirect involvement. These studies generally compare individuals who are experiencing direct involvement (e.g., participation on a works council or union-management committee) to those who are indirectly involved (communicate with those on councils or committees). As such, these studies provide a quasi-experimental comparison of the indirect involvement described in this chapter to the other, more direct forms of employee involvement. The findings are summarized in Table 6.2.

The members of the workers councils and management boards in Yugoslavia were compared to the other workers by Obradovic (1970). He surveyed 537 workers in 20 factories, comparing representatives and nonrepresentatives in factories using three levels of technology. After controlling for gender and level of education, Obradovic found that worker representatives had significantly higher work satisfaction, satisfaction with wages, satisfaction with physical working conditions, and control over how their jobs are performed. However, these findings varied according to the level of technology. In addition, worker representatives had significantly greater work alienation but were no different from nonrepresentatives in perceptions of promotional opportunities. The findings suggest that worker representatives are influenced by their participation, but there is no consistent pattern.

An interesting comparison of direct and indirect participation was presented by Juralewicz (1974), who experimentally manipulated participation in a Puerto Rican clothing factory. Three groups of four to seven members were assigned randomly to different levels of participation. One group frequently met directly with management to discuss changes in job procedures and work production. The second group had representatives meet with management and discuss these changes. The third group was simply informed about the changes. In contrast to the other studies reviewed

Table 6.2 Findings of Studies Comparing Representative and Direct Involvement

Study	Findings
Obradovic (1970)	More positive findings with direct involvement on most, but not all, job attitudes
Juralewicz (1974)	Representative involvement produced higher productivity than direct involvement, but no differences on attitudes
Nurick (1982)	More positive attitudes for direct versus representative involvement
Macy, Peterson, & Norton (1989)	Greater influence and more positive attitudes for direct versus representative involvement
Cooke (1990a)	Team-based QWL programs (direct involvement) were more effective than committee-based programs (representative)
Witt & Brkovic (1989)	Type of involvement is a moderator of employee attitudes
Hespe & Wall (1976)	Workers desire direct involvement for local issues and representative involvement for policy issues
Dickson (1980)	Direct involvement seen as more valuable than representative involvement
Lavy (1984)	Direct involvement associated with positive outcomes, and representative involvement with negative outcomes.
Lammers, Meurs, & Mijs (1987)	Direct and representative involvement had little impact on each other

here, the indirect form of participation (representatives) led to greater increases in productivity than direct participation or little participation. No significant effects were found in terms of job attitudes.

Nurick (1982) compared the impact of a quality of work life (QWL) program (see Chapter 3) on those directly involved with a QWL program to those only indirectly involved. Those respondents who were directly involved in the QWL project demonstrated significant increases during the period of the program (4 years) in job satisfaction, job involvement, trust, and a wide variety of influence measures. The indirect respondents (affected by the program but not directly involved) showed increases in several influence measures but few effects on the job attitudes.

In another test of direct versus indirect employee involvement, Macy, Peterson, and Norton (1989) examined the impact of a quality of work life (QWL) program (also reported in Chapter 3). The authors compared individuals directly involved with the

QWL program, as well as individuals at the same site but not involved in the program, with employees from another location. They found that respondents involved in the project reported positive increases in quality of work life, work environment, and interpersonal and structured participation. In addition, they reported increases in influence within several domains. The employees at the same plant (indirect participation) demonstrated some of these changes (in comparison to the control site), but not to the same extent as the direct involvement employees.

In a study of joint union-management programs, Cooke (1990a) examined the impact of employee involvement on employee-supervisor relations. In his analysis of 92 American plants, he compared team-based involvement programs and committee-based programs. The team-based programs provided direct involvement for employees, while the committee-based programs provided indirect, representative participation. Cooke's results (also reported in Chapter 3) indicated that the presence of teams was significantly and positively related to employee-supervisor relations. The representative participation (committee-based programs), however, had no impact on relations.

Workers' council members and nonmembers in Yugoslavia were compared by Witt and Brkovic (1989). These authors surveyed 134 employees of a tool factory, 25 of whom were members of the workers' council. Measures in the survey included job satisfaction and organizational commitment. The results indicated that members of the workers' council had a different pattern of attitudes. For example, perceived participation norms were more highly correlated with organizational commitment for council members than for other employees. The authors interpreted the results as suggesting that one's role (member or nonmember of the council) in self-management is an important moderator of employee attitudes.

In addition to these explicit comparisons of direct and indirect involvement, several studies have examined how the two forms of involvement are interrelated. A classic review of direct versus indirect involvement is presented by Hespe and Wall (1976). These authors reviewed the conceptual literature and pointed out that although employees may desire participation, it is not clear that they equally desire all forms of participation. They reviewed the literature up to that point and concluded that the evidence concerning indirect participation is insufficient. The authors then described 14 studies for which they examined the degree of participation, as well as the level of participation desired in local (day-to-day work decisions), medium (decisions affecting a department or group), and distant levels (top-management policy decisions). The findings indicated that workers feel they should have a great deal of input at the local level, less at the medium level, and the least amount of input at the distant level. In addition, the employees desired direct participation in situations involving local and medium participation and representative participation in distant decisions. The reactions toward participation also were moderated by individual and organizational differences.

In an interesting study of how direct and indirect participation interrelate, Dickson (1980) interviewed 77 top managers and 26 top shop stewards from 31 companies in Scotland. The purpose of the research was to determine how the two types of employee participation interact: Are they independent, complementary, or do they covary together? The results indicated that direct participation was seen as significantly more valuable than indirect participation by both managers and shop stewards but that the shop stewards were more positive about indirect participation. In addition, the evaluations of both types of participation were related, so an individual who perceived one as valuable would also be likely to perceive the other as valuable. The managers indicated that the two forms of participation are very dissimilar processes and therefore cannot be substituted for each other. The shop stewards, however, perceived them as equivalent in terms of outcomes and, therefore, substitutable.

Lavy (1984) surveyed 272 managerial and nonmanagerial employees about their perceptions direct and indirect participation. He found that direct participation tended to be associated with positive outcomes, such as perceived influence and greater acceptance of company policy. Indirect participation, however, was associated with negative outcomes, such as slow decision making and superiors not wanting to take responsibility.

Lammers, Meurs, & Mijs (1987) examined how direct participation interrelated with indirect participation (via works councils) in Dutch firms. These authors were interested in determining whether direct (shopfloor) participation would affect representative participation. They assessed the amount of direct employee participation in 16 firms and 14 hospitals in the Netherlands and

Belgium. In addition, they asked respondents to evaluate the amount of influence of the works councils. Lammers et al. (1987) found that, in general, the estimations of direct and indirect participation were independent, with each form of participation having little impact on the other.

Summary

Like the earlier research, the findings comparing representative and direct involvement indicate that indirect participation has little or no impact on the individuals or the organization. The most interesting comparisons are those between the representatives of the employees and the employees who are represented. Although effects are found for the representatives (who experience direct participation), these effects do not generalize to the remainder of the employees.

Comparative Research Across Nations

Although a great deal of research has described individual examples of representative participation around the world (Strauss, 1982), very little of it has examined *differences* across national boundaries. Because there are so many varieties of legislated representative participation, we would expect significant differences across countries. This section reviews the studies that examined such differences.

One comparative study comes out of the international research project on decision making in organizations (Decisions in Organizations [DIO], 1979; Heller, Drenth, Koopman, & Rus, 1977, 1988; Koopman et al., 1981). These researchers compared representative participation across Great Britain, Yugoslavia, and the Netherlands.

In their research the DIO group used a common methodology based on the Influence Power Continuum, a scale that outlines six possible levels of employee participation in decision making. More specifically, employees were asked to indicate whether management gave them (1) no information, (2) fairly detailed information, (3) opportunities to give advice, (4) opportunities to give advice that is taken into consideration, (5) joint decision making, or (6) complete control. The respondents were asked how much influence they had on operational issues, tactical issues, and strategic issues. The authors had several hypotheses concerning how sharing influence might lead to more positive attitudes and other outcomes for lower level employees.

In their studies the researchers compared perceptions of participation across seven companies and three countries. They found that the level of participation varied from Level 2 to Level 3. In general, employees were given detailed information and sometimes had opportunities to give advice. The highest levels of participation were found in Yugoslavian companies. Although the Netherlands requires works councils, few differences were found between the Dutch and British companies, except the British showed more variation. In addition, the degree of influence overall was higher for decisions involving personnel problems and worker conditions than for decisions dealing with production and standards.

A second multinational research project was conducted by the Industrial Democracy in Europe Research Group (IDE, 1979, 1981b, 1981c). IDE examined participation practices in 12 European countries to determine whether these varying practices had an impact on patterns of decision making and influence sharing. In this research the authors distinguished between de jure participation, which is the formal (written) description of how the participation is supposed to exist, and de facto participation, which describes how the participation actually existed. IDE surveyed a total of 134 organizations, involving nearly 9,000 interviews. In these interviews they investigated who influenced decisions in 16 areas.

The authors found that although de jure participation varied considerably across national borders, de facto participation varied little. The actual perceived influence of workers was similar and low, with the modest exception of Yugoslavia. The data showed that, in general, workers felt they had little influence over their work, with Yugoslavian workers perceiving somewhat greater influence. The differences across countries were minor (about 1 point on a 5-point scale), compared with the differences in influence between workers and management (about 2 to 3 points on a 5-point scale). Worker representation bodies (such as works councils) had little impact on these perceptions.

The IDE (1981b) also examined how the workers evaluated the various forms of representative participation across the 14 countries. They found that the respondents generally had positive attitudes concerning the consequences of the representative participation, with virtually no differences between workers, forepersons, and middle managers. Differences across the various countries were modest, with the Yugoslavian and West German respondents the most satisfied and the Israelis the least satisfied.

Tannenbaum, Kavcic, Rosner, Vianello, and Wieser (1974) compared 52 industrial plants in five countries: Yugoslavia, Israel, the United States, Italy, and Austria. The authors compared the plants in terms of the influence of various groups (board, managers, workers). They found that the Yugoslavian system and the Israeli kibbutz tended to be more participative than those in the other countries, although the differences were not dramatic. Plants in the other three countries did not vary as much, although American plants tended to have more participation than the Austrian plants, which in turn had greater participation than the Italian plants. In addition, American and Israeli plants tended to have more informal participation than those in the other countries.

In taking a somewhat different perspective, Cotton, McFarlin, and Sweeney (in press) and McFarlin, Sweeney, and Cotton (in press) examined how the values and assumptions of managers in different countries influence the form (direct vs. indirect) of participation. These authors interviewed and surveyed managers in the same organization across four different countries: the United States, the Netherlands, Great Britain, and Spain. Although facilities in the four countries had similar products and nearly identical technology, the managers approached employee involvement in very different ways. Three major themes emerged from the interviews: basic philosophy, degree of emphasis on formal programs, and orientation toward the individual.

Basic philosophy referred to why the managers would support employee involvement. In northern Europe, participation is seen as a goal, not as a *means* toward a goal. Management therefore has no motivation to provide opportunities for participation beyond those already required by law. Where participation programs existed, the American approach was much more formal, long term, and programmatic than the European efforts. The European managers, in contrast, tended to favor a more informal, *evolutionary* approach in which changes were made in small increments. Finally, the American managers focused on programs that were intended to apply across the board to all workers in a particular unit. The European managers almost universally focused on individual differences as a moderator; that is, such efforts would be successful with the *right* manager and the *right* employees.

Summary

The findings across the national boundaries indicate that, despite the variety of laws legislating worker involvement, few differences actually exist. With the exception of Yugoslavia, there is little variation across nations, despite some countries (Germany, the Netherlands) requiring both works councils and board representatives, while other countries (Great Britain, the United States), require nothing. Although Yugoslavia did demonstrate greater influence among the workers, it must be emphasized that these levels were, nevertheless, modest and that the gain was small. The differences that do exist across nations seem to be more in terms of how participation is viewed.

Implementation of Representative Participation

Because most examples of representative participation have been legislated by national governments, little has been written about how to implement this form of employee involvement. However, there have been a few discussions.

With the changes that will be occurring in Europe in the future, two issues become clear. Should employee participation be required throughout the unified Europe, and what form should that participation take? Various proposals contemplate requiring some form of codetermination for all large companies across Europe (BNA, 1991; Kapstein, Riemer, & Melcher, 1990).

Schloss (1990) examined the involvement practices in Germany, France, and the United Kingdom to assess what changing one of these forms might mean for the United Kingdom. She found that although a single form might be required across the country, board of director representation and works councils can take different forms across different companies or plants. For most sites the works council handles day-to-day issues, while the labor union and worker representatives are involved with long-range issues. One difficulty with the councils is finding employees, especially white-collar employees, to participate. Many councils are having to fill some council positions with full-time representatives. This is especially true for the position of chair for councils in larger companies.

The only other article to deal with implementation issues of worker councils is that of Knowles (1989), who focused on the use of employee councils for small companies. In his report the author argued that small businesses can benefit from the assistance of a council to explain and promote programs to the work force. Knowles recommended fair representation, commitment from top management, and sufficient information as the keys for such councils to be successful.

One common problem with worker representatives on the board of directors is that the representatives often are unprepared for their roles. It is unrealistic to expect employees to be able to move from their ordinary jobs to the board without some type of training. Although some countries (e.g., Sweden and Norway) provide training for worker-directors, most directors feel unprepared for their new positions (Stern, 1988).

One difficulty with both board representation and works councils is the place of the labor union. Ramondt (1987) described how the Dutch have established essentially a dual system, with the unions operating independently of the works councils. Backhaus (1987) gave an example of the problem of combining the labor union with codetermination. As described earlier, the British Post Office gave union representatives half of the seats on its corporate board in 1978. In reaction to this, a number of managers began to weaken the position of the board by reducing their communication with the board. The experiment was a failure, partly because the unions had to fulfill two very separate roles (Backhaus, 1987).

A final issue with the implementation of representative participation (or any other form of employee involvement) is the context of national differences. Managers and employees across different countries have different perspectives and assumptions about employee participation (Cotton et al., in press; McFarlin et al., in press). Therefore, representative participation is probably more effective in some cultures than in others. Erez (1986) tested these types of differences among supervisors in Israel. She found that direct participation was more effective among the kibbutz, while indirect involvement was more effective in the public sector. The implication is that the culture of the organization (and society) may well determine whether representative participation or direct employee involvement would be better.

Regardless of the culture, reports indicate that when representative participation is mixed with other forms of involvement (e.g., board representation and work redesign in Scandinavia), success seems more likely (Jain & Giles, 1985). It seems reasonable, therefore, that adding other forms of employee involvement to representative participation would be more effective than assuming that the representative participation will thrive alone.

Overall Conclusions

The intention of the legislation in Western Europe has been to integrate worker interests into organizational decision making (T. H. Hammer, personal communication, March 26, 1992). Its effectiveness in terms of these goals is not addressed in this chapter. If the intention is to improve employee attitudes and/or productivity, the findings concerning representative participation indicate that this approach to employee involvement is not very fruitful. As Warner (1976) commented over 15 years ago, "mere forms are *not* sufficient in themselves to guarantee 'real' workers' control . . . the problems of 'alienation' in the work force cannot be magically solved by simply installing workers' councils" (p. 404). Warner argued for a "contingency theory of industrial democracy, with appropriate organizational designs for each national-contingency setting" (p. 405). I have to agree.

Representative participation as a method to improve attitudes or productivity has two basic problems. First, it is clear that attempts to increase employee influence through national legislation are not effective. As one critic of the Yugoslavian experiment in self-management commented, "Free and equal participation in decision making does not mean equal influence in decision making. No system of self-management, no matter how perfectly conceived and strictly implemented in practice, can provide equal influence of all employees in the distribution of social power" (quoted in Warner, 1990, pp. 26-27).

Second, even if overall employee influence is increased through representation, there is no evidence that any positive effects trickle down to the individual employees. Even where employee representatives may have significant employee power, this power has little impact on the employees being represented.

Overall, then, it appears that the greatest value of representative participation is symbolic. If one is interested in changing employee attitudes or in improving organizational performance, representative participation would be a poor choice.

7 Job Enrichment

Most of the methods described in this volume require changing systems. Whether they be quality of work life programs, gainsharing programs, or works councils, they require that entire organizations, or at least plants or departments, be altered. Job enrichment, on the other hand, can involve only a single job performed by one individual. In this sense it is the most "micro" approach to be discussed. Because of this micro focus, several of the other approaches (quality of work life, self-directed work teams) typically incorporate some job enrichment in their programs. In fact, Rousseau (1977) discussed a synthesis between job design and sociotechnical systems.

I do not attempt to review all aspects of job design. There is too much to include in just one chapter. More comprehensive reviews can be found in Aldag and Brief (1979), Davis and Taylor (1979), Griffin (1982), and Hackman and Oldham (1980). As the title of this chapter indicates, I focus on job enrichment—redesigning jobs to provide greater participation and greater involvement. In this way the job itself produces internal motivation and job satisfaction (Hackman & Oldham, 1980). I do not discuss industrial engineering, human factors, or physiology (e.g., Campion, 1988; Campion & Thayer, 1985). Therefore, this chapter focuses narrowly on just one aspect of job design.

In Dachler and Wilpert's (1978) typology, job enrichment is formal involvement because job enrichment is a conscious effort to increase the autonomy and responsibility of job incumbents. It falls within the direct involvement category, as the participation is face to face. The level of influence, or access, is high; a major part of enriching jobs is providing autonomy within the jobs. Finally, the social range is small because individual jobs, not departments or entire plants, are enriched. This is not to say that many people would not be involved, because thousands could have the same job. However, the change could influence a single employee.

In contrast to most of the other chapters in this book, this chapter focuses on theoretical models and empirical tests of those models. The other approaches to employee involvement typically have been inductive, with models developed to explain managerial practices. With job enrichment, however, theoretical models like those of Herzberg and Hackman and Oldham have served to stimulate research and practice. Because of this impetus, there probably has been more research concerning job enrichment, especially carefully designed, academically respectable research, than any of the other approaches to job involvement. Therefore the chapter is organized around the major theoretical models, and an impressive amount of research is reviewed.

Job Enrichment at AT&T

In the late 1960s a group of researchers decided to change the way many workers at AT&T experienced their jobs.[6] Over a period of several years, they enriched dozens of different jobs, increasing the autonomy, responsibility, and feedback for thousands of workers. They carefully compared what happened with these workers and found that the job enrichment produced a variety of positive outcomes.

Concerned with high turnover among their personnel, management at AT&T decided to follow the ideas of Frederick Herzberg and enrich those jobs where the problems seemed worst. Although the company was following the theory of Herzberg and the studies predated the job characteristics model developed by Hackman, Oldham, and Lawler, the actions that it took would fit the latter model as well.

What did management do to the jobs? Consider the responsibility of answering complaints to the phone company. Previously this assignment had been as routine and simple as possible. Each correspondent would receive letters to answer from the supervisor, write out responses (following careful and detailed guidelines), and give them to the supervisor to check and mail out. The jobs were changed in a number of ways. Correspondents were told to sign their own names to their letters (this had been done before only for highly experienced workers). The work of more experienced workers was reviewed less frequently than before by the supervisor. All workers were told that they would be held fully accountable for the quality of their work. Production (the number of letters produced) was discussed only in general terms. Correspondents were encouraged to answer the letters in their own way, rather than following the form-letter approach. Particular individuals were appointed as "experts" on certain subjects and were available for others to consult about their area of expertise.

What impact did these changes have on the workers and their work? After an initial drop (for 2 months), customer satisfaction increased significantly and remained above previous levels. Both turnover and absenteeism dropped. In addition, substantial cost savings were achieved.

Another job, that of compiling phone directories, is certainly not an exciting duty. This tedium was confirmed by the fact that turnover on this task approached 100% a year. Prior to the job enrichment, clerks working on the directories would have their work repeatedly verified by other clerks. After the job enrichment change, the more experienced employees checked their own work. In addition, certain clerks were asked whether they would like to focus on just one directory and to follow through on all the steps necessary for "their" directory. The clerks talked directly to salespeople, to the printer, and to other departments. Where the directory was too large for one person, individuals were assigned letters of the alphabet and treated "their" letters as their own directory.

These changes in the directory clerks' jobs produced several positive outcomes. First, the clerks developed more positive attitudes about their work. Second, because of the improvements in productivity, only half the work force was necessary to accomplish the same work.

Overall, these experiments in job enrichment were received positively by top management at AT&T. In fact, some experiments were so successful that they were terminated early and were spread to additional jobs. The success of the formal experiments generated hundreds of additional projects involving thousands more enriched jobs. The workers and AT&T were extremely happy with the job changes and what was produced.

Herzberg and Other Early Research on Job Enrichment

In a thumbnail sketch of the history of job design, Griffin (1987) described the major phases as focusing on job specialization (Frederick W. Taylor), job enlargement in the early 1950s, job enrichment and Herzberg in the late 1950s, the job characteristics model of the 1970s and 1980s, and the information processing perspective of the late 1970s. Several of these models focus on job design, not employee involvement or participation. Therefore, I concentrate primarily on Herzberg's two-factor model of job enrichment and the job characteristics model of Hackman and Oldham.

Herzberg's motivation-hygiene theory, or two-factor theory, came out of an extensive study on job attitudes by Herzberg, Mausner, and Snyderman (1959). These authors found that the processes producing satisfaction are very different from those causing dissatisfaction. They concluded that satisfaction and dissatisfaction are not simply opposite ends of the same continuum, but are separate phenomena. Therefore, one concern might produce satisfaction, but the absence of it would not necessarily produce dissatisfaction.

In his research, Herzberg developed lists of factors (motivators) that lead to satisfaction and other lists (hygiene factors) that lead to dissatisfaction (Herzberg, 1966). In general, the motivators tend to be related to recognition, achievement, responsibility, and the work itself. The hygiene factors tend to include the context in which the job occurs, such as company policy, administrative practices, supervision, and interpersonal relations (Miner, 1980). For example, pay (a hygiene factor) might be claimed as a cause of dissatisfaction, but recognition (not higher pay) would be cited as an antecedent of satisfaction.

Herzberg (1968) argued that trying to motivate workers with hygiene factors (e.g., pay, work conditions) is inherently ineffectual because it requires escalating the rewards. As workers become accustomed to the pay and working conditions, an increase in these conditions is required to maintain the positive reactions. This increase leads to a continual racheting up of these factors. In contrast, a responsible, challenging job with recognition can continue to be motivating, as the responsibility and challenge will not dissipate. However, activation theory (Scott, 1966) posits that the impact of job enrichment dissipates over time, therefore requiring repeated enrichment (Gardner, 1990; Gardner & Cummings, 1988).

Research on the Two-Factor Theory

The research originally conducted by Herzberg and his associates (Herzberg et al., 1959) consisted of asking subjects to describe a time when they felt exceptionally good or exceptionally bad about their jobs (p. 35). In addition, the impact of these attitudes was assessed on such outcomes as performance, social relationships, and attitudes about the organization.

The data collected by Herzberg et al. (1959) showed that intrinsic job characteristics (achievement, responsibility, recognition) were related to experiences of satisfaction and that contextual factors (pay, supervision, working conditions) were related to experiences of dissatisfaction. Perceptions of satisfaction, in turn, were related to improvements in performance.

In their assessment of quality of work life programs, Cummings and Molloy (1977) reviewed 28 studies involving the restructuring of jobs, most coming from out of Herzberg's two-factor theory. Although some of the studies involved changes in the reward systems, organizational structure, or group process, the major changes were in terms of autonomy, task variety, and feedback. Of the 24 studies that assessed some aspect of performance (e.g., quality, costs, productivity), 16 found a majority of positive results, 7 had evenly mixed results, and only 1 reported no positive results. Of the 21 studies examining job attitudes, 15 found positive results, 4 found mixed or null results, and 2 found mixed and negative results.

In the years since Herzberg et al.'s research, a number of studies (e.g., Herzberg, 1966; Hinton, 1968; House & Wigdor, 1967; Paul, Robertson, & Herzberg, 1969; Schwab & Heneman, 1970) have replicated their methodology. Although positive results from job enrichment have been found (e.g., Davis & Cherns, 1975; Ford,

1969, 1973; Maher & Overbagh, 1971), criticisms of the two-factor theory led authors to try alternative approaches to testing the theory. These efforts have been generally unsuccessful (Miner, 1980).

In addition to the lack of positive findings, there have been criticisms of Herzberg's two-factor theory, as well as research supporting it (Hinton, 1968; House & Wigdor, 1967; King, 1970). The major theoretical (and empirical) criticism is that the two-factor theory oversimplifies the relationships between job characteristics and job attitudes. A primary example is the inability to distinguish completely between motivators and hygiene factors. Pay, for example, typically is seen as a hygiene factor, yet pay can be used as a means of recognition, a motivator. A related criticism is that the theory has not been stated in explicit terms, so multiple versions of the theory exist (King, 1970).

Most of the criticisms of the two-factor theory are concerns about its methodology. Vroom (1964) argued that Herzberg's methodology introduces a self-presentation bias into the results. Most of the motivators that Herzberg found were factors internal to the job or the job incumbent (e.g., responsibility, achievement), while most of the hygiene factors were external, provided by the organization. As Vroom pointed out, people generally attribute positive things to themselves and negative aspects to others. Therefore, it would be expected that respondents would tend to attribute good experiences to internal factors and bad experiences to external factors. A second methodological problem is the amount of interpretation required of the rater. Because of this measure, a rater's hypothesis might have more impact on the data than the respondent's perceptions (House & Wigdor, 1967, p. 372).

Other Research on Job Enrichment

Existing concurrent with Herzberg's two-factor theory was a relatively diverse literature on job enrichment. Definitions were not clear (Schwab & Cummings, 1976), and a number of terms were employed interchangeably (e.g., *job enlargement, task complexity, job enrichment, job scope*). For the most part the terms have referred to both horizontal expansion (adding tasks), as well as vertical expansion (adding responsibility; Lawler, 1986).

Herzberg et al. (1959) began one stream of research on the two-factor theory, while Turner and Lawrence (1965) began a different stream, focusing on job attributes and individual differences. These authors developed the Requisite Task Attributes Index (RTA) for measuring these attributes, based on six job attributes: variety, autonomy, responsibility, required interaction with others, optional interaction with others, and knowledge and skills required. These job attributes, plus the social organization (consisting of emergent norms and values), would determine worker responses (p. 11).

Turner and Lawrence examined these predictions on workers in 47 different jobs. Although they found a relationship between the task attributes and absenteeism, there was no effect for job satisfaction. The authors investigated further and found strong links between task attributes and both outcomes for workers in small towns but no effects for workers in large cities. Turner and Lawrence hypothesized that this difference might be due to greater alienation from work that can be found in the city culture.

Turner and Lawrence's book generated considerable interest and research (e.g., Susman, 1973), the first review of this literature being conducted by Hulin and Blood (1968). Their review of the existing literature indicated that a simple relationship between job enrichment and job satisfaction is not well supported. Building on Turner and Lawrence's ideas, Hulin and Blood proposed a more complex model, in which the relationship between the job and satisfaction depended on individual factors, such as norms about work. Workers from small towns with middle-class work norms would respond positively to enriched jobs, but workers from urban areas without this Protestant work ethic would be frustrated by these types of jobs.

Pierce and Dunham (1976) reviewed the literature from Hulin and Blood through 1975. In their paper, Pierce and Dunham summarized research on simple effects of job enrichment, as well as research examining interactions between job enrichment and individual factors and research examining interactions between job enrichment and other (organizational) variables. Their summary of studies that actually manipulated the design of jobs concluded that positive effects were found but that the possibility of Hawthorne effects or other problems in conclusions was high. The review of individual differences found evidence that they are related to reactions to job enrichment. The authors also expressed concerns about how job characteristics were measured.

Steers and Mowday (1977) reviewed a variety of conceptual models concerning task design, including Herzberg's two-factor model, Turner and Lawrence's (1965) model, the job characteristics model, and others. They concluded that major conceptual and empirical problems remained in the two-factor model and in Turner and Lawrence's model. They also determined that the job characteristics model had been supported in terms of job attitudes but not performance.

Summary

The general consensus within the academic community seems to be that Herzberg's two-factor model was interesting but not accurate. Several problems exist in the model itself. First, it is difficult to conceptually or empirically differentiate motivators from hygiene factors. Second, social desirability issues would tend to predict that people would choose internal factors as motivators and external factors as hygiene factors. Third, the model does not address the issue of individual differences; not everyone wants enriched jobs.

Although the model may not have been accurate, it was effective in stimulating research concerning job enrichment. Several points can be made about this research. First, a large number of successful case studies demonstrate the impact of job enrichment on attitudes and performance. However, most of this research falls into the "anecdotal story" classification, without pretests or comparison groups. Second, the research forced investigators to realize that individual differences exist in reactions to job enrichment. Not all people want to have a challenging, responsible job; some people want boring jobs with no accountability. All of this research served to set the stage for the job characteristics model and the explosion of research it stimulated in the 1970s and 1980s.

Hackman and Oldham's Job Characteristics Model

One of the best known and certainly most thoroughly tested models of job enrichment is that of Hackman and Oldham (Hackman & Lawler, 1971; Hackman & Oldham, 1975, 1976, 1980; Hackman, Oldham, Janson, & Purdy, 1975). Although more complete sum-

Job Characteristics Model

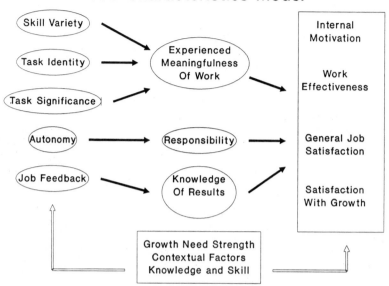

Figure 7.1. Job Characteristics Model

maries of the model can be found in the references above, a brief overview is presented here.

Hackman and Oldham posited that the degree to which jobs are motivating can be assessed through five core job characteristics: skill variety, task identity, task significance, autonomy, and job feedback (see Figure 7.1). *Skill variety* refers to the degree to which a job requires a variety of different activities. *Task identity* is the degree to which the job requires completion of a whole, identifiable piece of work. *Task significance* is the extent to which the job has a substantial impact on others. *Autonomy* is the limit to which the job provides substantial freedom, independence, and discretion. *Job feedback* describes the degree to which carrying out the work activities provides the individual with direct and clear information about his or her performance (Kulik, Oldham, & Hackman, 1987).

To the extent that a job contains these five characteristics, three psychological states are produced: experienced meaningfulness of the work, experienced responsibility for outcomes of the work, and knowledge of the actual results of the work activities. To the degree that these psychological states are present, high internal work motivation exists. As a caveat to this general model, Hackman and Oldham (1980) also included three moderating variables: knowledge and skill, growth need strength, and contextual satisfaction. The above model will prove effective only to the extent that the individual has the knowledge and skill to do the task, has the desire for interesting and challenging jobs (high growth need strength), and is satisfied with the external aspects of the job (pay, working conditions, supervision, etc.).

There has been a great deal of discussion of the model, and a large number of empirical studies have examined the model. The number of studies is remarkable, considering the general paucity of empirical research concerning the other forms of employee involvement. This richness of research is due primarily to the fact that Hackman and Oldham (1975) developed a questionnaire to measure the various aspects of their model and the fact that the model focuses on perceptions about jobs, rather than objective differences. Therefore, it is relatively easy to test the model by comparing across different people and different jobs.

Literature Reviews
of Job Enrichment Outcomes

A number of authors have reviewed the literature concerning the job characteristics model. Although the reviews often focused on different aspects of the theory or on methodological issues, I summarize them together to give an overview of the research on this model.

Griffin, Welsh, and Moorhead (1981) reviewed the research concerning job characteristics and performance. They found that the outcomes of 13 studies were contradictory. Part of the difficulty was that no two studies measured performance in the same fashion. The authors argued that even if the findings had been consistent, the variety of performance measures would have made any conclusions suspect.

In a comparison of four methods of motivating performance, Locke, Feren, McCaleb, Shaw, and Denny (1980) reviewed 13 studies of job enrichment. These were all of the studies they could find that did not combine job enrichment with other factors (such as technology, incentives, selection, training, etc.). The authors found that the median percentage of performance improvement in these studies was 17%. Improvements in performance were found in 92% of the sample. When the methodologically poorer studies were removed, the median improvement dropped to 8.75%. These findings were comparable to their results for goal setting as a means to improve performance but were worse than those of money as a motivator.

Kopelman (1985) reviewed the results of 30 interventions of job enlargement and enrichment, focusing on their impact on a variety of outcomes. He found a median increase in productivity of 6.4%; however, 11 of the 30 studies measuring productivity found negative or null effects. The author also found that as more job characteristics were changed, the effect on productivity grew. A comparison with examples of job simplification found that job simplification produced performance improvements comparable with job enrichment. Absenteeism was examined in nine studies of job enrichment, with an average improvement of 14.5%. Satisfaction was measured in 24 experiments, with improvements reported in 20 of the studies. Kopelman also registered concern with the durability of these effects, noting declines in some studies continuing over 1 year.

The most comprehensive review of the job characteristics model was conducted by Fried and Ferris (1987), who reviewed nearly 200 studies. Weak (but often significant) relationships were found between job characteristics and job performance and absenteeism. Other analyses indicated that the various job characteristics demonstrated moderate to strong relationships with overall job satisfaction and internal work motivation.

A meta-analysis of research examining the relationship between job characteristics and job satisfaction was performed by Loher, Noe, Moeller, and Fitzgerald (1985). (Meta-analysis is a statistical method for summarizing a large number of similar studies.) These authors combined the data from 24 studies to find an overall correlations between .32 to .46, averaging about .39.

In a meta-analysis of several types of organizational development interventions, Neuman, Edwards, and Raju (1989) examined the impact of job enrichment on overall job satisfaction and other job attitudes. The authors summarized 20 findings from seven studies involving more than 1,400 subjects. Their analyses demonstrated a corrected mean correlation between satisfaction and job enrichment of .27 and between other attitudes and job enrichment of .11. These findings were weaker than those of most of the other interventions that were reviewed.

Fried (1991) examined the relationship between measures of job characteristics on the Job Diagnostic Survey (JDS) and various outcome measures of performance and/or satisfaction. The number of samples and the number of subjects employed in the analyses varied across the different measures of job characteristics, but at least eight samples and 1,000 subjects were examined in each analysis. The results suggest a reliable link between the measures of the job characteristics and job satisfaction and a less reliable link between these measures and work performance.

The reviews tend to find positive, but not overwhelming, links between job characteristics and job satisfaction. Weaker results typically are found between job characteristics and performance or other behavioral outcomes (absenteeism and turnover). However, because of my more specific aim in this chapter, I present a review of selected studies.

Selected Job Enrichment Studies

Studies of the job characteristics model are too numerous to review them all in this chapter. In addition, most of the research is cross-sectional and correlational, comparing the reactions of people in different jobs. As Wall and Martin (1987) pointed out, there is still a need for field experimental studies. Therefore, I restrict my review to those studies examining actual jobs in real organizations, not laboratory studies. I also restrict it to studies involving either some type of intervention to change jobs or a longitudinal study where jobs were changed (some being enriched) for other reasons. Finally I include only those studies with a pretest-posttest design or (preferably) some type of quasi-control group. Many case studies of job enrichment exist (e.g., Ford, 1973; Weed, 1971); however, their methodology is problematic at best (Fein, 1974). These restrictions reduce the number of studies considerably. The results of the selected studies are summarized in Table 7.1.

The jobs of quality inspectors in an electronics factory were enriched in a study by Maher and Overbagh (1971). Attitudes and performance were measured 3 months before the change and

Table 7.1 Selected Studies of Job Enrichment

	Findings			
Study	*Job enrichment*	*Job attitudes*	*Performance*	*Absenteeism*
Maher & Overbagh (1971)		+	0	
Lawler, Hackman, & Kaufman (1973)	+	0 –		
Frank & Hackman (1975)	0	0	0	
Locke, Sirota, & Wolfson (1976)		+ 0	+	+
Hackman, Pearce, & Wolfe (1978)	+	+	0	–
Orpen (1979)	+	+	0	+
Bhagat & Schassie (1980)	+	+		
Griffeth (1985)	+	+		
Luthans, Kemmerer, Paul, & Taylor (1987)	+	+ 0	+	
Rosenbach & Zawacki (1989)	+	+		+
Wall, Corbett, Martin, Clegg, & Jackson (1990)		+	+	
Griffin (1991)	+	+ 0	+	

NOTE: In terms of improving job enrichment, attitudes, performance, and reducing absenteeism, + means improvement, 0 means no change, and – means decrement.

again 9 months after the change. The authors found that satisfaction with aspects of the job and the company improved, while other attributes, such as the physical working conditions, remained unchanged. Improvements in performance also were recorded. More than 1 year after the job enrichment, however, the satisfaction and performance of some inspectors began to drop. In response to this drop, further enrichment of their jobs was carried out, and their attitudes and performance improved. The improvements in job attitudes and performance were observed up to 5 years after the job enrichment.

Lawler, Hackman, and Kaufman (1973) examined the enrichment of telephone operators' jobs. The operators were surveyed about 2 weeks before the changes were made and again 6 months later. Results from the questionnaires indicated that the degree of variety and autonomy of the jobs increased, but no effects were found in terms of general satisfaction, job involvement, or internal motivation. In fact, their satisfaction with making friends on the job *decreased*. Lawler et al. suggested that these effects may have been due to changes in the supervisors' behavior. The supervisors reported decreased feelings of job security after the intervention, and the operators reported that supervisors began to oversupervise their subordinates.

Another interesting example of a job enrichment failure is described by Frank and Hackman (1975). These authors described the change to semiautonomous modules in the stock transfer department of a bank. Although job characteristics were related to job attitudes and performance, implementation of modules produced no change in perceived job characteristics or in job attitudes or performance. Management thought they were making major modifications, but the jobs themselves changed very little.

Locke, Sirota, and Wolfson (1976) described a job enrichment intervention in a government agency. Several units within the agency had their jobs enriched, while matched control units had no changes in their jobs. Locke et al. found that performance increased, turnover and absenteeism decreased, and job attitudes improved for the experimental units versus the control units. In spite of these positive results, Locke et al. argued that job enrichment had little impact. They argued that the performance effects were due to a more efficient use of work effort and that the other effects were due to a combination Hawthorne effect (Roethlisberger & Dickson, 1939) and an expectation of extrinsic rewards.

Hackman, Pearce, and Wolfe (1978) studied the impact of job changes carried out on clerical jobs in a bank. These job changes were stimulated by changes in technology, and the workers and managers involved were not aware of the motivating aspects of the job changes. The authors measured the job characteristics, job attitudes, performance, and absenteeism both 2 months before and 5 months after the intervention. The results showed that individuals who reported their jobs as becoming enriched had increased job satisfaction, while those who reported their jobs as becoming "de-enriched" had decreased satisfaction. Satisfactions with job security, pay, supervision, and co-workers were unaffected by these changes. Performance (rated by supervisors) and absenteeism also were unaffected by the job changes. Contrary to predictions, enriched jobs led to higher absenteeism for individuals who were high in growth need strength.

Orpen (1979) reported a true field experiment where clerical employees in a federal agency were randomly assigned to have their jobs either enriched or unchanged. Orpen assessed the job characteristics, job satisfaction, job involvement, performance, absenteeism, and turnover both before and then 6 months after the intervention. The results indicated that the manipulation altered perceptions of most of the job characteristics of those in the experimental group. In addition, the enriched group demonstrated higher satisfaction, job involvement, and intrinsic motivation, and lower absenteeism and turnover than the control group. However, no effects were found for performance or productivity.

In another naturally occurring quasi-experiment, Bhagat and Schassie (1980) examined the impact of a manufacturing organization going from a 5-day to a 4-day work week. The shortened work week led to changes in the characteristics of many jobs, some becoming more enriched, others becoming less enriched, and others remaining unchanged. Job perceptions were assessed prior to the changes and again 2 months after the change. Respondents were grouped on the basis of their perceptions of job characteristics. The results indicated that general satisfaction and internal work motivation rose for the enriched jobs, dropped with the de-enriched jobs, and did not vary for the unchanged jobs. Other facets of satisfaction (pay, security, supervisor) were unaffected by the changes in the jobs.

Both participation and job enrichment were examined in a study of part-time receptionists by Griffeth (1985). Employing a 2×2 experimental design, the author manipulated both job enrichment and participation. Half of the workers were selected randomly to generate ideas for enriching their jobs. Then half of the workers were selected randomly to employ these ideas to have their jobs enriched. Griffeth found that the enriched jobs were seen as being more enriched and that enrichment also improved several measures of job satisfaction and reduced voluntary turnover. The participation influenced only one measure of satisfaction.

In the only study to examine employee behavior directly, Luthans, Kemmerer, Paul, and Taylor (1987) analyzed the effects of a job enrichment intervention on department store salespersons. In the experimental design, 15 salespersons from three departments had their jobs enriched, while 17 salespersons in three other departments experienced no change. Job attitudes and job perceptions were collected from the experimental group prior to the intervention and again 4 weeks later. After answering the questionnaire for the second time, the experimental salespersons were told that the job enrichment program had ended and that all efforts to change the jobs would cease. Employee responses indicated that the salespersons perceived their jobs to have changed. In addition, observational data were collected on both the enriched and the nonenriched salespersons prior to the intervention, after the intervention, and after the intervention was withdrawn. The observational data showed that functional behaviors of the experimental group increased and that dysfunctional behaviors decreased after the intervention. These behaviors then returned to the baseline after the intervention was withdrawn. The behaviors of the control group showed little change over time. Measures of satisfaction also increased after the job enrichment, but the improvement was not significant for all types of satisfaction.

Employing a public-sector sample, Rosenbach and Zawacki (1989) examined the impact of a job enrichment experiment among two groups of military security guards. After measuring job attitudes, the guards and their supervisors went through a 2-hour workshop on job enrichment and then held brainstorming sessions to generate ways to enrich their jobs. After the meetings but before any changes were made, the questionnaire was administered again to check for a possible Hawthorne effect. No changes were found. The questionnaire was administered a third time after the implementation of the changes. The results indicated that the autonomy and feedback of the jobs were significantly enriched and that overall satisfaction and satisfaction with supervision significantly increased. Absenteeism, when compared with that of other groups having similar jobs, was significantly lower.

Employing a time series design, Wall, Corbett, Martin, Clegg, and Jackson (1990) examined the impact of enriching jobs involving advanced manufacturing technology. In addition to performance, job attitudes were measured before and after the enrichment. The authors found that the job enrichment improved performance, especially for those jobs that tended to have more performance problems. Significant improvements in intrinsic job satisfaction and perceived job pressure also were found.

In one of the longest longitudinal studies, Griffin (1991) examined the impact of job enrichment on bank tellers over a 4-year period. The tellers were surveyed before the intervention, 6 months after it began, and again at 24 months and 48 months. In addition, one group of tellers at another bank did not have their jobs changed and therefore were used as a control group. Differences were found over time with those tellers who had their jobs changed but not with the control group. Griffin found that perceptions of the job characteristics changed after the intervention and continued at the new level throughout the 4 years. Job satisfaction and organizational commitment significantly increased after 6 months but then dropped back to the original level after 24 and 48 months. Interestingly performance did not change initially but then did significantly increase at 24 and 48 months. The attitudinal effects were short-lived, but performance effects endured.

Overall these selected studies tend to be positive in terms of job attitudes. Of 13 studies, only 2 found no effects for some measure of satisfaction with the job (Frank & Hackman, 1975; Lawler et al., 1973), and 1 study found an increase followed by a drop after 1 year (Griffin, 1991). In spite of these overall positive results, Griffin's findings are troublesome because most studies did not measure satisfaction for more than 1 year. In terms of performance the studies are much less positive. Of nine studies examining performance, six found positive results, but questions have been raised concerning individual studies (e.g., Locke et al., 1976). The most interesting result in terms of performance comes from the Wall et al. (1990) study, which found that performance increased primarily in jobs that had difficulty in maintaining good performance. It may well be that improvements in performance from job enrichment are due to job incumbents improving the design of their jobs.

Moderators

A considerable amount of research concerning the job characteristics model has focused on how variables may moderate the job characteristics-job satisfaction link (Kulik et al., 1987; O'Connor, Rudolf, & Peters, 1980). Most of this research has concentrated on individual variables as moderators, most commonly growth need strength.

White (1978) reviewed 29 studies that examined individual differences and job enrichment. He divided the research into three streams, coming out of the Vroom (1960) research on participation and personality, the Hulin and Blood (1968) review, and the job characteristics model. White concluded that any moderator effects were modest and inconsistent and that reliable effects would hold only for narrowly defined constructs and specific situations. He recommended that the line of research be dropped. However, later reviews employing meta-analysis were more optimistic about growth need strength as a moderator.

Spector (1985) conducted a meta-analysis of 20 data sets, testing the impact of higher order need strength as a moderator between job characteristics and a variety of outcomes. He found significant differences between low and high need strength groups for such outcomes as satisfaction with promotion, supervision, co-workers, growth, the work itself, and with general satisfaction and performance. Although significant effects were found, the data contained few indications of workers with low need strength being adversely affected by enriched jobs.

In addition to reviewing the overall relationship between job characteristics and job satisfaction, Loher et al. (1985) examined the impact of growth need strength as a moderator between job characteristics and job satisfaction. They found a stronger relationship between job characteristics and job satisfaction for individuals with high growth need strength than for those with low growth need strength.

The meta-analyses by Fried and Ferris (1987) described above also examined the impact of growth need strength. These analyses suggested that growth need strength moderated the relationships between job characteristics and job satisfaction and performance.

Some of the inconsistencies in the findings on growth need strength might be due to problems in the research, not in the theory. O'Connor et al. (1980), for example, described some design issues that might have obscured moderator effects. Graen, Scandura, and Graen (1986) reviewed 26 studies of growth need strength as a moderator and criticized much of the research for concentrating on static, cross-sectional research. They argued that any outcomes would be reactions to the job enrichment and so should be measured after the changes in the job.

Researchers also have examined other individual mediators of the job characteristics-job satisfaction link. Individual variables that have been studied include job orientation (Sales, Levanoni, & Knoop, 1989), need for achievement (Evans, Kiggundu, & House, 1979), need for autonomy (Stone, Mowday, & Porter, 1977), locus of control (Sims & Szilagyi, 1976), work-related values (Stone, 1976), and job tenure (Kemp & Cook, 1983).

The job characteristics model specifies another moderator between job characteristics and job attitudes: work context. Typically this moderator has been operationalized as how satisfied workers are with other aspects of the work situation. Oldham (1976) and Oldham, Hackman, and Pearce (1976) examined this moderator and found strong positive results. However, Abdel-Halim (1979) and Katerberg, Hom, and Hulin (1979) found little evidence that context moderated reactions to job enrichment. Ferris and Gilmore (1984) examined organizational climate as the work context and found that it did moderate the relationship between job characteristics and satisfaction. Overall, it is not clear whether there is sufficient evidence for context as a moderator.

Finally a number of authors have discussed and/or examined the impact of other variables on job characteristics. Rousseau (1977) and Pierce (1984) each examined the impact of technology on perceptions of job design. Oldham and Hackman (1981) employed job characteristics and the attraction-selection framework to explain the reactions of employees to organizational structure. Umstot, Bell, and Mitchell (1976) compared the impact of goal setting and job enrichment on performance and satisfaction. Occupational level and job characteristics were examined by Sims and Szilagyi (1976). Muthukrishnan and Sethuraman (1985) studied how job design moderates the relationship between financial incentives and performance. Phillips and Freedman (1984) investigated how situational constraints and job characteristics influenced job incumbents' attitudes. The findings concerning these individual variables can be found in the studies.

In summary, many auxiliary variables have been studied within the job characteristics model. The evidence seems to be relatively positive that growth need strength moderates the relationship between job characteristics and job attitudes. Positive (although not overwhelming) evidence also can be found for growth need strength as a moderator with performance. Contextual factors have received mixed support as a moderator between job characteristics and satisfaction. Finally a number of other variables have been examined, but the research has been insufficient to draw firm conclusions.

Critiques of the Job Characteristics Model

Despite the enormous popularity of the job characteristics model in the 1970s and 1980s, a number of concerns have been raised about the model. Many of these apply to just this model, but other criticisms also can be leveled against job enrichment overall.

One of the more influential critiques of the model was made by Roberts and Glick (1981). They argued that a number of problems can be found with Hackman and Oldham's model. First, the model is sometimes vague and confused, making explicit tests of its effectiveness difficult, if not impossible. For example, Campbell (1988) pointed out that the concept of *task complexity* is ill-defined in the model. Second, the model focuses only on those individuals who would want enriched jobs (high in growth need strength); it ignores individuals who would not want such jobs. Third, much of the empirical literature compares responses on one part of a questionnaire with responses on another part of the same questionnaire. Relationships of this type are open to criticisms of common-method variance. Fourth, there is often an inconsistency between how the theory is conceptualized and proposed and how the research is operationalized. Fifth, a number of problems with the Job Diagnostic Survey have been identified, but little instrument development has occurred. The authors urged that tighter theoretical linkages be developed, that more attention be given to contextual variables, and that more longitudinal/causal research be conducted.

Perhaps the most damning critique has come from Salancik and Pfeffer (1977, 1978). These authors argued that most (if not all) of the concepts in the job characteristics model do not exist as objective physical realities, but rather are simply perceptions influenced by the social context. In short, "Salancik and Pfeffer believe that task perceptions and attitudes are largely socially constructed realities derived from social information available to the individual in the workplace" (Griffin, 1987, p. 84). As such, most of the job characteristics research is open to the knee-jerk criticisms of "perception-perception findings" or "common-method variance" espoused by some reviewers.

A review by Thomas and Griffin (1983) and studies by Kilduff and Regan (1988), Griffin (1983), Griffin, Bateman, Wayne, and Head (1987), Jex and Spector (1989), and White and Mitchell (1979) suggest that Salancik and Pfeffer's criticisms have some basis; that is, some portion of the perceptions concerning job characteristics are influenced by social information. However, evidence supporting the job characteristics model also was found. Algera (1983) found that the outcomes predicted by the model are related to objective measures of task characteristics (observers' ratings). In addition, Glick, Jenkins, and Gupta (1986) found a real relationship between job characteristics and effort but also determined that the relationships between job characteristics and overall satisfaction were inflated by common methods effects. It appears that an objective reality of the job influences perceptions; however, those perceptions also are biased by the social environment.

Related to the social cues hypothesis is the question of causality between job characteristics and job satisfaction. O'Reilly and his colleagues (Caldwell & O'Reilly, 1982; O'Reilly, Parlette, & Bloom, 1980) argued that it is not task perceptions that determine job satisfaction, but rather satisfaction that influences perceptions about one's job. Unfortunately the only study that could indicate causality was a laboratory study in which people were to imagine they had the job.

A final problem with the job characteristics model and job enrichment in general is the argument by Staw and his colleagues (Staw, Bell, & Clausen, 1986; Staw & Ross, 1985) that job attitudes are significantly influenced by dispositional factors; that is, some people are disposed to like their jobs, while others are not, and changing, enlarging, or enriching their jobs will not substantially change these reactions. Staw et al. (1986) based this argument on data showing moderate correlations between adolescent dispositions and adult job attitudes. In addition, Staw and Ross (1985) found that regardless of changes in pay or jobs, the best predictor of job attitudes was job satisfaction measured 5 years earlier. The dispositional hypothesis received additional support from Arvey, Bouchard, Segal, and Abraham (1989), who found that identical twins raised apart had similar levels of job satisfaction.

Gerhart (1987) reexamined the dispositional hypothesis, employing a design similar to that of Staw and Ross (1985) but incorporating a younger sample and objective as well as self-report measures of job complexity. He found that job attitudes in 1979 predicted attitudes in 1982 but that changes in job complexity provided additional predictive power. Newton and Keenan (1991) further compared the impact of dispositional and situational influences on job attitudes. Although they found evidence that attitudes generally tended to be stable, job changes had a significant impact on job attitudes. It appears that job satisfaction probably has a dispositional component (which may be genetic), but job aspects also contribute to job attitudes.

The Job Diagnostic Survey (JDS)

In addition to attacks on the job characteristics model, there have been numerous studies and disputes concerning the Job Diagnostic Survey (JDS), the instrument designed to assess the variables from the model (Hackman & Oldham, 1975, 1980).

A number of studies have conducted factor analyses of the Job Diagnostic Survey to determine whether the five job characteristics are actually different. These studies have found conflicting results (see Fried & Ferris, 1987, pp. 299-300; Harvey, Billings, & Nilan, 1985). In response to these problems, Idaszak and Drasgow (1987) revised the JDS, rewriting the items that were reverse-scored. Their findings, as well as those of Idaszak, Bottom, and Drasgow (1988), indicated that the new format was an improvement. Kulik, Oldham, and Langner (1988) also compared the original and revised JDS formats. They found that the revised format had some advantages but, overall, was no better than the original.

A common concern with the JDS is its validity: Does it measure what it is supposed to measure (Aldag, Barr, & Brief, 1981)? Gerhart (1988) examined this issue by comparing responses on the JDS by job incumbents with descriptions of the jobs from the *Dictionary of Occupational Titles*. He found that responses to the JDS were significantly related to the more objective data.

Another related criticism of the job characteristics model and the JDS is that they is conceptually deficient (Schwab, 1980); that is, although what the model measures is useful, other important factors are not assessed (Griffin, 1987). Stone and Gueutal (1985) empirically developed a measure of job characteristics that included many aspects not measured by the JDS (such as serving the public and physical demand). Zaccaro and Stone (1988) compared this empirically derived measure with the JDS and found that the additional dimensions explained more of the variance of several measures of satisfaction.

Other authors have argued that additional factors should be addressed. For example, Cordery and Wall (1985) asserted that most approaches to work redesign have ignored the role of the supervisor. O'Brien (1983) maintained that skill use also be incorporated. In yet another appraisal, Kiggundu (1983) found moderate support for the integration of task interdependence into the job characteristics model.

Numerous factors that might influence responses to the JDS also have been studied. These include contextual factors (Greenberg, Wang, & Dossett, 1982), culture (Brinbaum, Farh, & Wong, 1986; Orpen, 1983), positive mood (Kraiger, Billings, & Isen, 1989), cognitive ability of the respondents (Stone, Stone, & Gueutal, 1990), and the ability of observers to assess job characteristics (Cellar, Kernan, & Barrett, 1985).

Another approach was taken by Sims, Szilagyi, and Keller (1976), who developed their own perceptual measure of job characteristics—the Job Characteristic Inventory (JCI). The JCI examines six dimensions of job characteristics, assessing variety, autonomy, task identity, feedback, dealing with others, and friendship opportunities. Sims et al. (1976) reported on the development of the instrument and tested it on two samples. The JCI was used also by Sims and Szilagyi (1976) and by a variety of other authors (e.g., Pierce & Dunham, 1978). The research comparing the JDS and JCI was reviewed by Fried (1991). He found that the task identity and job feedback scales tended to be interchangeable but that the measures of skill variety and autonomy produced divergent results.

Summary

The job characteristics model is easily the most comprehensively tested approach to employee involvement discussed in this book. Despite this statement, we are still not certain of many aspects of the model.

First, the data are positive that job characteristics are related to job satisfaction and that job enrichment efforts typically produce improvements in job satisfaction. It should be noted that all facets of job satisfaction are not influenced; job characteristics typically are related to intrinsic job satisfaction or satisfaction with the job itself.

The research also demonstrates that job characteristics are unreliably correlated with measures of performance. In addition, job enrichment interventions often have no impact on performance. In short, it appears that performance may be related to job enrichment, but this is not always the case.

The evidence also suggests that individual differences (primarily growth need strength) and contextual differences (how satisfied the individual is with the job) moderate the job enrichment–job satisfaction relationship. Other factors also may have an impact, yet there is insufficient research to demonstrate these effects.

Much of the theorizing and research in the 1980s was aimed at finding alternative explanations for the findings above. It is likely that common-method variance is a problem with many of the findings. Correlations between one part of the JDS (job characteristics) and another part of the JDS (job satisfaction) may be inflated. This is why the field studies I reviewed are so important. They provide a better test of the model than simple correlational studies. Another problem is that the intervening psychological states (e.g., experienced meaningfulness) seldom are measured in tests of the model.

There are several alternative explanations for the research findings. The social information processing model (Salancik & Pfeffer, 1978), the dispositional hypothesis (Staw & Ross, 1985), and the deficiency of the JDS (Stone & Gueuthal, 1985) demonstrate that other factors can add to the explanation of job satisfaction and, perhaps, performance. However, even though they have knocked the job characteristics model around, it has not been overthrown.

Implementation of Job Enrichment

The issues concerning implementation come primarily from Herzberg's two-factor theory and Hackman and Oldham's job characteristics model. Unless there is a major difference in the advice the models make, I do not make references to the models but concentrate instead on their recommendations.

Methods for Enriching Jobs

Although individuals vary in terms of their motivators, Herzberg (1966) provided several general suggestions for how to enrich jobs. Table 7.2 outlines the methods he suggested. As the table shows, these suggestions also correspond to those coming from the job characteristics model. Although the models have several theoretical differences, their applications are very similar.

Table 7.2 Methods of Enriching Jobs: Suggestions From the Two-Factor and Job Characteristics Models

---

Two-factor model[1]

---

1. Remove some controls while retaining accountability.
2. Increase the accountability of individuals for their own work.
3. Grant additional authority to an employee in his or her activity.
4. Give a person a complete, natural unit of work.
5. Make periodic reports directly available to the worker rather than to the supervisor.
6. Introduce new and more difficult tasks not previously handled.
7. Assign individuals specific or specialized tasks, enabling them to become experts.

Job characteristics model[2]

---

1. Vertical loading—Add responsibilities and controls previously reserved for management.
2. Form natural work units.
3. Open feedback channels.
4. Combine tasks.
5. Establish client relationships.

NOTES: 1. From Herzberg (1966).
2. From Hackman, Oldham, Janson, & Purdy (1975).

The above methods should have an impact on job attitudes and the outcomes related to attitudes (absenteeism and turnover), but what about performance? The lack of findings concerning enrichment and performance suggests that additional measures need to be taken. The research by Umstot et al. (1976) may propose a possibility. These authors compared the effects of job enrichment and goal setting within one environment. They found that job enrichment influenced job attitudes, while goal setting influenced performance. It seems reasonable that a program combining these two techniques might be more effective than job enrichment alone.

Taking a much wider perspective than this chapter, Campion and Thayer (1985, 1987) searched the job design literature and found four approaches to job design: the mechanistic (scientific management) approach, the motivational (job enrichment) approach, the biological (ergonomics) approach, and the perceptual/motor (human factors) approach. They argued that each approach focuses on a different set of outcomes and that each has its own costs and benefits. The authors suggested that when diagnosing a job and making recommendations for redesign, all four approaches be kept in mind and that the most appropriate model be chosen on the basis of the outcomes desired. Unfortunately the various approaches sometimes lead to conflicting outcomes, so that greater efficiency in the mechanistic approach might lead to lower satisfaction in terms of the job enrichment approach. This type of trade-off was examined empirically by Campion and McClelland (1991), who found that enriched jobs improved satisfaction and customer service, but they also required greater skills, training, and compensable factors. These types of costs also are found with most of the other approaches to employee involvement (e.g., quality circles, self-directed work teams, quality of work life).

Employee Participation in Job Enrichment

Job enrichment typically is viewed as a "top-down" form of organizational change (Beer, 1980). It is very possible that managers might identify a job, diagnose its problems, redesign it for greater enrichment, and then implement these changes without ever discussing it with the employees involved. Is this desirable?

Perlman (1990a, 1990b) and Campion and Thayer (1987) argued that it is more effective to involve employees in the work redesign. Reasons for a bottom-up approach are (a) the employees may be more knowledgeable about and more committed to the program, (b) they would have more information about what aspects of their jobs need the most enrichment, and (c) they could contribute suggestions that might improve performance as well. Staw and Boettger (1990) developed the concept of *task revision*, in which employees improve performance by correcting faulty procedures. When participation is part of job enrichment, the job redesign also can include aspects of task revision. This, in fact, is possibly the cause for performance improvements after job enrichment.

The empirical evidence on participation and job enrichment is mixed. Seeborg (1978) examined this hypothesis in a 2½-day simulation where supervisors, the plant manager, or the employees themselves enriched their jobs. The author found that satisfaction increased more when employees participated and that identical changes were seen as "better" when employees participated. However, in a study by Griffeth (1985) described earlier, the addition of participation in designing the job produced almost no effects.

An additional argument for having employees participate in redesigning their jobs is that it can help reduce resistance to the changes. Kotter and Schlesinger (1979) discussed diagnosing and dealing with resistance to organizational change. One of their recommendations to forestall resistance is to involve those who will be most affected by the change.

Job Enrichment Within a Context

Oldham and Hackman (1980) discussed how most attempts to enrich jobs are initiated within other systems, such as control systems, reward systems, and technological systems. They emphasized that enrichment does not occur in a vacuum and that the other factors present can obliterate positive outcomes.

The impact of related organizational systems also was discussed by Cascio (1978) and Kopelman (1985). Cascio addressed the influence of pay, performance appraisal, communications, selection, placement, and training, while Kopelman examined how the personnel system, the organizational control and operating systems, and the bureaucratic culture can determine the effectiveness of job enrichment. Lawler (1986) made similar arguments, focusing on how individual and technological factors can make job enrichment ineffective.

A common criticism concerning much of the theorizing and research on job enrichment is the focus on psychological rather than objective definitions of job characteristics (Schwab & Cummings, 1976). Although it is assumed that some objective characteristics exist, most authors have begun with the perception of the job incumbent. Unfortunately many factors other than the job can influence these job perceptions.

Much has been written and hypothesized about the possibility of social processing effects on job enrichment (Salancik & Pfeffer, 1978); that is, that social processes have an influence on reactions to job characteristics. However, almost none of this research has been applied to the implementation of job enrichment. It would seem reasonable that if an organization wants to strengthen the effects of job enrichment, the implementers would try to emphasize social cues to add to the impact of the job changes. In support of this idea,

Anderson and Terborg (1988) found that beliefs about a job enrichment intervention were related to support for the intervention.

Individual Differences

The issue of individual differences is one place where the two-factor model and the job characteristics model diverge in their recommendations. Hackman and Oldham's job characteristics model posits large individual differences; workers with high need strength will respond more favorably to job enrichment. Kulik et al. (1987) conceptualized the job characteristics model as a model of person-environment fit. In fact, where a person has a low desire for enrichment and his or her job is enriched, Wanous (1976) predicted that performance will be poor, absenteeism and turnover will be high, and the employee will feel overwhelmed.

The two-factor model, however, does not incorporate individual differences. In fact, Paul et al. (1969) recommended that job changes not be made selectively. "Some people, however, develop as they never could under the old conditions, and do better than others originally rated much higher. . . . Not all people welcome having their jobs enriched, certainly, but so long as the changes are opportunities rather than demands, there is no reason to fear an adverse reaction" (pp. 74-75). The key here is that Herzberg assumed that job enrichment is perceived as an opportunity from which employees could abstain and continue to refer matters to their supervisor. Unfortunately job enrichment is not always viewed this way.

One point brought up by Schwab and Cummings (1976) but often ignored in the academic literature is the interaction of job enrichment and ability on performance. As Schwab and Cummings pointed out, job enrichment requires a minimum level of ability. If a job is enriched beyond the job incumbent's ability, performance and motivation will decrease. Hackman and Oldham (1980) incorporated this idea into their model, specifying that employees must have sufficient knowledge and skill to perform the work effectively. However, this individual difference has been ignored in comparison to growth need strength.

Compensation

Compensation is another difficult issue with job enrichment. The first question (Oldham & Hackman, 1980) is whether pay should be increased because the job is enriched and now has greater responsibility. As Oldham and Hackman pointed out, some (Lawler, 1986) argue that employees will expect higher pay and be disappointed when it does not arrive. Others (e.g., Paul et al., 1969) argue, however, that enriching jobs does not lead to demands for higher pay. Unfortunately there is little research on this issue, only anecdotes.

The second question concerning compensation is how the pay should be administered: Should it be contingent on performance or on a salary approach? Oldham and Hackman argued that this approach will depend on the ability to measure performance and the level of trust between management and workers. If performance is measured well and trust is high, contingent pay is appropriate. Regardless, it is likely that some change in compensation will be necessary. For example, an interesting case study by Champagne and Tausky (1978) found that job enrichment reduced the ability of employees to make incentive bonuses that were already in place. The employees appeared to enjoy the enriched jobs, but in moving among more challenging jobs, they also reduced their efficiency and their wages.

Role of the Supervisor

As with the other types of employee involvement, the job of the supervisor is altered when his or her subordinate's job is enriched. By giving autonomy, responsibility, and feedback to the employee, the supervisor's job becomes very different. If the supervisors are not prepared and alternative job duties are not developed, they may act to sabotage (deliberately or accidentally) the job enrichment effort. This apparently is what happened in the study by Lawler et al. (1973). The supervisors, their time freed up by the enrichment of their subordinates' jobs, spent that time more closely supervising their subordinates. Oldham and Hackman (1980) provided a list of tasks (from Walters & Associates, 1975) that supervisors could assume.

Several authors have argued that managers also may need to have their jobs enriched (e.g., Brenner, 1987). Paul et al. (1969) argued that job enrichment will lead to the enrichment of the supervisors' jobs, as they have more time available to spend on more important work.

Problems to Avoid and Things to Do

In an insightful piece, Hackman (1975) expressed concern that job enrichment might become another management fad, successful at first, copied by everyone, and leading to many failures and eventual abandonment. Hackman outlined six ways that, in his experience, job enrichment programs go wrong.

The first problem is that jobs are rarely diagnosed first, with enrichment applied where it could be most useful. Instead most programs go to jobs that are easy to change, are not highly important, or are politically attractive. A second problem is that the work is sometimes not really changed. Even though the program is established and much activity takes place, you need to be sure that something actually has happened. A third problem is the existence of ripple effects. This problem leads to what Oldham and Hackman (1980) referred to as "vanishing effects." Although job enrichment is seen as a relatively safe type of intervention because of its restricted focus, management must be prepared for more wide-ranging consequences.

The fourth problem is that enrichment programs rarely are evaluated in a systematic fashion with hard data. This infrequency means that little is learned from the program and that further expansion depends on the sales ability of the program's champion. A fifth problem is that line managers, staff members, union officers, and others involved are not educated about the enrichment program, its rationale, and what to expect in terms of changes. Finally, traditional bureaucracy can creep into the job enrichment process, reducing its effectiveness. Hackman argued that if these problems in job enrichment programs can be avoided, the probability of success becomes much greater.

Ford (1971) outlined a list of prescriptions and a list of things to avoid. He focused primarily on appointing "key" individuals, who would act as champions for the program. He also suggested more personalized "family" workshops to introduce the enrichment without formal training programs. Finally, he recommended working with lower level management and taking a positive bias—when in doubt, changing the job and giving the responsibility.

Overall Conclusions

The theories in this chapter, although incomplete, are better developed than those in any other chapter. The research is both more extensive and more rigorous than that examining any of the other approaches. The recommendations actually have research support. In a sense this is the best that academe has to offer.

So what do we know? From the reviews and the empirical studies summarized in this chapter, it seems likely that enriched jobs increase the job incumbent's job satisfaction. However, the findings on performance are much less positive. When one looks at the job characteristics model or Herzberg's two-factor model, these findings are not surprising.

Because a job is more complex, and/or contains more responsibility, should we necessarily expect performance to improve? Hackman and Lawler (1971) proposed that when "employees can satisfy their own needs best by working effectively toward organizational goals, employees will in fact tend to work hard toward the achievement of these goals" (p. 262). However, as Schwab and Cummings (1976) suggested, any relationship between enrichment and performance would be very complex, probably not linear.

In addition, individual differences (growth need strength or a desire for enrichment) have proven to be moderators of the job enrichment-job satisfaction relationship. For job enrichment to be most effective, it helps to have workers who have high growth need strength, who desire this type of job. The ability to do the enriched job also appears as a necessary (but overlooked) requirement.

What do we not know? We have little research on the necessary process for enriching jobs. First, we have examples of successes and failures but little direct comparison between them. Second, we have no definitive idea why enriched jobs (sometimes) improve performance. Is it because the employees are more motivated and work harder or because they can change the job and work more efficiently? Third, is growth need strength the best way to assess the readiness for an enriched job? Should all workers be given enriched jobs, or should only those who have demonstrated this readiness be included? These issues have both theoretical and practical value.

Why are there still so many questions if there has been so much research? One reason is that research seldom answers a question without raising another one in its place. As more was learned about the job characteristics model, for example, more new issues were brought up. The second reason is the use of the Job Diagnostic Survey (JDS).

The JDS made possible the explosion of research on job enrichment in the 1970s and 1980s, but it also severely weakened this research. Because one questionnaire could measure all of the variables in the model, it became easy to test the model by using a cross-sectional, correlational design. Of the hundreds of studies testing the job characteristics model, 90% have been survey studies, comparing the responses of one part of the questionnaire with responses on another part. This is not bad research, but it drew researchers away from the more difficult, messier research of examining job enrichment interventions. Because of this uneven focus, we know much about the intercorrelations of responses to the JDS survey but little about what happens when trying to enrich a job. The other approaches to employee involvement (quality circles, gainsharing, self-directed work teams) did not have this advantage and so were forced to study actual organizations trying these approaches. Perhaps they were lucky.

8 Self-Directed Work Teams

One of the more radical approaches to employee involvement, and one becoming increasing popular in the last several years, has been self-directed work teams (also called autonomous or semiautonomous work groups). Companies such as Proctor & Gamble, Digital Equipment, General Mills, Federal Express, TRW, and others are reorganizing their employees into these teams. Recent articles such as "Who Needs a Boss?" (Dumaine, 1990), "The Payoff From Teamwork" (Hoerr, 1989), and "Supervisors, Begone!" (1988) in general business periodicals such as *Fortune, Business Week,* and *Industry Week* demonstrate the interest that organizations have developed concerning this form of employee participation.

A recent survey of 476 *Fortune* 1000 firms found that although only 7% of the work force is organized into self-directed teams, management at half of the companies questioned say they will be relying on them more in the years ahead (Dumaine, 1990). "Ten years ago, fewer than two dozen manufacturing plants in the U.S. organized work on a team basis. Today teamwork is used in several hundred offices and factories" (Hoerr, Pollock, & Whiteside, 1986, p. 71). Even though the numbers are small, this was probably the fastest growing approach to participation in the late 1980s and early 1990s.

Some authors, such as Lawler (1978, 1986), have argued that this approach to employee involvement is our best hope for meaningful competition against the Japanese and other global competitors.

Others (Kapstein & Hoerr, 1989) suggest that these teams might spell the end of the assembly line in manufacturing.

Employing the framework of Dachler and Wilpert (1978), *self-directed work teams* involve a formal system of employee involvement, direct employee participation, and a high degree of control. The content of the involvement is on day-to-day work decisions, and it involves groups of lower level employees. Essentially it can be defined as where frontline employees (typically blue-collar production or clerical employees) are given the opportunity to make decisions (as a group) over their day-to-day work operations.

The team involves all of the employees in a specific area or those working on a specific product or process (Cummings, 1978). The team may be any size but is generally not more than 12 to 15 employees. The work team makes the decisions that typically would be made by a supervisor or foreperson. In a production facility, for example, the work team might decide who will operate what machines, when breaks would be taken, what type(s) of maintenance would be performed, how often quality would be checked, and other routine decisions. The team also might interact with their suppliers and customers, regardless of whether these other groups are within the company or outside. In some companies self-directed work teams will take over many of the human resource functions as well, making performance appraisals, hiring and firing decisions, and electing supervisors.

Self-Directed Work Teams at Johnson Wax

Out of the 30 years that I've been working here, this is the best thing that ever happened to me. (team member)

The component manufacturing area in Building 52 is the noisiest department at Waxdale—Johnson Wax's huge United States production facility in Racine, Wisconsin.[7] Large presses stamp out millions of plastic shapes, each batch requiring an earsplitting thousands of pounds of pressure. These pieces will go on to become the nozzles of Pledge, Glade, or Off spray cans or the tops of Agree hair shampoo bottles.

The machines are expensive and difficult to cool down, so they operate 24 hours a day, 7 days a week. The teams that operate this area work in 12-hour shifts—3 days on, 2 off, 2 on, and then 3 days off.

Each shift starts with a 30-minute team meeting. During this meeting all types of production issues are discussed: what products are being run, who will be working what area, suggestions and adjustments in handling the molds, who has to stay late, and so on. They also review their mail, memos, and reports, discuss policies, and so on. There may be a discussion of more long-term issues, such as vacations, changes in policies, new products, or more extensive maintenance. The administrative resource person (a rotating position) sometimes leads, but often sits and listens, letting everyone who wants to get involved do so.

Throughout the day, as color changes or mold changes are needed or as other routine events occur, the 11 individuals on the team are required to make decisions that previously were made by the foreperson or unit manager. Different members of the team may interact with the tool room, with scheduling, truck drivers, engineers and electricians, management, or whomever else they need to contact outside of component manufacturing. In addition, the team members do their own cleaning and maintenance and must cover for people who are absent, on vacation, or involved in training.

Many organizational changes have been made as well in the component manufacturing area. First, a number of the team members have become resource persons. Second, the pay system has been changed to a pay-for-knowledge plan, wherein pay is dependent not on the job one does or seniority, but on the skills one can demonstrate. Third, the members of each team conduct performance appraisals on each other.

In addition to the production work, different members of the team are designated as resource people. These are rotating positions, a new volunteer taking over each year. Their roles (in addition to running machines as part of the team) are to pass on information regarding safety, quality defects, administrative details, and so on.

The pay system has proven to be popular with the team members. An employee starting in the component manufacturing area is paid about $13 per hour. As he or she learns to do more jobs, the pay goes up. However, the pay system has some difficulties. Because one's pay is dependent on what one knows, many of the employees are eager for training. In fact, the primary gripe when the teams began was the lack of sufficient training opportunities.

The peer performance appraisals began about 1 year after the teams were set up. When each member is to be evaluated, appraisal forms are distributed to all of the other members of the team. They are given a week to rate the individual on safety/housekeeping, teamwork/participation, work habits, communication, and technical skills. The operations facilitator compiles the evaluations, gives an overall rating, and then passes the information on to a pay committee and the ratings and comments back to the employee.

Initially some employees were worried about other team members "sticking it to them." The appraisals have tended to be more rigorous and have produced lower evaluations than those given previously by supervisors. However, the team members feel that the appraisals are more valid and prefer being evaluated by people who know their work (the team members) rather than someone who does not see their daily work (the unit manager). These evaluations force members to keep a check on their own performance. On one work team an individual was voted out of that group by his teammates.

Overall, the workers and management at Johnson Wax are happy about the change to self-directed work teams. The workers say they would never go back to the old way of working. Management is happy with the regular improvements in safety, quality, and productivity.

Despite the positive outcomes, problems have occurred as well. The major complaint has been the lack of communication across the teams. When teams do things differently, when equipment is left out of place, or when tasks are not done, the next team to work will gripe. Large differences also occur across the teams in the degree to which everyone participates and how hard the team works.

The team members generally enjoy the control they now have over their jobs. However, this control also has brought increased responsibility. Like management, now it is sometimes difficult for these workers to leave the job at the plant.

Research on Self-Directed Work Teams

Like the example above from Johnson Wax, the research on self-directed work teams has been relatively positive, but the long history of this form of employee involvement has not produced definitive answers. Self-directed work teams have been implemented around the world for almost 40 years in many industries. Although many academics, consultants, and managers are enthusiastic about these teams, not everyone has been convinced.

Self-directed work teams (or autonomous work groups or semi-autonomous work groups) have long been a part of the sociotechnical systems framework (Herbst, 1962; Susman, 1976; Trist, 1981). *Sociotechnical systems theory* is an open systems approach that tries to optimize the relationship between the social and technical systems of an organization (Beekun, 1989, p. 877). Because the sociotechnical approach favors flexibility, it provides few standard recommendations. However, one common suggestion has been to implement self-directed work teams (Kelly, 1978). Because of this suggestion, studies going back to the 1950s have investigated this form of employee involvement.

The following review has divided the relevant research into three groups, dependent on the information and the methodology involved. I first present the classic case studies, which have been described in detail. I then recount several reviews that describe many other, smaller case studies. The remainder of the studies are some type of quasi-experimental design comparing a department or facility with self-directed work teams to a similar group without such teams.

Case Studies

Most of the research examining self-directed work teams has looked for changes in productivity, job attitudes, or other outcomes after the work teams were introduced. The better controlled studies have pretests conducted prior to the introduction of the self-directed work teams and have tried to make few major changes beyond the teams.

The original study of self-directed work teams and the genesis of sociotechnical systems was an examination of British coal mining teams (Trist & Bamforth, 1951). The authors studied the impact of a modern mine where management had invested large amounts of machinery and had designed specialist jobs. To the surprise of management, these improvements led to *lower* productivity than that found in an old-fashioned mine, not the higher productivity expected.

Trist and Bamforth studied the work processes at the "old-fashioned" Durham mine and found that the workers and managers had worked out a system of job rotation. In addition, because they worked together as a group, the Durham miners could see how their fellow miners were doing and could adjust their own jobs accordingly. Although no statistical tests were presented by Trist and Bamforth, miners in the newer, more specialized roles appeared less satisfied, less productive, and more likely to be absent than the miners employing the traditional, self-directed work teams (Trist, 1981).

This study and its findings by the Tavistock Institute of Human Relations in London led to additional studies of self-directed work teams. Several of these (e.g., Trist, Susman, & Brown, 1977) were quasi-experiments and so are reviewed later. Another of the earlier case studies was that of Rice (1953, 1958), who introduced self-directed work teams in weaving sheds in India and found increased productivity. Although the findings were impressive, so many other changes (such as increased pay) also occurred that it is difficult to isolate the impact of the self-directed work teams. The mills were examined by Miller (1975) 17 years after Rice's initial work. He found that while one mill maintained the group cohesiveness and high productivity, these had disappeared in the other mill.

The success of Trist and his colleagues in Great Britain and of Rice in India led to a series of experiments involving sociotechnical systems in Norway (Emery & Thorsrud, 1964/1969, 1976). Four demonstration projects, most dealing with self-directed teams, were conducted in a variety of manufacturing settings (Bolweg, 1976). Three of the four interventions were judged to be successful, with improved attitudes at two sites and higher productivity at one location.

The best-known application of self-directed work teams in the United States occurred at the General Foods dog food plant in Topeka (Walton, 1977, 1982). This plant was conceived in 1968 and started up in 1971. From the beginning, self-directed teams were the foundation of the production process, with teams designed to perform most production and support tasks. A "team leader" was assigned to each team to facilitate group development and process. This was, to use Lawler's (1978, 1990, 1991) term, one of the first "new plant approaches."

In general, the Topeka plant produced positive outcomes. Studies by Schrank (1974), Lawler, Jenkins, and Herline (1974), and Walton (1977) found high levels of worker participation, involvement, satisfaction, and substantial production savings. Lawler et al. (1974) reported "the highest levels (of satisfaction and involvement) we have found in any organization we have sampled" (reported in Walton, 1977, p. 423). Walton (1977) cited savings in "the neighborhood of a million dollars annually, a figure significant in a plant with 100 or so personnel and involving a capital investment in the range of 10-15 million dollars" (p. 423). Walton (1982) reported that, through 1981, productivity had improved every year except one, and product quality was consistently one of the best in the corporation.

Despite (or perhaps because of) these positive effects, Walton (1977) and Zwerdling (1984) reported an erosion of the quality of work life by late 1976. Although the Topeka plant still was regarded as superior in terms of worker attitudes and productivity, the earlier optimism and enthusiasm had diminished. Lawler (1986), DeVries (1988), and others have reported a "mid-life" crisis with new plants employing self-directed work teams; it appeared that Topeka had hit this difficult age. In a later evaluation Walton (1982) argued that these changes were simply reality setting in. The Topeka plant did not produce Utopia, as some optimists thought, nor did it fail, as some pessimists predicted.

Another well-known example of self-directed work teams is the work in Sweden of Volvo and Saab. Because of high taxes, low unemployment, and generous sick leave and unemployment practices (Bednarek, 1990), these auto companies have had considerable trouble in recruiting and keeping Swedish workers. Volvo's plants, for example, suffer absenteeism of 20%, and almost one-third of its workers quit yearly (Kapstein & Hoerr, 1989). These difficulties with the workers have led Volvo and Saab to attempt a variety of work design innovations.

Volvo opened a plant at Kalmar in 1974, with teams of 15 to 20 employees assembling sections of passenger cars. Rather than having the cars move past the workers on an assembly line, the cars sat while the people worked on them, and then the cars moved to the next team on individual carriers. Each team was responsible for a particular, identifiable subassembly of the car— steering gear, electrical system, interior, and so on (Katz & Kahn,

1978; Thompson, 1981). These changes also have been introduced into other new Volvo plants and, in modified forms, in existing plants as well (Gyllenhammar, 1977a, 1977b).

Volvo has been relatively silent about precise figures, but an independent assessment of the Kalmar plant indicated higher productivity (Mroczkowski & Champagne, 1984). Another report stated that the plant reduced direct manufacturing work hours by 60% from 1977 to 1988, and by 1988 Kalmar was Volvo's lowest cost assembly plant (Sel, 1988). Aguren, Hansson, and Karlsson (1976, in Katz & Kahn, 1978) evaluated worker attitudes at Kalmar in 1976. They found that over 90% of the workers liked the team-work and job switching in the teams. In addition, these authors found that assembly workers perceived *greater* direct influence on the work than white-collar employees.

Volvo opened another plant in 1989 at Uddevalla, where it employs teams of 7 to 10 workers to do the final assembly for Volvo 740s. Like Kalmar, the plant has no assembly line. Recently Volvo claimed that the Uddevalla plant already has demonstrated higher productivity and quality with lower absenteeism and turn-over than its other plants (Kapstein & Hoerr, 1989). Other sources, however, have suggested that the plant is not productive enough to be competitive (Prokesch, 1991).[8]

Saab-Scania also has implemented self-directed work teams, the best known example being the engine plant at Sodertaelje, near Stockholm (Katz & Kahn, 1978). This experiment, begun in 1969, started with only two work teams. These proved successful, so work teams were incorporated into the design of a new engine factory in 1972. The new plant replaced assembly lines with teams of 10 or fewer people assembling each engine at their own pace.

The engine plant has been successful with self-directed work teams. The quantity of production and costs are comparable with those of conventional assembly methods. Absenteeism and turn-over are low, and employee attitudes are high. Unfortunately there is no basis of comparison or standard of reference for these find-ings. Although they are positive, it is not clear whether the find-ings would be superior to those for a traditionally designed plant.

In an unusual experiment, six auto workers from Detroit spent 4 weeks in jobs at the Saab engine assembly plant in Sodertaelje (Goldmann, 1976). Although they liked many aspects of the plant, the American workers had reservations about the self-directed work team system. They objected, for example, to the pace and high degree of concentration demanded of assembly workers. They felt that there is a trade-off between monotonous work that allows for thoughts about other interests and more interesting work that requires concentration and a higher level of energy. Although this experiment cannot be generalized to American employees (or even to American automobile employees) it provides some interesting insights.

Case Study Reviews

In addition to the well-known examples outlined above, a number of papers have reviewed other case studies examining the impact of self-directed work teams. Cummings, Malloy, and Glen (1977) reviewed 58 work experiments involving a variety of job changes, including employee participation. Cummings and Malloy (1977) reviewed 16 studies, all of self-directed work teams. Excluding the Topeka study, Rice's (1958) studies, and the Trist, Higgin, Murray, and Pollock (1963) studies, 11 studies examining self-directed work teams are in both reviews; that is, these studies involved greater autonomy on the part of the employees, an increase in task variety (e.g., job rotation), and the establishment of team meetings.

Cummings and Molloy's (1977) review found that 9 of the 10 studies measuring productivity showed increases, while 1 demonstrated a decrease. Five of the six studies that examined costs found decreased costs (one study had no change). Of the eight studies that surveyed employee attitudes, five found improved attitudes, one found lower attitudes, and two found that some attitudes improved though others worsened. Four studies examined turnover; three found lower turnover, while one found higher turnover after moving to self-directed work teams. Three studies examined quality and found that this variable improved in two and decreased in one.

Reviewing the impact of organization development interventions, Nicholas (1982) examined the effects of job design approaches on "hard" outcomes (e.g., productivity, absenteeism, turnover) in 15 studies. Although he consolidated job enlargement, job enrichment (Chapter 7), and sociotechnical systems, a few conclusions can be made. First, the sociotechnical studies influenced 50% or more of the measures, including measures of costs, productivity, and quality. Second, the sociotechnical interventions were more successful than the job enrichment efforts across every group of outcomes.

Pasmore, Francis, and Haldeman (1982) reviewed 134 studies of sociotechnical systems from the 1970s. They reported that 71, or 53%, of the studies described the use of self-directed work teams. The self-directed work teams were extremely successful in terms of employee attitudes, safety, and quality; 100% of the studies that measured these variables found improvements in them. The studies also reported considerable success in terms of other variables. Of those studies that examined productivity, costs, absenteeism, and turnover, 89% found improved productivity, 85% showed decreased costs, 86% found decreased absenteeism, and 81% demonstrated decreased turnover.

Pasmore et al. (1984) noted that the use of self-directed work teams represented over half of the studies reporting positive results. They concluded that much of the success with sociotechnical interventions could be attributed to self-directed work teams and the skill development that goes with the teams.

Pasmore et al. also noted that although self-directed work teams were employed by a majority of the studies, many characteristics of these teams were not incorporated. For example, feedback on performance, providing interaction with customers, providing managerial information to team members, allowing team members to choose their peers, and allowing team members to supply themselves were mentioned as features in fewer than 10% of the studies. It appears, then, that many of the self-directed teams may not have experienced extensive autonomy.

Beekun (1989) employed a meta-analysis to examine the overall impact of sociotechnical interventions in 17 studies. (As I discussed in Chapter 2, *meta-analysis* [Glass, McGaw, & Smith, 1981; Guzzo, Jackson, & Katzell, 1987; Hunter, Schmidt, & Jackson, 1982] is a quantitative method for reviewing the statistical effects across research studies.) In his meta-analysis, Beekun (1989) reviewed studies that involved the formation of teams, not all of which were self-directed. He divided the studies into three groups, dependent on the degree of autonomy given to the teams. Autonomous work teams had complete freedom in the choice of work scheduling, work partners, and work techniques. Semiautonomous work teams had much freedom but also had some external supervision. Nonautonomous work teams provided very little freedom, and the workers were directed externally.

Beekun found that studies involving the establishment of autonomous, rather than semi- or nonautonomous, work teams demonstrated larger increases in productivity. He also found that increases in monetary incentives and studies outside of the United States tended to produce larger increases in productivity.

Pearce and Ravlin (1987) also conducted a survey of studies involving self-directed work teams, focusing on studies published between 1970 and 1980. Surprisingly their sample did not overlap at all with Beekun (1989), and it overlapped only in terms of the Topeka study with the Cummings et al. (1977) review. Although Pearce and Ravlin (1987) found generally positive results from the 10 field experiments they reviewed, they tended to focus on which aspects of the implementation process influenced success. Their results indicated that teams with a heterogeneous composition and minimal status differences tended to be most effective.

Summary

The results of the case studies and the reviews are very encouraging, probably *too* encouraging. As Pasmore et al. (1982) commented, reports on self-directed work teams "have tended to report on successful projects almost exclusively, leaving the literature almost void of data concerning the potential pitfalls of the sociotechnical approach" (pp. 1197-1198). In addition, even with successful projects it is not always clear whether other variables were measured but not reported because the data were disappointing. Finally, this methodological design (pretest and posttest with no control group) has a number of limitations. The data are very encouraging, but these caveats are necessary.

Quasi-Experiments

Although most of the studies of self-directed work teams simply have examined outcomes before and after conversion to teams, several studies have tried to compare the teams to some type of control group. The control groups are often other employees at the same site who were not formed into teams or other facilities that had not converted. These studies allow us to be more confident in our conclusions about the impact of self-directed work teams.

In an interesting experiment, Morse and Reimer (1956) introduced greater participation in two divisions of a department and
less participation in two other divisions of the same department.
In the participation divisions, clerical work teams made decisions
about many of their daily work issues, work methods and processes, break periods, handling of tardiness, and so on. In the
authoritarian conditions, more detailed and restrictive work standards were developed for the various jobs by staff officials. In
addition, decision making was moved from lower level management (who could be influenced by the clerks) to middle and upper
level management.

Morse and Reimer measured a variety of attitudinal measures,
all of which demonstrated improvements in the autonomy divisions and decrements in the authoritarian divisions. Most, but not
all, of these shifts were statistically significant. In addition, voluntary turnover was higher in the authoritarian divisions. All of the
divisions showed improvements in terms of productivity over the
time of the experiment (18 months); however, the authoritarian
divisions demonstrated greater improvements in productivity than
the participative divisions. The authors suggested that the supe-
riority of the authoritarian divisions may not have lasted if the
experiment had continued.

Trist et al. (1963) reported on a comparison of two units of
British coal miners in the same mine—one unit traditionally structured and the other designed as a self-directed work team. The
self-directed unit demonstrated both higher productivity and lower
absenteeism than the traditional unit.

Trist et al. (1977) described a study involving American coal
miners. This study compared one coal mining section with self-
directed work teams to two other sections in the same mine with
traditional organizations. Trist et al. emphasized that making comparisons between the sections was difficult because they varied in
terms of environmental conditions, as well as the availability of
backup equipment in case of problems. In addition, there was
"contamination" of the experimental manipulations as the control
sections learned about self-directed work teams. Blumberg and
Pringle (1983) used these difficulties to describe how the use of
control groups can misfire in field research.

One of the major objectives for the autonomous section was to
improve safety at the mine. Trist et al. (1977) reported a substantial

drop from 1973 to 1974 in violations of the 1969 Coal Mine Health and Safety Act for the autonomous section but an increase in violations for the control sections. The autonomous section also reported a smaller increase in accidents from 1973 than that of the control sections. In addition, safety ratings by mining experts consistently gave the autonomous section the highest ratings (Goodman, 1982).

Additional objectives included job attitudes, productivity, and costs. Interviews and surveys of miners found significant positive effects in terms of job attitudes. Although there were indications of improvements, no unequivocal changes were found in terms of productivity. A downward trend in costs was found within the autonomous section versus the control sections; overall, the financial benefits slightly exceeded costs (Goodman, 1982). The self-directed teams appeared to improve safety and attitudes, but the results in terms of productivity and costs can best be described as unclear (Zwerdling, 1984).

Pasmore (1978) described a quasi-experiment involving two units of a food-processing company with similar technologies and a common top manager. Self-directed work teams were introduced in one unit, while the other received a more traditional job enrichment intervention (see Chapter 7). Employee attitudes and productivity were assessed at both units before and after the job changes. Pasmore found that both interventions improved job attitudes, including job satisfaction. Significant improvements in productivity (and cost savings) also were found in the unit with self-directed work teams, but no improvements were found in the job enrichment unit.

Kemp, Wall, Clegg, and Cordery (1983), Wall and Clegg (1981), and Wall, Kemp, Jackson, and Clegg (1986) reported on a project comparing self-directed work teams in a new British candy factory to other employees in the same facility on a different shift and to other employees at another facility making similar products for the same company. The authors found that employees in the self-directed work teams had significantly higher satisfaction with those aspects intrinsic to the job (e.g, amount of responsibility, opportunity to use abilities). This effect was found over a 30-month period. In addition, there was higher satisfaction with those aspects extrinsic to the job (e.g, physical conditions, rate of pay), but this dissipated over time. No effects were found for work motivation or performance. However, cost savings were achieved through the elimination of supervisory positions.

The impact of self-directed teams on perceptions of control and other attitudes was examined by Denison (1982). He compared four plants with self-directed teams to 16 plants without teams in the same company. The outcomes included a variety of attitudes, including overall satisfaction, and perceptions of control. Denison found that employees in the plants with self-directed teams had significantly higher levels of satisfaction, plus both the employees and lower level management perceived greater control. The latter finding is interesting because it indicates that the greater control of the workers did not come at the expense of their supervisors.

Ondrack and Evans (1987) described a study involving employees of the petrochemical industry in Ontario, Canada. In the county studied, three plants had been newly designed and constructed for self-directed work teams (greenfield sites), and two plants had been converted to teams (converted sites). The remainder of the plants were traditionally managed. Ondrack and Evans compared survey responses of employees from these three types of plants to determine what differences self-directed work teams might produce and whether differences occur between greenfield and converted plants.

The authors assessed job characteristics (skill variety, task significance, etc.) by using the Job Diagnostic Survey developed by Hackman and Oldham (1980). In addition, they measured overall job satisfaction and satisfaction with specific job facets (pay, co-workers, supervisors, security, etc.). The authors found no overall differences on the job characteristics between the self-directed team facilities and the traditionally managed plants. However, they did find that the new (greenfield) self-directed work team facilities produced significantly higher scores than the other plants on several job characteristics. The authors also found no differences in job satisfaction between the self-directed team plants and the traditional plants. Employees at the greenfield sites, however, had higher scores on some measures of job satisfaction, while employees at the converted plants had higher scores on other measures. The authors used these results to suggest that self-directed work teams will be more successful at greenfield sites and that the technology of the production process may serve as a ceiling for any effects.

A longitudinal study of self-directed work teams over a period of 12 months was conducted by Cordery, Mueller, and Smith (1991). These authors compared two mineral processing plants in Australia. One of the plants, a new greenfield site, employed self-directed teams, while the other was a traditional plant. Both plants refined the same ore, employed the same technology, the same shifts, and similar pay and personnel policies. Cordery et al. surveyed the employees on a number of measures, including perceived intrinsic job characteristics, work role autonomy, satisfaction with extrinsic factors, satisfaction with the job and participation, organizational commitment, and trust in management. In addition, they collected absenteeism and turnover data from the organization.

The employees were surveyed two times, 8 months and 20 months after the start-up of the new plant. One group of employees in the traditional plant were acting as a self-directed work group. Therefore, the authors compared three groups: the new self-directed plant, the self-directed work team in the traditional plant, and the remainder of the production workers in the traditional plant. No effects were found for time, nor were any differences found between the self-directed groups in the traditional and greenfield sites. The employees in the self-directed teams (in both plants), however, responded significantly higher in terms of intrinsic job characteristics, work role autonomy, extrinsic satisfaction, intrinsic satisfaction, and organizational commitment. No effect was found for trust in management.

In contrast to the attitude data, employees at the new plant with self-directed work teams demonstrated higher absenteeism and higher turnover. These measures were equivalent, however, for the self-directed team members and traditional shift workers at the traditional plant. Exit interviews and other data indicated that the absenteeism and turnover data could be attributed to external factors such as the availability of work elsewhere, the distance to travel to the new plant, and high overtime during the plant's first year of operation.

Summary

The quasi-experiments described above provide better controlled assessments of self-directed work teams. Many of the methodological threats to validity found in pre-post case studies can be eliminated through the use of control groups (Cook & Campbell, 1979). In addition, the problem of not reporting negative results is somewhat reduced. In light of the time and effort required to develop such designs, researchers would be unlikely to abandon such a study simply because the results were not positive.

Despite the greater control and lower probability of a selection bias in results, the studies reviewed above are relatively positive. Virtually all of the studies showed improvement in terms of employee attitudes and attitude-related behaviors such as turnover and absenteeism. The results for productivity were less consistent. It appears that self-directed teams did not increase productivity in a simple and direct fashion. However, indirect improvements often occurred, through the elimination of one layer of management, for example, or through changes in work methods via employee suggestions. These findings imply that productivity improvements may occur but that these will be dependent on the environment in which the teams are introduced. For example, the technology of the work may facilitate or inhibit the impact of self-directed teams (Emery, 1980).

Overall Research Summary

Overall, self-directed work teams appear to have been successful. I attempt, in Table 8.1, to summarize the findings described above. This task is difficult, because many studies examined different outcome variables, some studies focused on the process rather than outcomes, and sufficient detail about some of the studies was lacking. However, Table 8.1 presents summaries of the outcomes for three variables of organizational interest: productivity, satisfaction, and absenteeism.

At the bottom of the table are the totals for the three outcome variables. Although some negative findings have been reported, the vast majority of studies tended to find positive results for self-directed work teams. From a total of 156 findings, only 6 were negative (in terms of becoming worse), and only 17 were null findings.

As mentioned above, one concern is that many more attempts to implement self-directed teams have not been published. In addition, we must assume a bias such that positive findings would more likely be published. Is it possible that these conclusions are an artifact produced by a biased sample of findings?

This issue, labeled the "file drawer problem," was addressed by Rosenthal (1979). Rosenthal suggested that reviewers in the behavioral sciences calculate how many other studies would have to be sitting in file drawers to invalidate the review. In a process similar to meta-analysis, one can calculate an approximate overall

Table 8.1 Summary of Studies Examining Self-Directed Work Teams

	Productivity	*Of those studying:* Satisfaction	Absenteeism
Case studies (6 studies)	3 improved 1 no effect	2 improved	2 improved
Case study reviews (114 studies)			
Cummings & Malloy (1977)	9 improved 1 worsened	5 improved 1 worsened, 2 mixed	no data
Pasmore, Francis, & Haldeman (1982)	40 improved 5 worsened or no change	36 improved	18 improved 3 no change
Beekun (1989)	3 improved 1 worsened	1 improved	5 improved 3 no change
Pearce & Ravlin (1987)	1 no change	2 improved	no data
Quasi-experimental studies (8 studies)			
	2 improved 3 no effect	6 improved 1 no effect	1 improved 1 no change
Totals:	57 improved 7 no change[*] 5 worsened[*]	50 improved 3 mixed or no change 1 worsened	26 improved 7 no change
Number of null studies required to make findings random ($p = .50$)	981	928	487

NOTE: *It is not clear whether nonimprovement meant a negative effect or no effect, so three of the five were designated as worsened and two of the five as no effect.
The production category includes only studies that directly measured productivity. It does not incorporate studies that measured cost, waste, quality, or other variables that could indirectly influence productivity.

probability value for the studies and then use this value to estimate how many additional nonsignificant results one would need to produce an overall lack of results. Of course, the results in this table have not all been shown to be statistically significant. We can only estimate the number of null results, assuming that what are described as "significant improvements" would, in fact, prove to be statistically significant.

Given that caveat, we can calculate that somewhere in the neighborhood of nearly 1,000 studies finding no effects for productivity and 900 studies for satisfaction would have to be uncovered. Because it has been studied less often, only about 500 studies of absenteeism would be required. Can we assume that probably *not* 1,000 (or even 500) negative studies were never published? Yes, considering the fact that self-directed work teams have not been implemented widely, it is unlikely that there could be so many studies, all of which had null results. In short, despite our fears that only positive results tend to be published, the numbers are large enough to suggest that self-directed work teams are effective.

Several additional conclusions can be made from the data in Table 8.1. First, the pattern of results tended to vary somewhat across the different groups of studies. In general, the case study reviews portrayed the most positive results in terms of productivity, with less favorable results occurring with the well-delineated case studies and the better controlled quasi-experimental studies. However, satisfaction was consistently found across all three types of studies.

Second, the largest number of studies, by far, comes from the reviews of the case studies. Although a few case studies and quasiexperimental studies are well known and are given great weight, they are but a small fraction of studies that have been reported. Our optimistic conclusions are due in large part to the studies included in the published reviews.

A final conclusion comes not from the numbers but from the descriptions of these studies. As one reads about the variety of situations where self-directed work teams are implemented, it becomes apparent that virtually all of the studies reviewed involved manufacturing organizations. Although claims have appeared for the effectiveness of self-directed work teams in clerical and service facilities (Hoerr, 1988), there is little empirical evidence. With the growing concern about productivity in the service sector, research would be extremely useful.

Although this review indicates that self-directed work teams can have positive effects, it does not suggest that these effects will *always* be positive. Nor does it suggest what is required for the teams to be successful. These are the issues I discuss in the next section, on the implementation of self-directed work teams.

Issues in the Implementation
of Self-Directed Work Teams

Implementation issues are a major concern with self-directed work teams because major changes must be made, they are at a "micro" level, and they require the support of both management and workers to be successful. Although suggestions for socio-technical design have been made (Cherns, 1976), they have tended toward general principles, not specific issues. At the other extreme are detailed how-to books for setting up self-directed work teams (Orsburn, Moran, Musselwhite, & Zenger, 1990; Wellins, Byham, & Wilson, 1991). In the following sections I discuss issues significant in the implementation of teams.

Boundaries

The first issue, and one of the most important, is that of establishing boundaries (Cummings & Huse, 1989; Miller & Rice, 1967). Borders are necessary to specify an area within which to establish teams, to define the makeup of the team in terms of tasks and personnel, and to establish the limits of how far the team may operate. In specifying an area, it would be ideal to define a "set of interrelated jobs or activities that produce a relatively whole piece of work" (Cummings & Huse, 1989, p. 301). The makeup of the team is determined by what tasks have to be accomplished and what roles are necessary for the smooth functioning of the team. Establishing limits for the team may be impossible, but clarification is useful, or else the team may flounder in trying to establish those limits itself. Of course, all of these decisions are dependent on the environment within which the team operates (Emery & Trist, 1965; Susman, 1976).

Degree of Autonomy

Another major decision involves the degree of autonomy that the team will enjoy. Sundstrom, De Meuse, and Futrell (1990) distinguished between (a) *semiautonomous* teams, which are led by a supervisor; (b) *self-managing teams,* which elect their leader; and (c) *self-designing teams,* which have the authority to determine their own composition and external relations. Kelly (1978) employed the term "responsible autonomy," referring to the need for the group to have sufficient autonomy for optimum assignment of individuals to the jobs. Carnall (1982) made the point that too little autonomy will not produce the benefits that are sought, yet too much autonomy can create problems in coordination.

Autonomy may occur in two general areas: the actual work decisions and personnel relations. The production process will in large part determine the degree of control that team members have in day-to-day operational decisions. In a continuous-process production facility or a service facility, almost all operational decisions could be left to the team. However, in a facility where long-term decisions are made or capital expenditures are required, such autonomy may not be possible. In general, then, the autonomy of the team to make work decisions will depend in large part on the environment in which it operates (Susman, 1976).

The second area of control concerns personnel decisions involving the team and team members. Organizations generally give responsibility for basic personnel decisions to supervisors, on the assumption that they are more knowledgeable than anyone else in management about who would be best for the job or how individual employees are performing. It seems a natural extension to argue that the employees themselves should be as knowledgeable or more knowledgeable than the supervisor. A commonly raised concern is the objectivity of team members: Can they be fair in these decisions? One response is to ask whether the supervisor is always fair and impartial.

There is no reason to believe that team members could not be as effective and objective as the supervisor. However, this recommendation comes with two major caveats: (a) The team has had the necessary training, and (b) the team is operating as a mature, functioning group in other respects. Tasks such as hiring, firing, performance evaluation, and so on typically are conducted with mature teams, those that have been operating a minimum of 1 or 2 years.

Training

Training can be divided into two general areas (Lawler, 1986): task training and interpersonal skill training. Task training allows members of the team to rotate among different jobs. Ideally all members of the team would be able to do all of the jobs, forming what Herbst (1974) defined as a composite autonomous group. At minimum, there needs to be some overlap in job skills. In addition, new skills probably will be necessary for the team. If responsibilities such as quality, scheduling, purchasing, and so on are given to the team, training that deals with these matters also will be required.

Self-directed work teams also require interpersonal skill training—training that focuses on how the members act as a group (Barry, 1991; Huszczo, 1990: Wellins et al., 1991). First, there is general training on what self-directed work teams are and are not. Both first-level and management employees will need to learn how their jobs will change and the benefits (and drawbacks) of teams. Second, they will need training on group decision making, providing and accepting feedback, conflict resolution, and other aspects of group process. A collection of employees cannot simply be thrown together, be called a team, and be expected to function (Tjosvold, 1986). Third, employees will need training on the specific details of self-directed work teams in their organization: how the teams are composed, changes in pay and promotion policies, and so on.

Despite their self-directing nature, many authors (e.g., Manz & Sims, 1986) have argued that self-directed work teams still require external supervision. This supervision, however, is very different from the traditional role and requires training to be successful. Cummings (1978) suggested two functions for the new supervisory role: developing team members and helping the team maintain its boundaries. Manz and Sims (1987) argued that the external leader's behaviors should facilitate the team's self-management through self-observation, self-evaluation, and self-reinforcement. Regardless of how the supervisory role is defined, training will be necessary for the transition to this position (Manz, Keating, & Donnellon, 1990).

Pay System

Another area for decision is the pay system. As Kelly (1978) noted, most sociotechnical theorists have tended to overlook the importance of pay. Ideally the pay system should support and reinforce collective productivity by the workers, efforts at group maintenance, and the taking of responsibility by the workers. A seniority- or job-based pay system will not be highly effective with self-directed work teams. Most organizations that made the switch to self-directed work teams also changed their compensation, either to a team-based performance, a salary plus bonus, or a skill-based system.

All three of the above systems have advantages and disadvantages. A team-based performance system is theoretically the best for fostering group spirit and cohesiveness. However, many operations make this type of pay difficult. For example, it may be difficult to measure the performance of the team, as it is only partially responsible for its performance. Another problem is if the team is dependent on its slowest member for its overall performance (e.g., an assembly line), the team could put extreme pressure on that individual, pressure that could disrupt the team.

A salary plus bonus has the advantage that, depending on how the bonus is determined, it can be very easy to administer. However, individual and team bonuses can be difficult to assess. These also might produce competition either within or between work teams. A facilitywide or companywide bonus (such as profit sharing) would be simpler and more straightforward, but it is not always clear how much the individual or team can influence these types of bonuses. General Motors' new Saturn plant, which depends heavily on teams, has this type of pay. Employees moving to Saturn were promised 80% of their normal pay plus performance bonuses (based on Saturn's success) that could boost their pay. Many GM employees who did not transfer to Saturn cited the uncertainty of these bonuses as a major reason for their refusal.

Skill-based compensation is the most novel and increasingly the most popular approach (Lawler & Ledford, 1985). An employee who is just starting learns one job and is paid, say, $7 per hour. When he or she learns a second job, there is a $0.50 per hour raise; another job brings another raise, and so on. Jobs that are more difficult to learn bring larger raises. Ideally, when all employees know each of the jobs, they all are paid the maximum. This type of pay system is straightforward to compute and motivates the employees to learn several jobs, ensuring the job rotation and involvement necessary for self-directed work teams. However, as the example at Johnson Wax showed, this system puts considerable pressure on management to provide training and opportunities to upgrade. In addition, after about 10 years or so, ambitious employees will have learned all of the jobs. At this time they will be earning the maximum pay, and motivation may begin to suffer.

Physical Facilities

One of the issues that must be addressed when implementing self-directed work teams concerns how the physical layout is influenced by the teams. In exploring this issue, the flow of the work must be examined first. By setting up teams, the work flow may be very different from that of a normal facility. Therefore, the physical layout may need to be different. For example, the new Volvo plant in Uddevalla employing self-directed work teams does not have long assembly lines. Instead the new plant is clustered around team work areas. With an existing plant, these types of changes may prove to be very expensive. Firms often compromise by implementing self-directed work teams but not changing the work flow.

In addition to the technological requirements, physical factors also are needed to emphasize the team aspect: a group meeting room, markers to establish the team "territory," and so on. For example, the Volvo plant in Kalmar, Sweden, consists of a series of hexagons, giving each work group its own wall and windows (Gyllenhammar, 1977b). It is very helpful if the physical environment supports the team cohesiveness that the organization is trying to develop. Emery (1980) made the point that many greenfield sites with self-directed work teams involve automated technologies where there is little face-to-face interaction among members of the team. It is difficult to maintain a group awareness under such conditions.

Existing Facilities

One issue that becomes apparent in the transformation to self-directed work teams is the difference between changing an existing facility and developing teams at a greenfield site (a totally new facility). An existing facility has to decide what to do with the current first-line supervisors and employees who do not fit into this approach, as well as the general fear and resistance in any major organizational change. Moving to self-directed teams will eliminate, or at least dramatically change, the supervisor's role (Zenger, 1991). Part of the cost savings of this approach is often through the elimination of the supervisor layer of management. What happens to these people?

Different organizations have addressed this issue in distinctive ways. Some companies have, when possible, offered the former supervisors other jobs or have terminated them when other positions were not available. Other organizations have kept the supervisors in their jobs but have redefined the job totally, making the supervisor a resource person to which teams can go for assistance, rather than a boss. Yet other corporations have made the supervisor a member of the team, often making him or her the permanent or initial facilitator. One company estimated that, on average, about 25% of first-line supervisors leave after a company adopts self-directed work teams (Versteeg, 1990).

Regardless of the strategy, almost no one's job is transformed as much as that of the first-line supervisor (Zenger, 1991). It is not surprising, then, that much of the resistance toward self-directed work teams comes from lower level management. If top management wants self-directed work teams to be successful, it must prepare a reasonable future for the supervisors and sell the program to these individuals as hard as it sells it to the employees. Strong resistance from first-line supervisors should be anticipated, and preparations should be made.

In addition to the issue of supervisors, there is the question of what to do with employees who do not want to participate in self-directed work teams, who want to keep their old jobs. Some employees, anywhere from 10% to 20%, will prefer to keep their work the way it currently is designed. Even though it may be boring and monotonous, they would prefer it to the responsibility and higher expectations of self-directed work teams. In Hackman and Oldham's (1980) model of work redesign, these are individuals with low growth need strength. There is little research on these individual differences (Blumberg, 1980; Cummings & Griggs, 1976), but it is clear that some will prefer traditional jobs. What should be done with these employees? This question has been answered in different ways by different organizations.

Many organizations have implemented self-directed work teams incrementally and have allowed unhappy employees to transfer out of the changes. Complete introduction of self-directed work teams will take years. Older workers may be allowed to transfer ahead of the changes, eventually retiring before they have to change.

However, if the entire facility is being converted immediately and/or most of the workers are not close to retirement, moving them around may not be an option. If all areas are converting to self-directed work teams, companies generally insist that all employees participate. It must be made clear to the employees that future pay raises, promotions, and other rewards will depend on their ability to function in the new environment.

New Facilities

Lawler (1978, 1990, 1991) outlined the practices that make up what he labeled as a "New Plant." The major issue unique to self-directed work teams in a new facility is how to select the proper employees. This is a simpler, more straightforward issue than those of existing facilities. Because of this simplicity, most organizations prefer, when they are able, to begin self-directed work teams in new facilities (Emery, 1980).

If the organization is setting up self-directed work teams from the beginning, it will want to select employees who not only can do the work but also will operate well in a team environment (Bowen, Ledford, & Nathan, 1991; Wellins et al., 1991). Therefore, in addition to the traditional methods of selecting employees (specific job skills, training, general aptitude, intelligence), there is a need for selecting employees who work well with others, operate easily in a group, and so on.

There are, as yet, no widely accepted standardized tests for measuring these abilities, but organizations have tried to select prospective employees, often employing an assessment center approach (Cosentino, Allen, & Wellins, 1990; Feuer & Lee, 1988). For example, Motorola recently tried to develop a selection process to choose employees who work well in a group. In setting up its Georgetown, Kentucky, plant, Toyota employed an assessment center focusing on interpersonal skills (Cosentino et al., 1990).

When General Motors and Toyota Motors set up their NUMMI joint venture in Freemont, California, they employed some novel selection tests for returning UAW members. One test involved having workers try to build structures with Tinkertoy parts. Unknown to the employees, it was necessary for several people to pool their resources to be successful. Those who tried on their own would fail. NUMMI wanted to see which employees would work together and which would not.

The Union

A final issue (or complication) when implementing self-directed work teams is the presence of a union. Many managers expect that self-directed work teams can only be implemented at nonunion facilities. Although most facilities with teams are nonunionized, a growing number of firms with unions are employing teams. A union does not preclude the use of self-directed work teams, it simply makes implementation more complicated.

As with any major change in an unionized environment, the initial steps are to develop a positive relationship with the union and to involve the union as soon as possible in planning the changes to self-directed work teams. Management also will need to realize that, like first-line supervisors, the role of lower level union officials will change dramatically. Rather than going to a shop stewart to complain, an employee now will be more likely to go to his or her team. In addition, the grievance procedure of the union probably will be changed considerably. Grievances may not be lodged against management supervisors, but against fellow team members. Management must work with the union to help foresee and prepare for these changes.

Three Common Pitfalls

The discussion of the decisions and process issues above outlines most of the difficulties that organizations will face when implementing self-directed work teams. The purpose of this section is simply to list and highlight the most obvious. Many of these also have been listed by others (e.g., Peters, 1988).

A major problem is the resistance of lower and middle-level managers (Saporito, 1986). The focus and attention is typically on how production or clerical jobs have been changed, but managerial jobs have changed as much or more (Manz et al., 1990), and these managers often will feel betrayed by those above them (Simmons & Mares, 1982). Be prepared for fear, resistance, and sometimes warfare.

A second problem concerns inadequate training for all concerned. This is a common problem with team building (Harris & Nicholson, 1989). I visited one plant where management was upset about the performance of their "teams." Self-directed teams had been created by management's announcing that teams existed, with no training, structural changes, or any other changes occurring. Employees, when interviewed, asked what "teams" were; they did not know. A 2-hour session on teams, conflict resolution, group decision making, and so on is not training. The members of self-directed teams in many companies devote about 15% to 20% of their time in training, the equivalent of 1 day each week (Lee, 1990).

A third problem is the lack of support from top management. As with any major organizational change, the support of powerful advocates is necessary (Burke, Clark, & Koopman, 1984; Garcia & Haggith, 1989; Stayer, 1990). Top management must take an active role for self-directed teams to be successful. There has to be support in order to overcome management resistance, to gain funds for training, to give support to the teams as they develop, to make decisions on new pay systems and other structural and rule changes, to avoid empire building, and to be sure that the teams truly are autonomous. This is probably the primary problem, for without top management support, the other problems may prove insurmountable.

Overall Conclusions

Self-directed work teams are the farthest example of pushing direct, day-to-day decision making to the people on the floor. As such, they are probably the most difficult change from a traditional structure. Moving to self-directed teams will be arduous, painful, and drawn out.

Despite concerns about a positive bias, the research evidence is relatively positive. Organizations that have experimented with self-directed work teams have found them to be an effective way to improve productivity and employee attitudes. Of course, we cannot be sure what percentage of the time they will prosper, what factors are necessary for success, and whether the teams were the only reason for these outcomes.

I have tried to outline some of the more important decisions, issues, and problems when implementing self-directed work teams. This is a major organizational change, altering the jobs of many people in the organization. It should not be attempted casually and requires the full support of top management. I believe that self-directed teams offer great promise for management, but the journey will be long and difficult.

9 Employee Ownership

One of the most visible and formal approaches to employee involvement is employee ownership. With the explosive growth of employee stock ownership plans (ESOPs) in the last 15 years, this has become a much more popular form of involvement. It is estimated that employees own more than $150 billion in stock (Bernstein, 1991; Blasi & Kruse, 1991). If all (or most) of the employees own a piece of the company, they should have greater influence, become more involved, and work harder. Right? Sometimes.

In terms of Dachler and Wilpert's (1978) typology, this form of employee participation is formal, and it has a combination of both direct (face-to-face) and indirect involvement. The amount of influence that employees have is often high (although it can vary tremendously), and the involvement typically includes the entire organization.

As in the previous chapters, I first present an example of this form of employee involvement. Then I describe the varieties of employee ownership, review the research concerning ownership outcomes, and discuss the major issues when implementing this approach to involvement.

Employee Ownership and More at Quad/Graphics

Employees at Quad/Graphics, a printing company in Pewaukee, Wisconsin, like to talk about the family feeling, the sense of being part of something at the company.[9] This philosophy is evident in the classes they take, the parties they have, even *Quad/News*, the community (not company) newspaper. It is obvious that Quad/Graphics is not the typical place to work.

The employees own 37% of the company through an employee stock ownership plan. Each year they receive a statement of their own account and have a shareholders' meeting to elect the board of directors. In this way, when the company does well, so do they. But there is lots more.

Employees at Quad/Graphics are expected to act like owners. When someone is wasting materials, employees are apt to say, "You're hurting our profit sharing." The mentality is that "What we do as individuals has an impact on company performance." To reinforce this attitude, the presses are directed by lead press workers, not supervisors, and each press is expected to be modified and improved by each crew. Each work team gets a monthly financial report indicating how they have done. In addition, each year, Harry V. Quadracci, founder and president, and all of the managers take off 3 days for a retreat called the Spring Fling. The employees run the company in their absence. After all, they own part of the company.

Employees at Quad/Graphics are expected to learn. First, they learn their job, with most employees starting at the entry level— the "jogger" on the printing press, for example. In addition, each new employee is given a mentor, whose job is to help explain how things operate at Quad/Graphics. The learning continues, forever, on the job and in formal classes that employees take on their own time in an old schoolhouse.

As far as the employees are concerned, Quad/Graphics is a major success. For example, much of the profits from Quad/Graphics goes back to the employees indirectly. There is an on-site child center and an on-site sports center. On-site college courses are offered, and a campground and recreational park are there for employees to use year round.

Quad/Graphics is also a success in the traditional business sense. It has grown from 11 employees in 1971 to more than 5,000 in 1991. It has grown from 1 press in a 20,000-square-foot building to 52 presses in seven facilities in Wisconsin, New York, Georgia, and California. It has won numerous quality and service awards from the magazines it prints, has been named to the 100 best companies to work for in America, and has made many people very wealthy.

Quad/Graphics is not for everyone, however. It is a very unstructured company, and some people are more comfortable with a more traditional, pyramid-shaped organization. In addition, it can be risky having your entire pension tied into the fortunes of one company, even Quad/Graphics. Therefore, about 80% of the employees also have a 401K retirement plan as well. However, the ownership plan is a big attraction for people to join the company.

Quad/Graphics integrates several forms of employee involvement: employee ownership, self-directed work teams, and informal participation. Its success shows that this type of combination may be the most effective approach to employee involvement.

Forms of Employee Ownership

Although they all encompass companies where a substantial number of employees own the firm, there are several very distinct forms of employee ownership. These different forms come out of different traditions, have different aims, and operate in very different ways.

Toscano (1983b) identified three general types of employee ownership: direct ownership, employee stock ownership plans, and worker cooperatives. *Direct ownership* is a typical company where employees individually own stock. *Employee stock ownership plans* (ESOPs) are created when the company establishes a specified benefit plan in which employees acquire stock as part of their benefits. The *worker cooperative* is a group of individuals working in a company who own and personally operate the organization.

Direct Ownership

Most publicly held corporations have some employees who own some of the shares. In this strict sense, they are employee-owned companies. However, for all intents and purposes, there is no link between the employee-owned stock and company strategy, employee behaviors, or any other potential outcome.

For employee ownership to be an important factor, two conditions must be met. First, the employees must have sufficient control over the company to influence significantly its strategy and decisions. If only one employee owns one share of several million shares, employee ownership exists, but it is trivial. Second, individual employee owners must perceive a significant stake in the company, feel they have some influence. Pierce, Rubenfeld, and Morgan (1991) labeled this as "psychological ownership."

In light of the conditions above, direct ownership can be very important in smaller firms, where the percentage of stock owned by current employees can be large enough to influence the corporation and the employees feel involved. Another possible situation is where larger companies offer stock options to most or all of their employees, a trend that is increasing (Weber, 1991).

Not a great deal of attention has been paid to direct ownership. Some exceptions are a study by Goldstein (1978) of a company in Australia, the privatization of formerly state-owned companies in Great Britain (Wright, Thompson, & Robbie, 1989), and studies in the United States where workers buy their companies to maintain their jobs (see Bradley & Gelb, 1985; Hammer, 1986; Stern & Hammer, 1978).

Interestingly many of companies bought by the employees to save jobs either fail and disappear or become successful and degenerate (evolve?) into more traditional public companies. For example, Toscano (1983a) described the Vermont Asbestos Group, a company that was owned by 78% of its work force when it was first created in 1975. As it became successful, stock prices for the company rose from $50 per share to over $2,000 per share. Many of the workers sold their stock to outside investors, and it eventually became a more traditional company.

The problem is that there is no way to draw a line between the employee-owned corporation and the publicly owned corporation where some of the stockholders are also employees. How do we distinguish the employee-owned firm from others that also have employee ownership but the employee owners lack the psychological ownership or have little impact on the company? Because of the difficulty in identifying these employee-owned companies, most researchers and practitioners have focused on other forms of employee participation. Therefore, I focus on the other, more frequently studied forms of employee ownership.

Employee Stock Ownership Plans

Employee stock ownership plans (ESOPs) are far and away the most popular form of employee ownership. The ESOP began in

1958, when Louis Kelso, a San Francisco lawyer, helped the employees of a West Coast newspaper take over their company. They bought it with a loan, using an existing stock bonus plan as collateral. Kelso described these ideas in his 1958 book *The Capitalist Manifesto* (Kelso & Adler, 1958).

ESOPs really took off in 1974, when Senator Russell Long of Louisiana pushed a series of tax incentives for ESOPs through Congress. These incentives made contributions to the ESOP tax deductible. Additional tax breaks passed by Congress in 1984 and revised in 1989 meant that lenders could deduct half of the interest they received on a loan to a qualified ESOP, so ESOPs could borrow at below-market rates. In addition, companies could deduct both the cash they gave their ESOPs to pay off the principal and interest on the loan and the dividends paid on stock held by the ESOP (Binns, 1990; Riley & McSweeny, 1987; Rosen, 1990).

An ESOP works by creating an employee stock ownership trust. This trust has to meet all of the federal requirements of any benefit plan as laid out by the Employee Retirement Income Security Act (ERISA). Unlike most other retirement plans, an ESOP must invest primarily in the company's stock. The ESOP can borrow money to buy stock, which, if the company pays back, is deductible. This allowance gives the company a nice way to borrow money more cheaply.

Companies contribute either stock or cash to buy stock for the trust and allocate the stock to employees. Complete vesting in the plan typically takes between 5 and 10 years. Employees often cannot take physical possession of the shares until they quit, retire, or die, but they can (in some plans) vote or tender the stock they own in their account.

Stock that is owned by the trust but not allocated to a individual employee is voted by the trustee of the trust. Supposedly this trustee should act as an independent stockholder. However, the trustee typically is appointed by the board of directors.

Overall, there are several major differences between ESOPs and direct ownership companies. First, employees do not need to invest their own money; the firm gives them shares. Second, employees do not choose to invest in the company; this is an automatic benefit they receive. Third, employees do not directly hold the stock; it remains in the trust until they quit, die, or retire. Fourth, workers typically cannot sell their stock while they are still employed at the company. Fifth, ESOP employees typically have more limited voting rights than employees who directly own stock.

ESOPs have become very popular, growing from a handful in 1974 to around 10,000 now, covering more than 10 million employees (Farrell, Smart, & Hammonds, 1989; Pierce & Furo, 1990). As of 1989, at least 40 of the *Fortune* 500 had 10% or more of their stock owned by employees (Long, 1990), and some 27% had at least 4% of their shares in workers' hands (White, 1991).

Worker Cooperatives

Worker cooperatives are the most democratic form of employee ownership. In a cooperative, only employees can be owners, although employees are not always owners. In addition, employees usually own equal shares of the company, and each person has one vote in the decision-making process.

Among the best-known cooperatives are the Mondragon cooperatives in Spain (Johnson & Whyte, 1977; Whyte & Whyte, 1988; Woodworth, 1986). These cooperatives, located in the Basque region, began in 1956 with one cooperative that produced small stoves. By the late 1980s, they had grown to more than 100 organizations employing more than 19,000 people, including Spain's largest refrigerator manufacturer, one of Spain's leading manufacturers of machine tools, an agricultural cooperative, a fishing co-op, a number of stores, and a bank (Whyte & Whyte, 1988; Zwerdling, 1984).

In terms of governance, the general membership of each cooperative in the Mondragon group meets once a year to elect a board of directors, which hires the rest of the management. Each member gets one vote. Despite the ownership structure, most jobs are designed in traditional ways, with little opportunity for input. Annual profits are divided into three parts: 10%-15% is used to benefit the community, 15%-20% goes into a reserve fund, and 70% is distributed to members in proportion to the hours worked and their rate of pay. This profit sharing is not paid out in cash, however. It goes into a fund, and interest on it is paid to the members (Zwerdling, 1984).

The best-known cooperatives in the United States are plywood firms in the Northwest (Greenberg, 1984; Zwerdling, 1984). These began back in the 1920s and still operate today. In these cooperatives, each of the workers gets one vote, and they vote in companywide elections on everything from choosing the board of directors and company officers to formulating corporate policies such as sick leave, purchasing equipment, and making real estate investments. Every worker makes the same pay and gets an equal share from the profits each year (Zwerdling, 1984).

Many other worker cooperatives also exist in the United States (Jackall & Levin, 1984), as well as in Europe and Israel (Long, 1990). I do not include examples of what have been labeled as "social ownership" (Russell, Hochner, & Perry, 1979), such as the cooperatives in Yugoslavia and the kibbutz in Israel. These organizations are not owned by the employees, but by society as a whole. These organizations are examined in Chapter 6 as examples of representative participation.

Research on Employee Ownership

Considerable research has been conducted on the impact of employee ownership on the effectiveness of the organization, the attitudes of the employees, and other outcomes. This research has produced both positive (Conte & Tannenbaum, 1978) and negative conclusions (O'Toole, 1979). In addition, interest has been growing within the economics discipline about the performance of employee-owned firms (e.g., Jones, 1985; Jones & Svejnar, 1982b). Finally, the collection of data has accelerated over the last 15 years as ESOPs have become increasingly popular.

In the following sections, I first review the literature investigating organizational performance as an outcome of employee ownership. Then I examine the impact of ownership on employee attitudes. Finally, I discuss the research concerning how employee ownership operates to influence these outcomes.

Organizational Performance

A number of authors have made the claim that employee-owned companies are more productive or more profitable than other firms in their industry. For example, it has been argued that employee-owned companies generate superior earnings and long-term stock-price gains (White, 1992). However, the research evidence on organizational performance, as in most of the previous chapters, is mixed (Jones & Pliskin, 1991). I present a few of the better known case studies and then the surveys and comparative studies where employee-owned firms are compared with traditional companies.

Case Studies

Bradley, Estrin, and Taylor (1990) presented data on the performance of the John Lewis Partnership, Britain's largest employee-owned firm. This retail firm has been employee owned since 1929. Bradley et al.'s analysis shows employee costs and earnings to be consistent through the 1970s and 1980s. In addition, the partnership's performance relative to its competitors demonstrates that it has been one of the top retail firms in the United Kingdom over the last two decades. The authors concluded that this longitudinal data, in conjunction with the cross-sectional findings from other studies, demonstrates that employee-owned firms perform just as well as the best conventional firms.

Another case study of performance, the Mondragon system in Spain, has been described by Johnson and Whyte (1977), Whyte and Whyte (1988), Woodworth (1986), and many others. Over the last 35 years, not one of the 89 Mondragon business start-ups has failed, employment has increased, layoffs have been avoided, and profits and sales have increased at healthy rates (Woodworth, 1986, p. 396). Mondragon also has strengths in its employment security, its capacity to invest for the future, and its group management (Whyte & Whyte, 1988, pp. 218-222). In an economic analysis of the Mondragon cooperatives, Thomas (1982) concluded that "productivity and profitability are higher for cooperatives than for capitalist firms" (p. 149).

Many more case studies, such as those above, argue that employee ownership is comparable or superior to traditional firms. I do not review these, but instead move on to discuss surveys and comparative studies of employee-owned firms. In these studies employee-owned companies are contrasted with industry averages or similar, traditional firms.

Surveys and Comparative Studies

The first survey of employee-owned companies was conducted by Conte and Tannenbaum (1978). These authors surveyed 98 employee-owned companies, 30 involving direct ownership, and 68 involving ESOPs. Interestingly they found that the firms with direct ownership had higher levels of employee influence. Profit data were available for 30 of the companies. Overall, the profits of these companies were 1.5 times those of the average for their industries, but this difference was not statistically significant. In looking at the predictors of profit, Conte and Tannenbaum found the only significant predictor to be the amount of equity owned by the workers.

Long (1980) examined the impact of ownership on profitability in three employee-owned companies (trucking firm, knitting mill, and furniture firm). Although all were employee owned, they had very different ownership structures. The trucking firm possessed the greatest degree of employee ownership, followed by the knitting mill, and then the furniture firm. The trucking company and knitting mill went from substantial losses before conversion to employee ownership, to consistent profits after conversion. The furniture firm also demonstrated an increase in profitability, but not as large. However, differences in situations and industries made direct comparisons impossible.

Another survey of 229 ESOP firms was conducted by Marsh and McAllister (1981). These authors found that the average productivity (compensation/sales) of the employee-owned companies increased annually about 0.75% from 1975 to 1979. The productivity averages for companies in the same industries averaged a *negative* 0.74% over that same period. In addition, the highest productivity was found in ESOPs with 100 to 1,000 employees.

Rosen and Klein (1983) explored the capacity for employee-owned firms to create jobs. These authors examined data on 43 of the 108 employee-owned companies they contacted. Their results indicated that employee-owned firms grew much faster than average, producing an employee growth rate of 2.78%, compared with 1.14% for conventional firms. This difference translated into a growth rate three times higher than that of the average conventional firm.

Granrose, Applebaum, and Singh (1986) compared employee-owned supermarkets to conventional supermarkets in Philadelphia. The employee-owned supermarkets originally had been owned by the same chain that owned the conventional stores but had converted to avoid being closed. In 1981, before conversion, the employee-owned supermarkets had significantly lower profits and higher unit labor costs than the conventional supermarkets. In 1983, after conversion, the employee-owned stores had significantly lower unit labor costs than the conventional markets and significantly higher profits than some of the conventional stores.

Rosen and Quarrey (1987) compared 45 ESOP companies to 238 conventional companies, chosen to be comparable in terms of business line, size, and location. Because most of the ESOP companies were closely held, profit statements were not available. Therefore, the authors compared the companies in terms of growth. Rosen and Quarrey found that during the 5 years before converting to employee ownership, the future ESOP companies grew 1.21% faster in terms of employment and 1.89% faster in terms of sales. After converting to employee ownership, however, the ESOP companies grew 5.05% faster in terms of employment and 5.4% faster in terms of sales. In addition, 73% of the ESOP companies significantly improved their performance after converting to employee ownership (p. 127).

In another well-known survey examining the impact of employee ownership, the U.S. General Accounting Office (GAO) (GAO, 1987: Hanford & Grasso, 1991) compared 111 companies that established ESOPs from 1976 through 1979 to a comparison group matched by size and industry without ESOPs. The GAO report concluded that ESOPs have little impact on either profits or labor productivity. However, ESOPs with employee involvement programs did demonstrate greater productivity than before they converted to ESOPs.

Park and Rosen (1990) focused on the performance of leveraged ESOP firms. These authors examined 38 ESOPs that acquired considerable debt to buy the company, and they compared them to the averages of companies of comparable asset size in the same industry. Park and Rosen found that the leveraged ESOPs had much greater debt than the average company but that gross profits, financial efficiency, and solvency were comparable.

The last two studies on organizational performance focus on a different outcome: survival. Jones (1979) presented a survey of worker cooperatives formed in the United States over the last century. Examining a sample of 32 firms, he found that the survival rate of cooperatives (including those sold) exceeded 50% over a 55-year period, a higher survival rate than conventional firms. He also found that most cooperatives were smaller than comparable conventional firms, although exceptions existed. Assessments of firm efficiency and profitability were few and crude, suggesting that some cooperatives were very effective, while others were less so.

Estrin and Jones (1992) tested the hypothesis that, over time, worker cooperatives tend to fail or to degenerate into traditional firms. Employing a sample of 283 French cooperatives, the authors examined survival from 1970 to 1979. They found that the worker cooperatives demonstrated a low mortality rate during the 1970s, and about 40% of these firms were 30 or more years old. In addition, little evidence was found of cooperatives degenerating into traditional firms.

Summary

The findings concerning organizational performance are summarized in Table 9.1. Overall, the findings are positive, but not entirely consistent. This result is similar to that of other reviews (Jones & Pliskin, 1991). Although no studies found employee-owned companies to have lower performance than conventional firms, several studies found no differences.

In addition, any positive conclusions require several cautions for this optimism. First, employee-owned companies often are identified through press reports and other types of publicity; these reports probably tend to focus more on successful companies than on unsuccessful companies. Second, there is considerable self-selection in terms of the firms surveyed and studied; a failing ESOP is probably unwilling to be studied in great detail. For these reasons, the negative findings from the GAO survey, which was the broadest, are disheartening. Finally, many employee-owned companies are privately held (for example, 81% in Marsh and McAllister's 1981 survey), making access to overall measures such as profitability difficult, if not impossible, to obtain. In spite of these difficulties, there seems to be evidence for a cautious conclusion that employee-owned firms sometimes (but not always) perform better than conventional firms.

Employee Attitudes and Behavior

Tannenbaum (1983) and others have proposed that employee ownership should positively influence a variety of employee

Table 9.1 Studies Concerning Employee-Owned Firm Performance

Study	Number of firms	Form of ownership	Findings
Bradley, Estrin, & Taylor (1990)	1	Direct	One of the top firms in its industry for decades
Woodworth (1986)	89[*]	Co-op	No firm failures; higher than average job, sales, and profits growth
Conte & Tannenbaum (1978)	30	ESOP and direct	Profits 150% higher (but not significant)
Long (1980)	3	N/A[**]	Increased profitability after conversion
Marsh & McAllister (1981)	229	ESOP	Productivity increases compared to average decreases
Rosen & Klein (1983)	43	N/A	Job growth about 3 times average
Granrose, Applebaum, & Singh (1986)	2	N/A	Higher profits, reduced costs
Rosen & Quarrey (1987)	45	ESOP	Increased sales and job growth after conversion and higher than conventional firms
General Accounting Office (1987)	111	ESOP	No effects on profitability or productivity
Park & Rosen (1990)	38	ESOP LBO[***]	Average profitability and financial efficiency
Jones (1979)	32	Co-op	Higher than average survival
Estrin & Jones (1992)	283	Co-op	Higher than average survival

NOTE: *The 89 co-ops were part of the Mondragon group; **N/A means information not available; ***LBO refers to a leveraged buyout.

attitudes and attitude-related behaviors. This hypothesis has been tested widely, with mixed results. I first examine the studies of worker cooperatives and then discuss those studies involving ESOPs and direct ownership.

Worker Cooperatives

A study by Russell et al. (1979) examined the amount of influence and job attitudes of employees in worker-owned refuse collection cooperatives in the San Francisco area. These authors found that the perceived influence of worker-owners was comparable to that of forepersons and supervisors in private firms. After controlling for other factors, analyses demonstrated that worker-owners had more positive reactions than other workers on one measure of organizational identification and one measure of job satisfaction. Other items, however, demonstrated no differences. In addition, the findings indicated that although worker-owners were better off, another class of employees—nonowner-workers—was not as well off.

The impact of ownership on attitudes was tested in the plywood cooperatives by Greenberg (1980). In comparing four employee cooperatives and one larger, conventional plant, the author found significant differences in overall job satisfaction. In addition, several measures of perceived influence were highly correlated (.29 to .46) with job satisfaction. Although these results are very positive, one confound between the samples was that the income of the employees in the cooperatives was 30% higher.

The impact of employee ownership on absenteeism was explored by Rhodes and Steers (1981). These authors hypothesized that ownership should lead to stronger perceptions of participation and equity, which would lead to greater commitment and to lower absenteeism, tardiness, turnover, and grievances. Comparing a plywood cooperative to a conventional plywood facility, Rhodes and Steers found that respondents in the employee-owned firm perceived greater influence and pay equity, as well as greater organizational commitment. Turnover and grievances were lower at the employee-owned facility; however, absenteeism and tardiness were higher. The authors explained the last differences as due to a control system in the conventional plant (threatening dismissal), while the employee-owned facility had no such system.

An organizational fit analysis was tested by Oliver (1990), who hypothesized that positive employee attitudes, such as commitment and involvement, would be greater for certain types of employees in an employee-owned firm. Surveying a petrochemical company in the United Kingdom, Oliver examined the relationships between demographic variables and organizational commitment, identification, involvement, and loyalty. Most of the demographic variables were unrelated to the employee attitudes, but values were significantly related. Participatory values, in particular, were significantly related to commitment, identification, and involvement. Individuals with strong values for participation possessed more positive attitudes. In addition, instrumental values (valuing job security, income, and work conditions) were *negatively* and significantly related to commitment and involvement, a finding that provides some evidence that fit can be an important mediator.

ESOPs and Direct Ownership

A before-and-after design was employed by Tucker, Nock, and Toscano (1989) to examine the impact of an ESOP on job satisfaction, organizational commitment, and perceived influence. All employees of a small (40 employees) graphics company were surveyed 6 months before and 9 months after the ESOP plan began. Both satisfaction and commitment rose over time, with commitment having the larger increase. Perceived influence showed little change after the ESOP. One possible confound is that the ESOP was accompanied by economic growth, which could have been responsible for the improved attitudes.

Long has conducted a variety of studies examining employee attitudes in employee-owned companies. In one study, Long (1978a) examined retrospectively the attitudes of nonmanagerial employees from a trucking firm that had been purchased by its employees 6 months before. Long found that majorities of the employees reported increased job satisfaction, job security, communication with management, and perceived job effort. Those employees who held stock in the company reported significantly higher satisfaction, integration, involvement, commitment, and perceived job effort than nonstockholders. Of course, these questions asked respondents to remember how they felt before buying the firm. In addition, causality is an open question.

In another study Long (1980) compared the trucking company to a knitting mill and a furniture firm, all three of which fell on a rough continuum from most employee-owned (trucking) to least (furniture). Long found that job attitudes and employees' perceptions of influence improved most in the trucking company and least in the furniture firm. However, Long presented no direct, quantitative comparisons among the companies.

Negative results were found in a study by Long (1981) examining the conversion of an electronics firm to employee ownership. The degree of influence and desires for influence were measured 7 months before conversion, about 7 months after, and about 18 months after conversion to employee ownership. Perceived influence increased (nonsignificantly) in the first wave after employee ownership but then dropped back to earlier levels 18 months after the conversion. In addition, desires for influence dropped after converting to employee ownership.

In another analysis of this same company, Long (1982) examined the impact of employee ownership on integration, job involvement, commitment, motivation, and general satisfaction. None of these demonstrated a significant change after conversion to employee ownership. When Long conducted a finer analysis, examining non-managerial employees who perceived no changes in participation after conversion, he found that the attitudes actually became more negative. Several reasons are given for these findings. First, there was a large influx of new employees after the conversion, changing the sample substantially. Second, the primary mechanisms for participation were representatives on the board, an employee council, and quarterly shareholder meetings. As the findings in Chapter 6 indicate, such indirect forms of participation are generally less effective than more direct mechanisms.

The impact of employee ownership on job satisfaction and absenteeism was examined by Hammer, Landau, and Stern (1981). Their results indicated that voluntary absenteeism dropped after conversion to employee ownership but that involuntary absenteeism increased. Job satisfaction had no impact on absenteeism.

Granrose et al. (1986) presented an interesting study comparing employee-owned supermarkets and conventional supermarkets, with and without quality of work life (QWL) programs. The results indicated that employees in the employe-owned supermarkets perceived themselves as participating more in daily decisions and in long-term decisions. The existence of QWL programs in the conventional supermarkets did not increase perceptions of participation. Job and life satisfaction were higher in the employee-owned supermarkets than those without QWL programs, but no differences were found between the employee-owned and traditional firms with QWL programs. The authors suggested that the most effective situation would be a combination of employee ownership plus QWL programs.

Buchko (1988) examined the impact of employee ownership on absenteeism and grievances. Inspecting these variables over 6 years for a media firm, the author found that absenteeism did not change; however, grievances increased after conversion to employee ownership. Buchko presented several explanations for this last finding.

Rooney (1988) surveyed 61 conventional and employee-owned firms to determined how much participation workers actually had in 12 different areas (e.g., setting wages, hiring/firing, work rules, investment decisions, etc.). Each area was assessed with a 5-point scale: *no participation* (1), *employees informed/consulted* (2), *collective bargaining* (3), *co-decided on joint board* (4), and *a majority of employees decides* (5). With a possible range from 12 to 60, the modal response of the firms was 12. Among the firms where a majority of shares were owned by employees, only 49% had scores of 24 (informed/consulted) or more, and only 12% had scores of 48 (co-decided) or more. In short, even with majority employee ownership, most companies did not inform/consult employees on all 12 issues, and the vast majority did not have significant employee input into decisions.

Summary

The findings regarding employee attitudes are summarized in Table 9.2. Like the performance results, they are mixed. The few studies of worker cooperatives found generally positive results. The studies of ESOPs and direct ownership found primarily positive, but also negative and null, results. To add to the confusion, most conversions to employee ownership are accompanied by a variety of other events (changes in worker population, financial rewards, sales and profits, etc.). Examples of positive changes in attitudes or the lack of changes can often be explained by these confounding effects. Overall, positive attitudes generally are found to be related to employee ownership. The attitude (satisfaction, commitment, etc.) may vary, however, and in several cases the conversion to employee ownership actually produced more negative attitudes.

Why Employee Ownership Should Have an Impact

Most of the research on employee ownership has focused on the mechanisms by which ownership may influence worker attitudes and/or firm performance. Two general theories explain any positive effects arising from employee ownership. One theory sees employee ownership as a financial investment and argues that employee-owners are more satisfied and more productive because

Table 9.2 The Impact of Employee Ownership on Employee Attitudes

Study	Perceived influence	Outcomes Job satis- faction	Organi- zational commitment	Other outcomes[*]
Worker cooperatives				
Russell, Hochner, & Perry (1979)	+	+ 0	+	
Greenberg (1980)	+	+		
Rhodes & Steers (1981)	+		+	Higher absenteeism
Oliver (1990)				Relation between values and attitudes
ESOPs and direct employee ownership				
Tucker, Nock, & Toscano (1989)	0	+	+	
Long (1978b)	+	+	+	
Long (1981, 1982)	0	0	0	
Granrose, Applebaum, & Singh (1986)	+	+ 0		
Hammer, Landau, & Stern (1981)				Both higher and lower absenteeism
Rooney (1988)	0			
Buchko (1988)				No effect on absenteeism; more grievances

NOTE: *Findings indicate how employee ownership workers responded.

of the financial rewards they receive from the company (French, 1987; French & Rosenstein, 1984a). The other theory views the impact of employee ownership in more psychological terms, arguing that positive outcomes are due to a sense of "psychological ownership" created by financial, but especially psychological, factors (Long, 1978a, 1989; Paul, Ebadi, & Dilts, 1987; Pierce et al., 1991). In the following pages I review the research concerning the impact of these moderating factors on productivity and employee attitudes.

Productivity

The GAO (1987) study of ESOP outcomes examined a variety of possible moderators, including the average value of an employee's holding, the size of stock dividends paid to employees, and the degree of employee influence on corporate decision making. The only significant variable was the degree of employee influence. Productivity was positively related to employee participation in corporate decision making.

As described above, Rosen and Quarrey (1987) found that employee-owned companies grew faster than conventional firms. In addition, they found that employee involvement was also important. "ESOP companies that instituted participation plans grew at a rate three to four times faster than ESOP companies that did not. Also impressive was the correlation between performance and the actual routines of participation—for example, the number of meetings held in which workers and management could develop corporate plans and resolve difficulties" (Rosen & Quarrey, 1987, p. 128). Unfortunately the authors presented no explicit results to buttress these conclusions.

In a very different setting—worker cooperatives—Jones (1987) examined the impact of worker-directors (see Chapter 6) and employee ownership on productivity. In this study financial ownership was the value of assets of individual members of a sample of 50 British cooperatives during 1978. Jones found that the presence of worker-directors had a positive impact on productivity. However, he found that the degree of financial participation (ownership) was *negatively* related to productivity.

In a cross-national survey, Estrin, Jones, and Svejnar (1987) examined worker cooperatives in France, Italy, Spain, the United Kingdom, and the United States. Their analyses focused on common variables for their samples from France, Italy, and the United Kingdom. Examining the impact of five economic measures of employee participation (profit sharing, capital stake per employee-owner, percentage of employees owning stock, etc.), the authors found that these variables had a significant effect on productivity. The strongest and most reliable effects were found for the amount of profits allocated to employee-owners. The degree of worker participation in decision making was related to productivity in the British and French samples and in part, but not in all, of the Italian sample. Overall, consistent effects were found for both financial commitment and worker involvement in worker cooperatives across three countries.

Conte and Svejnar (1988) compared companies with profit sharing, companies with ESOPs, and producer cooperatives in the plywood industry in terms of productive efficiency. In their sample of 40 firms, efficiency was assessed as a function of total hours worked, fixed investment, sales, and several other factors. These authors then examined the impact of profit sharing, percentage of stock owned by nonmanagerial employees, and measures of participation on productive efficiency. The measures of employee participation (participation programs or participation in setting wages) were positively related to productive efficiency. The amount of stock owned by nonmanagerial employees (directly and through an ESOP) was significantly and *negatively* related to efficiency.

Employee Attitudes

Probably the best-known study examining how an ESOP influences worker attitudes was conducted by Klein and her colleagues (Klein, 1987; see also Rosen, Klein, & Young, 1986a, 1986b). These authors examined three possible models that could explain more positive attitudes in employee-owned firms. The attitudes could be due to the ownership per se (intrinsic satisfaction model), the financial benefits of ownership (extrinsic satisfaction model), or the increased worker participation and influence (instrumental satisfaction model).

Klein assessed worker influence, employee attitudes, and financial outcomes of 2,804 employees in 37 employee-owned firms. The primary variables included satisfaction with the ESOP, organizational commitment, turnover intentions, employee ownership philosophy, perceptions of work influence, and stock return. The results indicated that employees are most satisfied and most committed when the company makes large contributions to the ESOP, when management has a strong employee ownership philosophy, and when there are extensive communications by management.

These results support the extrinsic and instrumental models, but not the intrinsic model, of satisfaction. Klein argued that the most likely explanation was that positive employee attitudes were due to the rewards that employee ownership provided. Although management philosophy and work influence were related to positive attitudes, the direction of causality was not clear. Klein used these findings to suggest more research on compensation and benefit plans.

A follow-up analysis by Klein and Hall (1988) employing the same data set examined predictors of individuals' satisfaction

with their ESOP. Whereas the original study (Klein, 1987) analyzed the data at the company level, this later analysis examined
both company and individual characteristics to predict individual
responses. The results indicated that satisfaction with the ESOP
was related to company characteristics (e.g., philosophy of management, size of contribution, ESOP age). In addition, individual
characteristics (e.g., salary, tenure, education) were related to satisfaction. Finally, a number of interactions between ESOP characteristics and individual characteristics were significant.

An interesting study by Long (1978b) tried to distinguish between employee ownership by individuals (owning stock in the
company) and participation in decision making. As the author
pointed out, these two situations are expected to covary, but this
is not necessarily so. In his study of a trucking firm (see Long,
1978a), Long measured whether respondents owned stock and
how much influence they felt they had on a variety of issues. In
addition, a number of outcome variables (involvement, commitment, satisfaction) also were measured. Long found that the correlation between stock ownership and perceived influence was
only .14. Stock ownership was significantly related to involvement and commitment, but perceived influence was significantly
related to integration, involvement, satisfaction, and motivation.

A number of studies have examined the impact of degree of
ownership on employee attitudes: Is there a relationship between
the number of shares employees own and their attitudes about the
company or employee ownership? French and Rosenstein (1984b)
compared the value of shares held in the firm to several attitudes
for employees of an employee-owned plumbing and heating company. These authors found that although ownership alone was not
a predictor of the employee attitudes, the interaction between
ownership and position in the corporate hierarchy predicted organizational identification, and the interaction between ownership and white-collar/blue-collar status predicted how well the
employee understood the employee ownership plan. Surprisingly
the relationship between ownership and organizational identification was stronger for lower level employees.

Hammer and Stern (1980) examined the perceptions of workers
and managers of their roles in an employee-owned firm. Surveying a furniture firm that was converted to avoid liquidation, these
authors found no correlation between the number of shares owned

and the employees' perceptions of ownership. Stockholders among the employees perceived themselves as owners of the firm more than nonstockholders, but both blue-collar and white-collar workers perceived management as owners of the company more than themselves. In short, legal ownership was not related to psychological ownership. In another study described above, Hammer et al. (1981) found that absenteeism behavior was influenced by conversion to employee ownership. However, there was no relationship at the individual level between ownership and individual absenteeism.

Another study examining the impact of stock ownership on employee attitudes was conducted by Long (1982). He compared employees making high stock purchases to comparable employees making low stock purchases. Few differences were found between the groups.

In the study described above by Buchko (1988), he assessed the degree of employee ownership in terms of amount of stock. Buchko found that this measure of ownership was significantly related to organizational commitment but not to absenteeism. Although the positive finding is encouraging, it should be noted that the computation of ownership incorporated both organizational tenure and salary, which probably would be related to commitment.

Sockell (1985) examined the impact of ownership on several union-related attitudes in three unionized, employee-owned firms. She found that stock ownership had no effect on perceived need for the union or on willingness to strike in two of the three companies. In the third company, ownership was negatively related to willingness to strike. Ownership was a significant predictor of attending union meetings in one firm and was a predictor of grievances filed in another firm.

Ettling (1990) surveyed 903 respondents from 29 ESOPs that were at least 2 years old and had more than 30 employees. The survey assessed economic conditions that should lead to a sense of psychological ownership (such as stock value change), plus ownership satisfaction, job satisfaction, pay satisfaction, organizational commitment, internal work motivation, and intentions to leave the organization. Stock value change (a measure of financial rewards from the ESOP) significantly predicted only satisfaction with ownership. However, a variable that summarized the economic policies leading to psychological ownership significantly predicted ownership satisfaction, pay satisfaction, organizational commitment, and intentions to quit. In addition, a number of interactions were significant. The interactions indicated that where psychological ownership was low, rising stock prices could lead to more negative employee attitudes.

Investigating a somewhat unique situation, Lengnick-Hall (1991) examined the impact of ownership stake on employee attitudes in a Midwest utility. Because of changes in ESOP laws in 1986, the utility altered its ESOP, directly benefitting long-term employees, slightly benefitting moderate-tenure employees (6 to 15 years), and eliminating benefits for short-term employees. Therefore, three groups of employees with very different ownership stakes in the ESOP existed within the same company. The findings werè consistent with the studies above: The degree of ownership was unrelated to employee satisfaction (except satisfaction with the ESOP) and organizational commitment.

Summary

The research above is summarized in Table 9.3. This table compares the findings in terms of the financial ownership and psychological ownership hypotheses. This is a gross oversimplification, but it can serve to abstract the findings.

As the table shows, considerably more research has addressed the financial ownership hypothesis, and the research findings concerning this are extremely mixed. Some research indicates that measures of financial stake (e.g., size of contribution by company) are related to employee attitudes and/or organizational performance, yet the most obvious measure (amount of stock owned) shows few positive effects. Proponents of the financial perspective argue that the number of shares is an inadequate measure because in ESOPs (the firms most commonly studied) the shares are part of a retirement pension, and so profits are not paid directly to the employee. In addition, the range of values for the amount of stock also may be too limited within one company. It might be necessary to survey across a variety of ESOPs to test this hypothesis adequately. Third, it is also true that the direct incentive is small. Although any savings and improvements an employee makes will increase his or her profits, he or she will get only a very tiny percentage of that profit.

Table 9.3 Tests of the Financial and Psychological Ownership
Hypotheses

Study	Form	Findings
Performance[**]		
General Accounting Office (1987)	ESOP	No support for financial hypothesis; some support for psychological
Rosen & Quarrey (1987)	ESOP	Support for financial hypothesis
Jones (1987)	Co-op	No support for financial hypothesis; support for psychological
Estrin, Jones, & Svejnar (1987)	Co-op	Support for financial hypothesis; support for psychological
Conte & Svejnar (1988)	ESOP and co-op	No support for financial hypothesis; support for psychological
Klein (1987)	ESOP	Support for financial hypothesis; support for psychological
Employee attitudes[***]		
Klein (1987)	ESOP	Support for financial hypothesis; support for psychological
Klein & Hall (1988)	ESOP	Support for financial hypothesis
Long (1978b)	Direct*	Support for financial hypothesis; support for psychological
French & Rosenstein (1984a)	ESOP	Partial support for financial hypothesis
Hammer & Stern (1990)	Direct	No support for financial hypothesis
Long (1982)	Direct	No support for financial hypothesis
Sockell (1985)	ESOP and direct	Small support for financial hypothesis
Ettling (1990)	ESOP	No support for financial hypothesis; support for psychological
Buchko (1988)	ESOP	Some support for financial hypothesis
Lengnick-Hall (1991)	ESOP	No support for financial hypothesis

NOTE: *Direct refers to direct ownership, Co-op to worker cooperatives; **Performance refers to financial performance or productivity; and ***attitudes refers to all types of employee attitudes.

There is less research but more consistent evidence that perceptions of involvement or some type of employee participation program is related to more positive employee attitudes and/or organizational performance. However, this relationship is based on only seven studies covering all types of employee ownership.

The evidence seems to suggest that some combination of both financial and psychological ownership is probably most effective.

It makes sense that financial ownership without a sense of ownership would be ineffective, yet simple participation may not be enough. The inconsistency in the performance and employee attitude outcomes described above could be attributed to inadequate financial or psychological ownership.

Implementation of Employee Ownership: The ESOP

Because of the tax advantages they offer, most companies converting to employee ownership employ ESOPs. Worker cooperatives will continue to be formed and to exist, but at a relatively low rate. Because of this environment, almost all of the literature focusing on setting up employee ownership comes at it from the perspective of organizing an ESOP. My discussion also takes this perspective.

Benefits and Drawbacks of ESOPs for Management

Management may desire the ESOP for a number of reasons, most of them unconcerned with the philosophy of employee involvement. In the past the most popular reasons for employee ownership were either a company was failing and workers were about to lose their jobs or the owner(s) of a small company wanted to sell part or all of the company yet put control of the company into friendly hands. Until the 1980s these two reasons explained most ESOP plans.

In the last decade, however, two additional reasons led to the explosive growth in ESOPs. First, the ESOP provides considerable tax benefits, making it a valuable financial tool (Binns, 1990; Block, 1991). In fact, there has been considerable discussion of ESOPs, not as a means of involving employees, but as an excellent way of raising funds (e.g., Nassau & Schwartz, 1989; Riley & McSweeny, 1987).

Second, the ESOP is an effective takeover defense, allowing a company's management to place considerable chunks of stock out of the reach of corporate raiders (Curtis, 1990). When employees vote their stock, they tend to side with management against outside antagonists. In addition, the stock in the employee stock ownership trust (ESOT) that is not parcelled out to employees is voted by a trustee, usually appointed by management.

As the reader can see, as much as managers may discuss the potential benefits of employee ownership on productivity, quality, and so on, the impetus for setting up ESOPs is typically external, not internal.

Management concerns with employee ownership have come from two directions. First, employee ownership presents a contradiction to the way organizations typically are run in capitalist societies. This disruption can produce problems for management. A study by Stern and Hammer (1978), for example, found that a majority of the union leader respondents had negative opinions about employee ownership. A study by Bellas (1972), for example, found that managers in employee-owned companies had lower job satisfaction than managers in conventional firms. Any type of radical change, such as conversion to employee ownership, will produce concerns.

Although employee ownership generally is seen as a somewhat unusual arrangement, some evidence indicates that it is becoming more accepted. Egan, Herrmann, and Jones (1989) surveyed undergraduates at three universities to find their opinions about employee ownership. These authors found that students preferred firms entirely owned by both managerial and nonmanagerial employees and firms owned equally by employees and other people. The least preferred firms were those owned entirely by nonemployees (stockholders).

The second type of ESOP drawbacks for management involve pragmatic issues with the implementation. First, ESOP legal fees can be high, making it undesirable for small firms (Emshwiller, 1991a; Rosen, 1983). Second, the tax benefits are useful only if the company makes a profit. Third, the tax benefits are mandated by Congress and can be eliminated at any time. With the negative press in the last several years about ESOPs (Farrell & Hoerr, 1989; Hoerr, Stevenson, & Norman, 1985; Nasar, 1989), it is possible that Congress might abolish some of the tax incentives.

Benefits and Drawbacks of ESOPs
for Employees

The major benefit of the ESOP for employees is that it can be used to save jobs if the company or a facility is to be shut down. However, in one study of the reasons why employees voted for employee ownership, Hochner and Granrose (1985) found that individual attitudes (entrepreneurial spirit) seemed to be a major cause.

In addition to saving jobs, of course, are the *possible* benefits to employees of increased participation in decision making—greater commitment, job satisfaction, and so on. In many ESOPs the employees felt that this possibility turned their work life around (see examples in Kirkpatrick, 1988; Rosen et al., 1986a, 1986b; Taplin, 1989).

With these advantages, however, come several disadvantages for employees. First and most important, the ESOP is a pension plan for employees in which the majority (or sometimes all) of the pension depends on the company's performance. If the company fails, the ESOP also fails, and the employees lose some or all of their pensions. A GAO study found that 30% of the ESOPs surveyed in 1981 had been terminated, a rate substantially higher than other pension funds. In addition, the average ESOP account balances were lower than traditional pension plans but were growing faster (Staff, 1991a). In other words, the ESOP is a calculated risk, with employees betting their pensions. Employees turning to an ESOP to save their jobs could possibly end up without jobs or pensions (Konrad, 1991; Lehnert, 1991; Mallory, 1991; White, 1991).

A second potential drawback for employees is that the involvement benefits associated with an ESOP are not guaranteed. In some ESOPs employees were ignored and even abused by management (Dentzer, Friday, & Cohn, 1987; Fisher, 1991). Blasi and Kruse (1991) labeled this situation the "feudal employee-ownership culture."

The Dan River ESOP, for example, was formed when the company went private to avoid being taken over by corporate raider Carl Icahn (Foust, 1987). To make the ESOP work, employees gave up their pension plan in return for a 70% share of the stock. However, they were given no voting rights with their stock. The top 26 managers plus outside investors bought a special class of stock that included voting rights. In addition, this special stock class appreciated in value faster than the stock purchased by the employees. Because of these problems and others, employees felt they were cheated, and productivity and profit improvement have been nonexistent.

Abuses like the Dan River ESOP occur because ESOPs increasingly are seen as financial strategies rather than methods of employee involvement. All of these financial advantages can be accomplished without management giving up power (Dunn & Daily, 1991: Emshwiller, 1991b). In fact, one article notes that an owner need not lose control even if he or she sells more than a majority interest. The president of an ESOP company summed it up well by saying, "You could sell 100% of your firm to an ESOP and still manage it the same way you always did" (Emshwiller, 1991b, p. B9). One way to do this is to have the founder name him- or herself as trustee of the ESOP. This individual then would vote most of the shares in a privately held company.

Because of these financial advantages, ESOPs have grown tremendously in the last decade, and the focus has been on the financial outcomes rather than on the more traditional employee-involvement outcomes. Recent writers in the popular business press have focused on the negative side of ESOPs (Becker, 1989; Blasi, 1988; Farrell & Hoerr, 1989; Nasar, 1989). The negative examples are piling up. Employees at South Bend Lathe bought the company through an ESOP and later went out on strike, against themselves. Employing a leveraged ESOP, Burlington Industries went private in 1987 to avoid a takeover. In 1992 the company tried to make a public offering, diluting the employees' stake in the company from 49% to 3% and reducing the value of their stock by more than 50%. The employees then prepared to unionize (Konrad, 1992) and sue the firm (Ruffenach & Anders, 1992). In some situations the employees are joined in their lawsuits by the Department of Labor (Fisher, 1991).

How to Manage the ESOP

From the research conducted on ESOPs and from successful case studies, some general recommendations can be made. First, decisions need to be made concerning the type and amount of contributions the company makes to the ESOP. Second, employees need to be educated about the ESOP and its implications. Third, it is advisable to incorporate some form of employee involvement when setting up the ESOP. Fourth, management needs to be committed to the ESOP as a method of employee involvement, not as a lucrative financial strategy. Although none of these recommendations are guaranteed to produce success, they generally are found in successful ESOPs.

Financial Policies

In setting up an ESOP, the company makes an initial contribution of stock or money for stock and then makes regular additional contributions for the employees. The research by Klein (1987) and

Rosen et al. (1986a) demonstrates that more effective plans (in terms of employee attitudes) have larger contributions by the company. Whether it is the greater financial reward for employees or the stronger demonstration of management's commitment that is important is irrelevant. Regardless of the reason, the company should "make regular, substantial contributions to the ownership plan. . . . most of the companies that scored the highest on our surveys contributed an amount equal to 10-25% of pay every year to their ownership plan" (Rosen et al., 1986a, p. 194).

Employee Education

In addition to making substantial contributions, it is also important to educate employees effectively about the ownership plan when it is first set up and to inform employees regularly about the ownership plan, how the company stock is doing, and so on. (Young, 1990). Research by Klein (1987) and Hammer and Stern (1980) demonstrate that companies that communicate what is going on to their employees tend to be more successful. If one adopts a financial perspective, it seems reasonable that employees will be motivated by employee ownership only when they understand how much money they are making. Expectancy theory (Porter & Lawler, 1968; Vroom, 1964) would predict that employees will be motivated by the financial aspects of employee ownership only when they can see the links between their performance and the increased outcomes of ownership. This is not easy. Joe Vittoria, chair of Avis, which converted to employee ownership in 1987, spent a good part of his time meeting with employees and keeping them informed about Avis's progress (Kirkpatrick, 1988). At the beginning it requires education for employees to better understand the ESOP itself, as well as begin participation programs, to help make the ESOP effective ("Once the ESOP," 1990; Vanderslice & Leventhal, 1987).

Employee Involvement

There seems to be general agreement that more successful ESOPs involve their employees in decision making (e.g., Eisman, 1989; Taplin, 1989). If employees are involved in some sense, they may have more positive attitudes and the organization may be more productive. In this respect one can look at the preceding chapters in this book for an idea of how the employees might be involved. It seems reasonable that direct, face-to-face participation with a significant amount of influence would be most effective. Eisman (1989) suggested that employees "who have the most expertise in a given area make the decisions about it" (p. 50). Representative forms of involvement, such as boards of directors, employee councils, and the like, probably are going to be less effective. The experiences of employee ownership failure (e.g., Long, 1981) often have this form of involvement for employees. It seems reasonable that more direct forms would be better.

Management Commitment

Related to the greater participation of employees is the need for commitment of management to the philosophy of employee ownership (Pierce & Furo, 1990). It is valuable for management to see the ESOP as a transference of control to the employees, not simply as a new financing program. It is also important for both management and the employees to have the same expectations concerning the transference of ownership. Examples where management and the employees did not have common expectations (e.g., Hammer, 1986; Johannesen, 1979) demonstrate the problems that exist when this does not occur. Rosen et al. (1986a) argued that management "treat people like owners, not employees" (p. 194). Largely symbolic actions, such as renaming employees as "associates" or reducing the status symbols of managerial rank, can be important. Eisman (1989) and Young (1990) advocated (a) personal commitment of top management to employee ownership and (b) written corporate values outlining this commitment. Like so many of the other forms of employee involvement discussed in this book, the commitment of management is necessary for success.

Employee involvement may be stimulated in a number of ways. Weirton Steel, a successful ESOP (Schroeder & Hoerr, 1989), employs work groups to foster employee involvement (Rosen, 1987). Quad/Graphics uses self-directed printing crews. Other companies operate using informal participation, saving the cost and hassle of formal programs. The form that the participation takes may be less important than firm commitment of management to the participation.

Overall Conclusions

As with other forms of employee involvement, the evidence concerning employee ownership is neither uniform nor incontrovertible. Some conclusions, however, can be drawn.

First, although the findings are mixed, it appears that employee ownership can (but not always) have a positive impact on organizational productivity and employee attitudes. Success is certainly not guaranteed, but the weight of the evidence suggests that employee ownership (plus employee participation) is more likely than not to have a positive effect.

One problem with much of the empirical data is that the samples tended to be self-selected or to include large percentages of companies that had been publicized in some way. This occurrence usually tends to limit studies primarily to successful employee-ownership firms. An additional problem is that the studies were either before-and-after designs, where typically many things occurred in addition to the conversion to ownership, or they contrasted employee-owned companies to "comparable" conventional firms. Of course, no firm is directly comparable to another, so the findings may be influenced by other variations between the companies. What would be ideal is combining these two designs into a design with a pretest and posttest for both the employee-owned company and a highly similar company (Cook & Campbell, 1979).

A second conclusion concerns the types of employee ownership. Although authors differentiate between forms of employee ownership, they seldom discriminate in terms of examining outcomes. It seems likely from the findings that worker cooperatives are more effective than ESOPs. Surveys and other comparative studies, however, seldom distinguish between cooperatives and ESOPs. Therefore, at this point it is only an interesting question. The difficulty, of course, is that large numbers of comparable cooperatives and ESOPs would need to be compared to test this hypothesis, and these organizations probably do not exist.

A third conclusion is that the effectiveness of ESOPs seems to be diminishing over time. Early studies and reviews of ESOPs tended to be relatively positive. More recent surveys (such as the GAO 1987 study), however, have tended to be less sanguine. In addition, the popular business press has become much more critical of ESOPs in the last several years. Why do these trends exist?

Many ESOPs in the late 1980s and early 1990s were created only to obtain cheap financing or to protect the company (actually the company's management) from hostile takeovers. Therefore, the overall population of employee-owned firms has changed; financial ownership still exists, but psychological ownership has decreased. The firms may be successful in terms of financing or avoiding takeovers, but they tend to fail in terms of the outcomes we have studied. This is bad news for ESOPs. It may be better for Congress to rescind some of the tax incentives and to leave ESOPs only for those companies that are committed to employee ownership and involvement.

Fourth, it seems obvious (now) that the most effective examples of employee ownership involve both a financial commitment and employee involvement. It is possible to do without one of these; the other chapters describe successful cases of employee involvement without ownership, and this chapter has identified examples of successful employee ownership without employee cooperation. For example, the Vermont Asbestos Group employee buyout was very successful in terms of saving jobs and profitability, yet the workers battled constantly with management until they finally sold out to an outside investor (Johannesen, 1979). In spite of these exceptions, it is clear that if one wants to maximize the likelihood of a successful employee-owned company, employees should be given a significant stake in the company, and employee involvement programs should be instituted.

Overall, it seems that employee ownership can be an effective strategy for committing and motivating employees. However, this is a relatively expensive way (in terms of lost government revenue) to encourage employee participation (GAO, 1986), and ownership does not guarantee employee involvement (Blasi, 1988). Ironically employee ownership seems to be most effective when it also incorporates employee involvement.

10 Overall Findings and Future Directions for Research

Overall Findings

It is now time to take the morass of findings from the preceding chapters and attempt to organize them. This chapter has two objectives. First, I want to summarize the findings from Chapter 3 through Chapter 9. At its simplest, I want to answer the question "What works and what does not?" Of course, the issues are never this simple. Second, I want to suggest new areas of research or to reemphasize areas of research that deserve more attention.

Research Findings

I tried to develop a table with simple pluses and minuses to indicate which forms of employee involvement were effective and which were not. For most forms, however, the outcomes were not this simple or straightforward. I ended up with the findings summarized in Table 10.1. In it I attempted to simplify (as much as possible) what has been found.

As a previous review of the participation literature indicated (Cotton, Vollrath, Froggatt, Lengnick-Hall, & Jennings, 1988), considerable variance exists in outcomes across the assorted forms of employee involvement. Overall, the most effective approaches are

Table 10.1 Findings for Different Forms of Employee Involvement

Strong effects	
Self-directed work teams	General improvements in productivity and job attitudes
Gainsharing plans	Improvements in productivity; some effects on employee attitudes
Intermediate effects	
Quality of work life	Improvements in labor-management relations; varying effects on productivity and employee attitudes
Job enrichment	General improvements in job attitudes; varying effects on productivity
Employee ownership	Cooperatives are linked to higher job attitudes and productivity; ESOPs have varying effects on job attitudes and productivity
Weak effects	
Quality circles	Improvements in attitudes about programs; few effects for productivity and employee attitudes
Representative participation	Few effects on productivity or employee attitudes

self-directed work teams and gainsharing programs. These two forms of employee involvement generally produce significant improvements in both productivity and employee attitudes.

The least effective forms of involvement are representative participation and quality circles. Representative participation has little impact on either productivity or employee attitudes. Of course, many advocates of this form of employee involvement typically focus on other outcomes, such as workplace democracy. Quality circles improve attitudes about participation, and they can improve productivity through suggestions. The empirical research shows, however, that, overall, there is little effect on either productivity or employee attitudes. In addition, quality circles demonstrate a low incidence of survival.

Quality of work life programs, job enrichment, and employee ownership are intermediate in terms of their effectiveness. Quality of work life programs improve labor-management relations and have, on occasion, improved productivity and job attitudes. However, these successes occurred in only about 50% of the studies. Job enrichment consistently improves job attitudes, but its impact on productivity is also about 50%. The effects of employee ownership vary according to whether one is discussing cooperatives or employee stock ownership plans (ESOPs). Because the vast majority of employee-owned companies are ESOPs, the impact of this type of ownership should be paramount. Unfortunately the record of ESOPs is spotty, with some studies finding improvements, others not. I put the greatest confidence in the GAO (1987) study that found that ESOP ownership plus a participation program leads to improved productivity but that ownership alone has no impact.

In terms of recommendations, then, it appears that the strongest recommendations would be given to self-directed work teams and gainsharing. Only qualified support would be given to quality of work life programs, job enrichment, and employee ownership. Without further evidence, it seems that little effort should be aimed at quality circles or representative participation.

Content of Employee Involvement

What inferences are we to draw from these findings? In comparing the types of involvement, it appears that four factors differentiate those forms that work from those that do not. First, the involvement needs to be focused, directed on one's everyday work, not deciding policy issues of the entire organization. The two forms with the broadest possible concentration—representative participation and employee ownership—were among the least effective. In this sense my conclusions differ markedly from the recommendations of Lawler (1988a) for high-involvement management.

Second, employees need to have a degree of control or power to make decisions. In the least effective forms—quality circles and representative participation—employee involvement denotes making recommendations to management. It is true that gainsharing also involves recommendations, but smaller and less expensive recommendations are either rubber-stamped by management or decided by a departmental committee made up of workers and management.

Third, although the focus of involvement may be narrow, it allows for changes and improvements instigated by the worker. This is why job enrichment is not as effective as self-directed work teams or gainsharing. Most job enrichment programs specify how the work is to be changed and restrict further changes within a management-designed format. The changes are primarily top-down and do not allow for bottom-up alterations. Self-directed work teams and gainsharing programs, however, assume that workers will continue to redesign and improve their jobs. This action is akin to the notion of action learning, described by Mohrman and Cummings (1989).

Fourth, the more successful forms of employee involvement require a major change in the work life of the employee. With self-directed work teams this requirement is moving from an individual job concentration to a team focus. For gainsharing programs it is the impact of compensation; the worker's pay varies, depending on the program. The weakest forms of involvement—quality circles and representative participation—demand little change in the employee's life. The moderately successful quality of work life, job enrichment, and employee ownership dictate a greater impact on the individual employees.

So what are the characteristics of the optimal employee involvement program?

1. Employees focus on their work and those factors that interact with their work.
2. Employees have the power to make at least some changes, not just recommendations, concerning their work.
3. The job changes are continuous and ongoing, allowing for further employee input. The modifications are not restricted to a single transformation or a short time frame.
4. The job changes are substantial for the employees, not minor or cosmetic changes.

Process of Employee Involvement

One interesting finding from summarizing these chapters is that although the outcomes differed across the various forms of employee involvement, the recommended processes for involvement were remarkably similar. Regardless of whether the discussions concerned self-directed work teams, gainsharing, or quality of work life, parallel suggestions arose for implementation. The points that follow summarize these suggestions for the involvement process.

Management commitment. Almost every writer describing every form has commented on the need for management commitment for employee involvement to be effective. In one survey of corporations with employee involvement programs, the number one factor necessary for success is support by top management (Dulworth, Landen, & Usilaner, 1990). The number two factor is support by middle management. Without such management commitment, it may be better not even to try. The negative findings about quality circles are a good example of this. It may be that quality circles could be more effective. As I pointed out in Chapter 4, however, quality circles are popular because they require little commitment from management; that is also why they tend to fail so often.

Employee education/training. All of these employee involvement approaches expect employees to do new tasks, to offer new ideas, and to make decisions they have not made before. Workers cannot be expected to step up and do this without some type of training. In addition, many programs (e.g., self-directed work teams) also require job skill training. Introducing employee involvement without preparing the workers is an effective way to fail.

Management education/training. For these employee involvement programs to be successful, managers also must change their perspectives and behavior (Saporito, 1986). In a survey of organizations implementing self-directed work teams, the number one problem area was in managers' willingness to change and give up authority (Zenger-Miller Company, 1990). Managers cannot be expected to make these changes without some type of education or training (Rosow & Zager, 1990). Often, however, managers (especially first-line supervisors) are overlooked when these innovations are made. This is another easy way to fail.

Summary

What, then, is the ideal employee involvement program? It should be a program that focuses on the employees' daily work, that gives employees the power to make changes and keeps those changes ongoing, and that has substantial job changes for the employees. The program should be implemented with top management support, and it should include education and training for both the employees and management. If all of these happen, the employee involvement should succeed.

Future Directions for Research

One of the interesting sociological findings in comparing the research on employee involvement is the variety of research demonstrated. For example, gainsharing has been studied primarily as an applied technique by consultants who specialize in setting up these types of programs. Therefore, much of the research consists of case studies describing one or more organizations that employed gainsharing and assessing the effectiveness of the program. From this research we can find that gainsharing tends to be effective, but there is little research on *why* gainsharing works or what factors promote or inhibit its effectiveness. In contrast, job enrichment has been studied by academics in organizational behavior. Outside of a few early case studies (Ford, 1973), authors have not examined outcomes but instead have concentrated on factors that influence perceptions of enrichment.

I have tended to spotlight just two possible outcomes from employee involvement (productivity and employee attitudes), and I have concentrated on manufacturing organizations because most of the research comes from this sector. In the discussion below, I identify additional outcomes that need to be examined, settings that need to be studied, and processes that need to be explored. There is much work yet to be done.

New Outcomes

Adaptability. One potential question is whether employee involvement increases the adaptability or flexibility of the organization, making the organization more capable of change. This improvement often is attributed to involvement (Heckscher, 1988: Helfgott, 1988), but there is little research on whether this actually occurs. Delaney and Sockell (1990) found that employee involvement programs were related to the degree to which groups support changes. Another study, by Castrogiovanni and Macy (1990), found that employee involvement increased the capacity of organizational information processing. Does employee involvement tend to make an organization more organic (Burns & Stalker, 1961) and thereby more flexible? In turn, is this greater flexibility responsible for increases in productivity found in some types of employee involvement? We do not know.

In conjunction with flexibility, employee involvement often is touted as a weapon in breaking down bureaucracy (Dumaine, 1991), explaining why some large companies can remain responsive and agile (Dumaine, 1992; Weber, 1992) and showing how to adapt to varying local markets around the world (Jacob, 1992). However, there is no research examining these types of outcomes. They sound good in recommendations to managers, but some empirical support would be worthwhile.

Mental health. Another outcome that is sometimes linked to job involvement is mental health, or a reduction of stress due to greater control in the job. Statistics demonstrate that workers in low-level, blue-collar jobs are more likely to be sick and more likely to die from a variety of physical diseases (Cooper & Smith, 1985). Research and logic also indicate that these types of jobs have little control (Fisher, S., 1985; Ganster & Fusilier, 1989). Finally, research has shown that a lack of control and repetitive work tend to produce stress (Cox, 1985; Ganster & Fusilier, 1989; Smith, 1985). A straightforward prediction, then, would be that improving the degree of employee involvement probably will improve mental health. For example, Kornhauser (1965) found that the most significant aspect of the job influencing mental health was the opportunity a job offers to use abilities and to provide a sense of accomplishment (p. 263).

A major difficulty with investigating mental health and employee involvement is the conflicting results among different studies (Spector, 1986). Several studies have found links between job design and mental health. For example, Caplan, Cobb, French, Harrison, and Pinneau (1975), Fraser (1947), Gardell (1977), and Karasek (1990) found poorer mental health among jobs with less control. Other studies, however, such as Margolis, Kroes, and Quinn (1974) and Karasek (1979), found no such relationship. It is likely that other variables moderate the job control-mental health relationship. These might include workload (Ganster & Fusilier, 1989; Spector, 1986), communication and social support (Sweeney, McFarlin, & Cotton, 1991; Williams & House, 1985), cognitive failure (Clegg & Wall, 1990; Clegg, Wall, & Kemp, 1987), and many others (e.g., Jackson, 1983). Regardless, more understanding (and therefore more research) is necessary.

Financial impact. A final outcome might be to estimate the dollar impact of employee involvement programs. Cascio (1982) demonstrated how this can be accomplished with human resource management practices, and Mirvis and Lawler (1977) estimated the financial impact of employee attitudes. This approach can be expanded to incorporate employee involvement. For example, Macy and Mirvis (1976) estimated the costs of various employee behaviors (absenteeism, accidents, and low quality) at a corporation and then estimated the benefit-to-cost ratio of a quality of work life program (Macy & Mirvis, 1982). To the extent that employee involvement programs influence these behaviors and attitudes, such programs have a measurable financial impact on the organization. To be able to assess this financial impact and report on it (Mirvis & Lawler, 1984) would be very useful in encouraging such programs.

New Settings

Service organizations. Davis and Luthans (1988) and others (e.g., Henkoff, 1991a) pointed out the need for new techniques to improve the quality and productivity of the American service industry. Although the *Fortune* 500 industrials increased sales per employee almost 30% from 1982 through 1990, the sales per employee for the *Fortune* 500 service companies actually *fell* 1% over this period. The service sector showed no increase in productivity from 1973 to 1988 (Davis & Luthans, 1988), and white-collar productivity was anemic as well.

The settings for most of the examples in this book have been in manufacturing. But we need to go beyond this, into service industries and white-collar jobs. A survey of gainsharing experience by Markham, Scott, and Little (1992) found that the vast majority of gainsharing programs were in the manufacturing and machinery/equipment industries (p. 36). The greatest productivity gains, however, occurred in the financial industry (p. 39). It appears that there should be considerable opportunity within service organizations. On the theoretical side, Chase and Hayes (1991) provided a framework describing four levels in a service firm's performance. Greater work force involvement is associated with a world-class service delivery.

Public sector. Another setting requiring research and application is the public sector. In the past a number of quality of work life programs have been sponsored in public organizations. Their success has not been great (Herrick, 1983a; Krim & Arthur, 1989). Currently there are movements to "empower" lower level participants in order to make government more efficient and responsive (Dwyer, Garland, DeGeorge, McWilliams, & Forest, 1992; Henkoff, 1991b). A major area of interest for empowerment is education, where local school teachers and principals may be given greater input into decision making (Bernstein & Howington, 1991; Henkoff, 1991c; Kantrowitz et al., 1991). These ideas for the public sector sound promising but lack coherent planning or structure. The experience from other types of involvement programs (e.g., the need for commitment, training, etc.) would seem to be useful here.

New Processes to Be Explored

Integrating content and process. A final direction for research is in exploring processes that have not been examined or in trying new approaches to examining the processes. This book is organized according to the *content* of the various employee involvement interventions. However, in each chapter I also have tried to address *process* issues for each form of involvement. By now it should be clear that most forms of involvement can produce positive effects and that any form can produce failures. Success is an interaction of an effective form of employee involvement and an effective implementation process.

Considerable (or at least some) research examines the content of the employee involvement interventions themselves. Extensive research and considerable writing examine process issues in organizational change. However, little research examines the interaction of specific forms of employee involvement program and the process of change. For example, how do different types of training influence the effectiveness of self-directed work teams? More interaction needs to occur between those interested in the process of organizational change and those interested in specific techniques, such as gainsharing or employee ownership (Doherty, Nord, & McAdams, 1989). Some forms of employee involvement (e.g., gainsharing, employee ownership) have virtually no research on how the process of implementation influences their effectiveness.

Some writers on organizational change have virtually no appreciation of the difference between quality circles and self-directed work teams. We need this type of integration and the synergy it may produce.

Integrating multiple forms of employee involvement. Job enrichment and quality circles are the most micro approaches to employee involvement. Therefore, they can be incorporated easily into the other approaches. In fact, the major theory employed in self-directed work teams—sociotechnical systems—is labeled as a theory of job design. It would seem reasonable that combining several forms of employee ownership would be more effective than a single ("purer") form. The example of Quad/Graphics in Chapter 9 illustrated different forms of employee involvement in one organization. The GAO (1987) study on ESOPs indicated that employee ownership plus employee participation were more effective than ownership alone. Is there any reason why we should stay with just one form at a time? Experimentation about which forms of involvement work well together seems to be a logical next step.

Overall Conclusions

I mentioned in Chapter 1 how this book makes two contradictory assumptions. The first is that all forms of employee involvement are related; the second is that they are all different. As the summary of findings discussed in this chapter shows, both assumptions are true.

The many forms of employee involvement are related in that the process of implementation is similar, whether you are instituting quality circles, a gainsharing program, or self-directed work teams. All of these forms of involvement require management commitment, as well as education for employees and management.

These forms of employee involvement vary in terms of their impact on productivity and employee attitudes. Therefore, you cannot address the issue of whether or not employee participation is effective; it depends on the form of participation you are studying. A success or failure with quality circles means little if you are interested in self-directed work teams.

The suggestions for future research give us a glimpse of the vast horizons of unanswered questions. Productivity and employee attitudes are relatively simplistic outcomes in comparison to organizational flexibility, economic benefits, and mental health. Yet many of the arguments given to encourage employee involvement center on these relatively untested outcomes. Employee involvement in the service and public sectors also shows promise. With only a minority of the workers in manufacturing and lower productivity in the other sectors of the economy, employee involvement needs to expand to new settings. Finally, there needs to be more integration of the content from employee involvement and process from organizational change and more attempts to fuse different forms of employee involvement.

11 Final Conclusions

This final chapter is not long, because I have made most of my points already (and my editor says I have run out of space). However, I would like to review some of the major points that came out of this review of the literature on employee involvement and participation.

My first conclusion is that some forms of employee involvement are effective in terms of some criteria, and others are less so. Success is determined by both the form of the employee involvement and the outcome studied. Trying to aggregate the literature on all of the different forms of participation and reaching an overall conclusion provide no insight whatsoever. A reviewer might as well summarize the findings on Maslow's theory, expectancy theory, and goal-setting theory and determine that there is little evidence for the effects of motivation on behavior.

The outcomes I chose for study were explicitly managerial: productivity and employee attitudes. Employing these outcomes, I found that quality circles and representative participation were relatively ineffectual. Had I chosen other outcomes, these forms of involvement might have been much more influential.

My second conclusion is that there are no guarantees with employee involvement. Even the most effective forms (e.g., self-directed work teams and gainsharing) will fail if they are not implemented effectively. This is no different from other types of organizational change (Macy, Bliese, & Norton, 1991). For example, goal setting requires that individuals be committed to the goal, understand the goal, receive feedback, and so forth, for goal setting to be effective (Locke & Latham, 1990).

My third conclusion is that American management has been involving employees more effectively in the last 5 years (Neumeier, 1992; O'Boyle, 1992; Wartzman, 1992), and this has helped improve productivity (Spiers, 1992). We should be feeling confident about the ability of employee involvement to have an impact.

My fourth conclusion, however, is that this confidence may be misplaced. Consider the following quote (Lesieur, 1958):

> We have learned that, if we push decision-making down in an organization as far as we possibly can, we tend to get better decisions, people tend to grow and to develop more rapidly, and they are motivated more effectively. . . . We recognize that no small group of management or no single manager can have all the answers. . . . I suspect that our conception of management as a manipulative, directive process is one day going to be supplanted by a very different notion that people are, after all, adults and capable of self-direction. (pp. 11-14)

This quote mirrors the current confidence in employee involvement and sounds as if it were spoken yesterday. However, it was written 35 years ago by Douglas McGregor (Lesieur, 1958). Effective employee involvement requires a shift in how management views its work. This type of "paradigm shift" (Kuhn, 1970; a term being used much too often) is slow and difficult.

As the research listed in earlier chapters demonstrates, employee involvement is not always successful. In addition, attempts often do not produce significant effects (Overman, 1990). Finally, the inevitable backlash against employee involvement also has begun (Kiechel, 1992). Therefore, although I feel that considerable success has been accomplished, the opportunity for backsliding is always present.

When I first started investigating employee involvement in the early 1980s, I truly had no strong opinions. Now, after years of reading and research, I firmly believe that involvement is capable of generating world-class improvements in American industry. The American worker is as capable as any other in the world and more capable than those of many other nations (Magnet, 1992). However, our success in global competition demands brainpower—

the ability to work smarter, not just harder (Reilly & DiAngelo, 1988; Stewart, 1991).

> The U.S. cannot match the wage rates of Taiwan and Mexico. It can potentially match anyone in its ability to provide an educated, creative work force. (Duffey, 1988, p. 94)

We can win in the global competition, but it will require a new approach to management, one incorporating employee involvement.

Notes

1. The material in this section comes from interviews and discussions with local PEL coordinators, members of the UAW-GM Human Resource Center, and PEL participants.

2. In December of 1992, the NLRB ruled against the labor-management teams at Electromation. However, the ruling was extremely narrow, and was not expected to resolve the legal dispute over such teams.

3. The material in this section comes from published accounts and discussions with plant personnel.

4. The material in this section comes from published accounts and discussions with plant personnel.

5. The material in this section comes from interviews with managers and workers and current and past members of the unit council and board of directors.

6. The material in this section comes from Ford (1969, 1973).

7. The material in this section comes from interviews with management and the teams.

8. After a change in top management, Volvo decided in October of 1992 to close the Uddevalla and Kalmar plants.

9. The material in this section comes from published reports plus interviews with managers and employees of Quad/Graphics.

References

Abbott, M. L. (1987). Looking closely at quality circles: Implications for intervention. *Clinical Sociology Review, 5,* 119-131.

Abdel-Hamin, A. A. (1979). Individual and interpersonal moderators of employee reactions to job characteristics: A reexamination. *Personnel Psychology, 32,* 121-137.

Accordino, J. J. (1989). Quality-of-working-life systems in large cities: An assessment. *Public Productivity Review, 12,* 345-360.

Ackoff, R. L. (1981). *Creating the corporate future.* New York: John Wiley.

Ackoff, R. L. (1989). The circular organization: An update. *Academy of Management Executive, 3*(1), 11-16.

Adair-Heeley, C. B. (1989). JIT methods and practices—measurements: The driving force for change. *Production and Inventory Management Review and Apics News, 9*(3), 28-29.

Adam, E. E. (1991). Quality circle performance. *Journal of Management, 17,* 25-39.

Adams, R. J., & Rummel, C. H. (1977). Workers' participation in management in West Germany: Impact on the worker, the enterprise, and the trade union. *Industrial Relations Journal, 8*(1), 4-22.

Adizes, I., & Borgese, E. M. (1975). *Self-management: New dimensions to democracy.* Santa Barbara, CA: ABC-CLIO.

Aguren, S., Hansson, R., & Karlsson, K. G. (1976). *The impact of new design on work organization.* Stockholm: Rationalization Council SAF-LO.

Aldag, R. J., Barr, S. H., & Brief, A. P. (1981). Measurement of perceived task characteristics. *Psychological Bulletin, 90,* 415-431.

Aldag, R. J., & Brief, A. P. (1979). *Task design and employee motivation.* Glenview, IL: Scott, Foresman.

Alderfer, C. P. (1987). An intergroup perspective on group dynamics. In J. Lorsch (Ed.), *Handbook of organizational behavior* (pp. 190-222). Englewood Cliffs, NJ: Prentice-Hall.

Alexander, C. P. (1988). Quality's third dimension. *Quality Progress, 21*(7), 21-23.

Algera, J. A. (1983). Objective and perceived task characteristics as a determinant of reactions by task performers. *Journal of Occupational Psychology, 56,* 95-107.

Alkhafaji, A. F. (1987). The importance of co-determination in corporate policy. *IM, 29*(3), 26-29.

Anderson, R. L., & Terborg, J. R. (1988). Employee beliefs and support for a work redesign intervention. *Journal of Management, 14*, 493-503.

Are work teams illegal? (1992, January 13). *Fortune*, pp. 14-15.

Arnholt, M. (1986). People, not machines, are the answer. *WARD'S Auto World, 6*(6), 38-39.

Arvey, R. D., Bouchard, T. J., Segal, N. L., & Abraham, L. M. (1989). Job satisfaction: Environmental and genetic components. *Journal of Applied Psychology, 74*, 187-192.

Asch, S. E. (1956). Studies of independence and conformity: I. A minority of one against a unanimous majority. *Psychological Monographs, 70* (Whole No. 416).

Aune, A. A. (1984). The Norwegian approach to productivity and company wide quality control. *Quality Circles Journal, 7*(4), 42-44.

Backhaus, J. (1987). The emergence of worker participation: Evolution and legislation compared. *Journal of Economic Issues, 21*(2), 895-910.

Bagwell, T. C. (1987, September). Quality circles: Two keys to success. *Quality Progress, 20*, 57-59.

Baloff, N., & Doherty, E. M. (1989, Winter). Potential pitfalls in employee participation. *Organizational Dynamics, 17*, 51-62.

Banas, P. A. (1988). Employee involvement: A sustained labor/management initiative at the Ford Motor Company. In J. P. Campbell & R. J. Campbell (Eds.), *Productivity in organizations: New perspectives from industrial and organizational psychology* (pp. 388-416). San Francisco: Jossey-Bass.

Bank, J. (1987). Teaching the Chinese about quality circles—A personal account. In M. Warner (Ed.), *Management reforms in China* (pp. 99-110). New York: St. Martin's.

Bank, J., & Jones, K. (1977). *Worker directors speak.* Westmead, UK: Gower.

Bank, J., & Wilpert, B. (1983). What's so special about quality circles? *Journal of General Management, 9*(1), 21-37.

Barkman, D. F. (1987). Team discipline: Put performance on the line. *Personnel Journal, 66*(3), 58-63.

Barra, R. (1983). *Putting quality circles to work: A practical strategy for boosting productivity and profits.* New York: McGraw-Hill.

Barrick, M. R., & Alexander, R. A. (1987). A review of quality circle efficacy and the existence of positive-findings bias. *Personnel Psychology, 40*, 579-592.

Barrick, M. R., & Alexander, R. A. (1992). Estimating the benefits of a quality circle intervention. *Journal of Organizational Behavior, 13*, 73-80.

Barry, D. (1991). Managing the bossless team: Lessons in distributed leadership. *Organizational Dynamics, 20*(1), 31-47.

Bartolke, K., Eschweiler, W., Flechsenberger, D., & Tannenbaum, A. S. (1982). Workers' participation and the distribution of control as perceived by members of ten German companies. *Administrative Sciences Quarterly, 27*, 380-397.

Batstone, E., Ferner, A., & Terry, M. (1983). *Unions on the board: An experiment in industrial democracy.* Oxford, UK: Basil Blackwell.

Beardsley, J. (1986). Beyond quality circles? *Quality Circles Journal, 9*(6), 10-14.

Beck, D. (1992, January/February). Implementing a gainsharing plan: What companies need to know. *Compensation and Benefits Review, 24*, 21-33.

Becker, G. S. (1989, October 23). ESOPs aren't the magic key to anything. *Business Week*, p. 20.

Bednarek, D. I. (1990, August 21). Job policies strain firms in Sweden. *Milwaukee Journal*, p. C6.

Beekun, R. I. (1989). Assessing the effectiveness of sociotechnical interventions: Antidote or fad? *Human Relations, 10,* 877-897.

Beer, M. (1980). *Organizational change and development: A systems view.* Santa Monica, CA: Goodyear.

Bellas, C. J. (1972). *Industrial democracy and the worker-owned firm: A study of twenty-one plywood firms in the Pacific Northwest.* New York: Praeger.

Benelli, G., Loderer, C., & Lys, T. (1987). Labor participation in corporate policy-making decisions: West Germany's experience with codetermination. *Journal of Business, 60*(4), 553-575.

Berman, S. J., & Hellweg, S. A. (1989). Perceived supervisor communication competence and supervisor satisfaction as a function of quality circle participation. *Journal of Business Communication, 26*(2), 103-122.

Bernstein, A. (1991, July 15). Joe Sixpack's grip on corporate America. *Business Week*, pp. 108-110.

Bernstein, A. (1992, May 4). Putting a damper on that old team spirit. *Business Week*, p. 60.

Bernstein, A., & Howington, P. (1991, January 28). Letting teachers call the shots. *Business Week*, pp. 54-55.

Bernstein, A., & Rothman, M. (1987, May 11). Steelworkers want to make teamwork an institution. *Business Week*, p. 84.

Bertsch, G. K., & Obradovic, J. (1979). Participation and influence in Yugoslav self-management. *Industrial Relations, 18*(3), 322-329.

Bhagat, R. S., & Schassie, M. B. (1980). Effects of changes in job characteristics on some theory-specific attitudinal outcomes: Results from a naturally occurring quasi-experiment. *Human Relations, 33,* 297-313.

Binns, D. M. (1990). ESOPs and the 1989 Budget Reconciliation Act: The impact on public companies. In K. M. Young (Ed.), *The expanding role of ESOPs in public companies* (pp. 189-194). New York: Quorum.

Blake, L. (1991). Group decision making at Baxter. *Personnel Journal, 70*(1), 76-82.

Blasi, J. (1988). *Employee stock ownership plans: Revolution or rip-off?* New York: Ballinger.

Blasi, J., & Kruse, D. L. (1991). *The new owners: The mass emergence of employee ownership in public companies and what it means to American business.* Champaign, IL: Harper Business.

Blinder, A. S. (1989, January 29). Want to boost productivity? Try giving workers a way. *Business Week*, p. 40.

Blinder, A. S. (1989/1990, Winter). Pay, participation, and productivity: A report on the evidence. *Brookings Review, 8,* 33-38.

Block, S. B. (1991, January). The advantages and disadvantages of ESOPs: A long-range analysis. *Journal of Small Business Management*, pp. 15-21.

Blount, J. (1990). Behind the lines. *Canadian Business, 43*(1), 62-67.

Blumberg, M. (1980). Job switching in autonomous work groups: An exploratory study in a Pennsylvania coal mine. *Academy of Management Journal, 23,* 287-306.

Blumberg, M., & Pringle, C. D. (1983). How control groups can cause loss of control in action research: The case of Rushton coal mine. *Journal of Applied Behavioral Science, 19*, 409-425.

Bocialetti, G. (1987). Quality of work life: Some unintended effects on the seniority tradition of an industrial union. *Group and Organization Studies, 12*, 386-410.

Boissoneau, R. (1989). New approaches to managing people at work. *Health Care Supervisor, 7*(4), 67-76.

Bolweg, J. F. (1976). *Job design and industrial democracy; The case of Norway.* Leiden, Netherlands: Martinus Nijhoff.

Bowen, D. E., Ledford, G. E., & Nathan, B. R. (1991). Hiring for the organization, not the job. *Academy of Management Executive, 5*(4), 35-51.

Bowman, J. S. (1989). Quality circles: Promise, problems, and prospects in Florida. *Public Personnel Management, 18*(4), 375-403.

Bozman, R., & Gibson, P. (1986). Implementing participative teams in the hospitality industry. *Quality Circles Journal, 9*(2), 10-13.

Bradley, K., Estrin, S., & Taylor, S. (1990). Employee ownership and company performance. *Industrial Relations, 29*, 385-402.

Bradley, K., & Gelb, A. (1985, September/October). Employee buyouts of troubled companies. *Harvard Business Review, 63*, 121-130.

Bradley, K., & Hill, S. (1987). Quality circles and managerial interests. *Industrial Relations, 26*(1), 68-82.

Brenner, O. C. (1987). Get middle managers back on the team with the job orientation dissatisfaction index. *NRECA Management Quarterly, 28*(3), 6-12.

Brett, J. M., & Hammer, T. H. (1982). Organizational behavior and industrial relations. In *Industrial Relations Research in the 1970s: Review and appraisal* (pp. 221-281). Madison, WI: IRRA.

Brinbaum, P. H., Farh, J., & Wong, G. Y. Y. (1986). The job characteristics model in Hong Kong. *Journal of Applied Psychology, 71*, 598-605.

Brockner, J., & Hess, T. (1986). Self-esteem and task performance in quality circles. *Academy of Management Journal, 29*, 617-623.

Brooks, G. E. (1986). VDTs and health risks: What unions are doing. *Personnel, 63*(7), 59-64.

Brower, M. J. (1983). Massachusetts: Lessons from efforts that failed. In N. Q. Herrick (Ed.), *Improving government: Experiments with quality of working life systems* (pp. 61-69). New York: Praeger.

Buch, K., & Spangler, R. (1990). The effects of quality circles on performance and promotions. *Human Relations, 43*, 573-582.

Buchko, A. A. (1988). The effects of employee ownership on employee behaviors. In *Academy of Management best papers proceedings, 1988* (pp. 181-185). Anaheim, CA: Academy of Management.

Bullock, A. (1977). Committee of inquiry on industrial democracy. *Report* (Cmnd 6706). London: Her Majesty's Stationery Office (HMSO).

Bullock, R. J., & Lawler, E. E. (1984). Gainsharing: A few questions, and fewer answers. *Human Resource Management, 23*, 23-40.

Bullock, R. J., & Perlow, R. (1986). The effects of gainsharing on fundamental job attitudes. *Academy of Management best papers proceedings, 1986* (pp. 229-233). Chicago: Academy of Management.

Bullock, R. J., & Tubbs, M. E. (1990). A case meta-analysis of gainsharing plans as organization development interventions. *Journal of Applied Behavioral Science, 26*, 383-404.

Burack, E. H. (1988). A strategic planning and operational agenda for human resources. *Human Resource Planning, 11*(2), 63-68.

Burda, D. (1990, November 12). Hospital teams find solutions, savings through quality management techniques. *Modern Healthcare, 20*(45), 44.

Bureau of National Affairs (BNA). (1991, November 4). EC draft on worker consultation draws criticism from trade unions. *BNA's Employee Relations Weekly, 9,* 1192.

Burke, W. W., Clark, L. P., & Koopman, C. (1984, September). Improving your OD project's chances for success. *Training and Development Journal*, pp. 62-68.

Burns, T., & Stalker G. M. (1961). *The management of innovation.* London: Tavistock.

Bushe, G. R. (1987). Temporary or permanent middle-management groups: Correlates with attitudes in QWL change projects. *Group and Organization Studies, 12*, 23-37.

Bushe, G. R. (1988a). Cultural contradictions of statistical process control in American manufacturing organizations. *Journal of Management, 14*, 19-31.

Bushe, G. R. (1988b). Developing cooperative labor-management relations in unionized factories: A multiple case study of quality circles and parallel organizations within joint quality of work life projects. *Journal of Applied Behavioral Science, 24*, 129-150.

Caldwell, D. F., & O'Reilly, C. A. (1982). Task perceptions and job satisfaction: A question of causality. *Journal of Applied Psychology, 67*, 361-369.

Callerman, T. E., & Heyl, J. E. (1986). A model for material requirements planning implementation. *International Journal of Operations and Production Management, 6*(5), 30-37.

Campbell, D. J. (1988). Task complexity: A review and analysis. *Academy of Management Review, 13*, 40-52.

Campion, M. A. (1988). Interdisciplinary approaches to job design: A constructive replication with extensions. *Journal of Applied Psychology, 73*, 467-481.

Campion, M. A., & McClelland, C. L. (1991). Interdisciplinary examination of the costs and benefits of enlarged jobs: A job design quasi-experiment. *Journal of Applied Psychology, 76*, 186-198.

Campion, M. A., & Thayer, P. W. (1985). Development and field evaluation of an interdisciplinary measure of job design. *Journal of Applied Psychology, 70*, 29-43.

Campion, M. A., & Thayer, P. W. (1987). Job design: Approaches, outcomes, and trade-offs. *Organizational Dynamics, 15*(3), 66-79.

Caplan, R. D., Cobb, S., French, J. R. P., Harrison, R. D., & Pinneau, S. R. (1975). *Job demands and worker health: Main effects and occupational differences.* Washington, DC: Government Printing Office.

Carnall, C. A. (1982). Semi-autonomous work groups and the social structure of the organization. *Journal of Management Studies, 19*, 277-294.

Cascio, W. F. (1978). *Applied psychology in personnel management.* Reston, VA: Reston Publishing.

Cascio, W. F. (1982). *Costing human resources: The financial impact of behavior in organizations.* Boston: Kent.

Case history: The benefits of gainsharing. (1987). *Small Business Reports, 12*(4), 90.

Castorina, P., & Wood, B. (1988, June). Why circles fail. *Journal for Quality and Participation, 11*(2), 40-41.

Castrogiovanni, G. J., & Macy, B. A. (1990). Organizational information-processing capabilities and degree of employee participation. *Group and Organization Studies, 15,* 313-336.

Cellar, D. F., Kernana, M. C., & Barrett, G. V. (1985). Conventional wisdom and ratings of job characteristics: Can observers be objective? *Journal of Management, 11,* 131-138.

Champagne, P. J., & Tausky, C. (1978). When job enrichment doesn't pay. *Personnel, 55*(1), 30-40.

Chase, R. B., & Hayes, R. H. (1991, Fall). Beefing up operations in service firms. *Sloan Management Review, 33,* 15-26.

Cheal, A. E. (1987, June). Electronic quality circles. *Quality Circles Journal, 10*(2), 58-60.

Cherns, A. (1976). The principles of sociotechnical design. *Human Relations, 29,* 783-792.

Cherns, A. (1986). The political dimensions of QWL. *International Journal of Manpower, 7*(4), 18-22.

Claire, S., & Wexler, J. (1985). Quality circles: Productivity with an OD perspective. In D. D. Warrick (Ed.), *Contemporary organization development: Current thinking and applications* (pp. 329-339). Glenview, IL: Scott, Foresman.

Clark, H. B., Wood, R., Kuehnel, T., Flanagan, S., Mosk, M., & Northrup, J. T. (1986). Preliminary validation and training of supervisory interactional skills. *Journal of Organizational Behavior Management, 7,* 95-115.

Clegg, C., & Wall, T. (1990). The relationship between simplified jobs and mental health: A replication study. *Journal of Occupational Psychology, 63,* 289-296.

Clegg, C., Wall, T., & Kemp, N. J. (1987). Women on the assembly-line: A comparison of main and interactive explanations of job satisfaction, absence and mental health. *Journal of Occupational Psychology, 60,* 273-287.

Cole, R. E. (1979). *Work, mobility, and participation: A comparative study of American and Japanese industry.* Berkeley: University of California Press.

Coleman, P. (1974). *Transactional analysis and successful management.* Elk Grove, IL: Advanced Systems.

Comen, T. (1989). Making quality assurance work for you. *Cornell Hotel and Restaurant Administration, 30*(3), 23-29.

Conger, J. A., & Kanungo, R. N. (1988). The empowerment process: Integrating theory and practice. *Academy of Management Review, 13,* 471-482.

Conte, M. A., & Svejnar, J. (1988). Productivity effects of worker participation in management, profit-sharing, worker ownership of assets and unionization in U.S. firms. *International Journal of Industrial Organization, 6,* 139-151.

Conte, M. A., & Tannenbaum, A. S. (1978). Employee-owned companies: Is the difference measurable? *Monthly Labor Review, 101,* 23-28.

Cook, M. H. (1982, January). Quality circles—They really work, but. . . . *Training and Development Journal, 36,* 4-5.

Cook, T. D., & Campbell, D. T. (1979). *Quasi-experimentation: Design and analysis issues for field settings.* Chicago: Rand McNally.

Cooke, W. N. (1989). Improving productivity and quality through collaboration. *Industrial Relations, 28,* 299-319.

Cooke, W. N. (1990a). Factors influencing the effect of joint union-management programs on employee-supervisor relations. *Industrial and Labor Relations Review, 43*(5), 587-603.

Cooke, W. N. (1990b). *Labor-management cooperation.* Kalamazoo, MI: UpJohn Institute.

Cooper, C. L., & Smith, M. J. (1985). Introduction: Blue collar workers are "At risk." In C. L. Cooper & M. J. Smith (Eds.), *Job stress and blue collar work* (pp. 1-4). Chichester, England: John Wiley.

Copenhaver, L., & Guest, R. H. (1982/1983). Quality of work life: The anatomy of two successes. *National Productivity Review, 1*(1), 5-12.

Copp, E., & Nielsen, K. (1989). Improving productivity through quality control. *Transmission and Distribution, 41*(12), 46-48.

Coppett, J. I., & Sullivan, C. H. (1986). Marketing in the information age. *Business, 36*(3), 13-18.

Cordery, J. L., Mueller, W. S., & Smith, L. M. (1991). Attitudinal and behavioral effects of autonomous group working: A longitudinal field study. *Academy of Management Journal, 34,* 464-476.

Cordery, J. L., & Wall, T. D. (1985). Work design and supervisory practice: A model. *Human Relations, 38,* 425-441.

Cordova, E. (1982). Workers' participation in decisions within enterprises: Recent trends and problems. *International Labour Review, 121*(2), 125-140.

Cosentino, C., Allen, J., & Wellins, R. (1990, March). Choosing the right people. *HRMagazine,* pp. 66-70.

Cotton, J. L., McFarlin, D. M., & Sweeney, P. D. (in press). A cross-national comparison of employee participation: Insights for American management. *Journal of Managerial Psychology.*

Cotton, J. L., Vollrath, D. A., Froggatt, K. L., Lengnick-Hall, M. L., & Jennings, K. R. (1988). Employee participation: Diverse forms and different outcomes. *Academy of Management Journal, 13,* 8-22.

Cotton, J. L., Vollrath, D. A., Lengnick-Hall, M. L., & Froggatt, K. L. (1990). Fact: The form of participation does matter—A rebuttal to Leana, Locke, and Schweiger. *Academy of Management Journal, 15,* 147-153.

Covey, S. R. (1989). Universal mission statement. *Executive Excellence, 6*(3), 7-9.

Cox, T. (1985). Repetitive work: Occupational stress and health. In C. L. Cooper & M. J. Smith (Eds.), *Job stress and blue collar work* (pp. 85-112). Chichester, UK: John Wiley.

Cummings, T. G. (1978, July). Self-regulating work groups: A socio-technical synthesis. *Academy of Management Review,* pp. 625-634.

Cummings, T. G., & Griggs, W. H. (1976, Winter). Worker reactions to autonomous work groups: Conditions for functioning, differential effects, and individual differences. *Organization and Administrative Sciences, 7,* 87-100.

Cummings, T. G., & Huse, E. F. (1989). *Organizational development and change.* St. Paul, MN: West.

Cummings, T. G., & Molloy, E. S. (1977). *Improving productivity and the quality of work life.* New York: Praeger.

Cummings, T. G., Molloy, E. S., & Glen, R. (1977). A methodological critique of fifty-eight selected work experiments. *Human Relations, 30,* 675-708.

Curtis, J. (1990). Using an ESOP as a takeover defense. In K. M. Young (Ed.), *The expanding role of ESOPs in public companies* (pp. 63-70). New York: Quorum.

Cutcher-Gershenfeld, J., McKersie, R. B., & Wever, K. R. (1988). *The changing role of union leaders* (U.S. Department of Labor, Bureau of Labor-Management, BLMR 127). Washington, DC: Government Printing Office.

Czaja, S. J., Cary, J. M., Drury, C. G., & Cohen, B. G. (1987). An ergonomic evaluation of traditional and automated office environments. *Office, Technology and People, 3*(3), 231-246.

Dachler, H. P., & Wilpert, B. (1978). Conceptual dimensions and boundaries of participation in organizations: A critical evaluation. *Administrative Science Quarterly, 23*, 1-39.

Dailey, D. A. (1986). Creativity and motivation: Keys to effective safety committees. *Professional Safety, 31*(12), 17-23.

Davenport, R. (1950). Enterprise for every man. *Fortune, 41*(1), 51-58.

Davies, R. J. (1978, April). Industrial democracy in Europe and its relevance for Canada: A critical review. *Labour Gazette*, pp. 133-138.

Davis, B., & Milbank, D. (1992, February 7). If the U.S. work ethic is fading, "laziness" may not be the reason. *Wall Street Journal*, pp. A1, A5.

Davis, L. E., & Cherns, A. E. (1975). *The quality of working life* (Vols. 1-2). New York: Free Press.

Davis, L. E., & Taylor, J. C. (1979). *Design of jobs* (2nd ed.). Santa Monica, CA: Goodyear.

Davis, T. R. V., & Luthans, F. (1988). Service OD: Techniques for improving the delivery of quality service. *Organizational Development Journal, 6*(4), 76-80.

Dean, J. W. (1985). The decision to participate in quality circles. *Journal of Applied Behavioral Science, 21*, 317-327.

Decisions in Organizations (DIO). (1979). Participative decision making: A comparative study. *Industrial Relations, 18*, 295-309.

Delamotte, Y. (1988). Workers' participation and policies in France. *International Labour Review, 127*(2), 221-241.

Delaney, J. T., & Sockell, D. (1990). Employee involvement programs, unionization, and organizational flexibility. *Academy of Management best papers proceedings* (pp. 264-268). San Francisco: Academy of Management.

Denison, D. R. (1982). Sociotechnical design and self-managing work groups: The impact on control. *Journal of Organizational Behavior, 3*, 297-314.

Dentzer, S., Friday, C., & Cohn, B. (1987, October 19). The foibles of ESOPs. *Newsweek*, pp. 58-59.

Deppe, J. (1990). The development of quality circles in the FRG. *International Journal of Quality and Reliability Management, 7*(1), 56-63.

DeToro, I. J. (1987). Quality circles and the techniques of creativity: A case history. *Journal of Creative Behavior, 21*(2), 137-140.

DeVries, D. L. (1988, August). Trials and tribulations of a booster of self-managing teams. Paper presented at the Academy of Management National Meeting, Anaheim, CA.

Dickson, J. W. (1980). Perceptions of direct and indirect participation in British companies. *Journal of Applied Psychology, 65*, 226-232.

Dillon, J. L. (1985). Quality circles, the Sperry approach. In Y. K. Shetty & V. M. Buehler (Eds.), *Productivity and quality through people: Practices of well-managed companies* (pp. 271-273). New York: Quorum.

Dilts, D. A., & Paul, R. J. (1990). Employee ownership of unionized firms: Collective bargaining or codetermination? *Business and Society, 29*(1), 19-27.

Doherty, E. M., Nord, W. R., & McAdams, J. L. (1989). Gainsharing and organization development: A productive synergy. *Journal of Applied Behavioral Science, 25,* 209-229.

Donahue, D. J. (1981). Reversing the decline in U.S. productivity growth. In V. M. Buehler & Y. K. Shetty (Eds.), *Productivity improvement: Case studies of proven practice* (pp. 108-112). New York: American Management Association.

Donovan, S. (1987). David Maus: 1987 credit union executive of the year. *Credit Union Management, 10*(11), 12-14, 18.

Doyle, R. J. (1983). *Gainsharing and productivity: A guide to planning, implementation, and development.* New York: AMACOM.

Drago, R. (1986). Participatory management in capitalist firms: An analysis of "quality circles." *Economic Analysis and Workers' Management, 20*(3), 233-249.

Drago, R. (1988). Quality circle survival: An exploratory analysis. *Industrial Relations, 27*(3), 336-351.

Drexler, J. A., & Lawler, E. E. (1977). A union-management cooperative project to improve the quality of work life. *Journal of Applied Behavioral Science, 13*(3), 373-387.

Duffey, J. (1988). Competitiveness and human resources. *California Management Review, 30*(3), 92-100.

Dulworth, M. R., Landen, D. L., & Usilaner, B. L. (1990). Employee involvement systems in U.S. corporations: Right objectives, wrong strategies. *National Productivity Review, 9*(2), 141-156.

Dumaine, B. (1989, February 13). How managers can succeed through speed. *Fortune,* pp. 54-59.

Dumaine, B. (1990, May 7). Who needs a boss? *Fortune,* pp. 52-60.

Dumaine, B. (1991, June 17). The bureaucracy busters. *Fortune,* pp. 36-50.

Dumaine, B. (1992, April 20). Is big still good? *Fortune,* pp. 50-60.

Dunford, R., & McGraw, P. (1986). Abandoning simple recipes and benefitting from quality circles: An Australian study. *Work and People, 12*(2), 22-25.

Dunn, C. P., & Daily, C. M. (1991). The fusion of privilege and power: ESOPs in theory and practice. *Employee Responsibilities and Rights Journal, 4*(1), 61-74.

Dwyer, P., Garland, S. B., DeGeorge, G., McWilliams, G., & Forest, S. A. (1992, January 20). The new gospel of good government. *Business Week,* pp. 66-70.

Eaton, A. E. (1990). The extent and determinants of local union control of participative programs. *Industrial and Labor Relations Review, 43,* 604-620.

Eden, D., & Japhet-Michaeli, M. (1991, August). *Participation in quality circles and high expectations: Impact on attitudes and output.* Paper presented at the National Meeting of the Academy of Management, Miami, FL.

Efraty, D., & Sirgy, M. J. (1990). The effects of quality of working life (QWL) on employee behavioral responses. *Social Indicators Research, 22,* 31-47.

Egan, D., Herrmann, D. J., & Jones, D. C. (1989). Evidence on attitudes toward alternative sharing arrangements. *Industrial Relations, 28,* 411-418.

Eisman, R. (1989). Do employee owners try harder? *Incentive, 163*(12), 49-54, 82-83.

Elizur, D. (1990). Quality circles and quality of work life. *International Journal of Manpower, 11*(6), 3-7.

Ellinger, C., & Nissen, B. (1987). A case study of a failed QWL program: Implications for labor education. *Labor Studies Journal, 11*(3), 195-219.

Elmuti, D. (1989). Quality control circles in Saudi Arabia: A case study. *Production and Inventory Management Journal, 30*(4), 52-55.

Elmuti, D., & Kathawala, Y. (1990). Effects of computer aided quality circles on organizational productivity and satisfaction. *Information and Management, 19*(1), 33-40.

Emery, F. (1980). Designing socio-technical systems for "greenfield" sites. *Journal of Occupational Behaviour, 1,* 19-27.

Emery, F. E., & Thorsrud, E. (1964/1969). *Form and content in industrial democracy: Some experiences from Norway and other European countries.* London: Tavistock.

Emery, F. E., & Thorsrud, E. (1976). *Democracy at work: The report of the Norwegian industrial democracy program.* Leiden, Netherlands: Martinus Nijhoff.

Emery, F. E., & Trist, E. L. (1965). The causal texture of organizational environments. *Human Relations, 18,* 21-32.

Employment Policy Foundation. (1991). *Quality at risk: Are employee participation programs in jeopardy?* Washington, DC: Author.

Emshwiller, J. R. (1991a, March 22). ESOPs: Profitable tax shelter for some, A cash-draining nightmare for others. *Wall Street Journal,* p. B14.

Emshwiller, J. R. (1991b, March 22). Will an ESOP work for your company? *Wall Street Journal,* p. B9.

Ephlin, D. (1986). Saturn's strategic role in industrial relations. *Survey of Business, 21*(4), 23-25.

Erez, M. (1986). The congruence of goal-setting strategies with socio-cultural values and its effect on performance. *Journal of Management, 12*(4), 585-592.

Estrin, S., & Bartlett, W. (1982). The effects of enterprise self-management in Yugoslavia: An empirical survey. In D. C. Jones & J. Svejnar (Eds.), *Participatory and self-managed firms* (pp. 83-107). Lexington, MA: Lexington.

Estrin, S., & Jones, D. C. (1992). The viability of employee-owned firms: Evidence from France. *Industrial and Labor Relations Review, 45,* 323-338.

Estrin, S., Jones, D. C., & Svejnar, J. (1987). The productivity effects of worker participation: Producer cooperatives in Western economies. *Journal of Comparative Economics, 11,* 40-61.

Ettling, J. (1990). Winning and losing with ESOPs: The design of effective employee stock ownership plans. In L. R. Jauch & J. L. Wall (Eds.), *Academy of Management best papers proceedings, 1990* (pp. 269-273). San Francisco: Academy of Management.

Evans, M. G., Kiggundu, M. N., & House, R. J. (1979). A partial test and extension of the job characteristics model of motivation. *Organizational Behavior and Human Performance, 24,* 354-381.

Ewing, J. C. (1989). Gainsharing plans: Two key factors. *Compensation and Benefits Review, 21*(1), 49-53.

Farnham, A. (1989, December 4). The trust gap. *Fortune,* pp. 56-78.

Farrell, C., & Hoerr, J. (1989, May 15). ESOPs: Are they good for you? *Business Week (Industrial/Technology Edition),* pp. 116-123.

Farrell, C., Smart, T., & Hammonds, K. H. (1989, March 20). Suddenly, blue chips are red-hot for ESOPs. *Business Week,* p. 144.

Fein, M. (1974). Job enrichment: A reevaluation. *Sloan Management Review, 15*(2), 69-88.

Fein, M. (1981). *Improshare: An alternative to traditional managing.* Norcross, GA: Institute of Industrial Engineers.

Fein, M. (1982a). Financial motivation. In G. Salvendy (Ed.), *Handbook of industrial engineering* (pp. 2.3.1-2.3.40). New York: John Wiley.

Fein, M. (1982b, August). *Improved productivity through worker involvement.* Paper presented at the National Academy of Management Meetings, New York.

Ferrari, S. (1986). Training for quality—The Italian experience of quality circles. *Journal of European Industrial Training, 10*(3), 12-16.

Ferris, G. R., & Gilmore, D. C. (1984). The moderating role of work context in job design research: A test of competing models. *Academy of Management Journal, 27,* 885-892.

Ferris, G. R., & Wagner, J. A. (1985). Quality circles in the United States: A conceptual reevaluation. *Journal of Applied Behavioral Science, 21,* 155-167.

Festinger, L., Schachter, S., & Back, K. (1950). *Social pressures in informal groups.* New York: Harper.

Feuer, D., & Lee, C. (1988). The kaizen connection: How companies pick tomorrow's workers. *Training, 25*(5), 23-35.

Fields, M. W., & Thacker, J. W. (1992). Influence of quality of work life on company and union commitment. *Academy of Management Journal, 35,* 439-450.

Fisher, A. B. (1985, November 11). Behind the hype at GM's Saturn. *Fortune,* pp. 34-46.

Fisher, A. B. (1991, May 20). Employees left holding the bag. *Fortune,* pp. 83-93.

Fisher, K. (1986). Management roles in the implementation of participative management systems. *Human Resources Management, 25*(3), 459-480.

Fisher, S. (1985). Control and blue collar work. In C. L. Cooper & M. J. Smith (Eds.), *Job stress and blue collar work* (pp. 19-48). Chichester, UK: John Wiley.

Fitzroy, F. R., & Kraft, K. (1987). Efficiency and internal organization: Works councils in West German firms. *Economica, 54,* 493-504.

Florkowski, G. W. (1990). Analyzing group incentive plans. *HRMagazine, 35*(1), 36-38.

Ford, R. N. (1969). *Motivation through the work itself.* New York: American Management Association.

Ford, R. N. (1971). A prescription for job enrichment success. In J. H. Maher (Ed.), *New perspectives in job enrichment* (pp. 211-224). New York: Van Nostrand Reinhold.

Ford, R. N. (1973). Job enrichment lessons from AT&T. *Harvard Business Review, 51*(1), 96-106.

Foust, D. (1987, October 26). How Dan River's ESOP missed the boat. *Business Week,* pp. 34-35.

Frank, L. L., & Hackman, J. R. (1975). A failure of job enrichment: The case of the change that wasn't. *Journal of Applied Behavioral Science, 11,* 413-436.

Fraser, R. (1947). *The incidence of neurosis among factory workers.* London: Industrial Health Research Board.

Freeman, C. E. (1985). Civilian personnel and the readiness equation. *Bureaucrat, 14*(3), 39-42.

Freiman, J. M., & Saxberg, B. O. (1989). Impact of quality circles on productivity and quality: Research limitations of a field experiment. *IEEE Transactions on Engineering Management, 36*(2), 114-118.

French, J. L. (1987). Employee perspectives on stock ownership: Financial investment or mechanism of control? *Academy of Management Review, 12,* 427-435.

French, J. L., & Rosenstein, J. (1984a). Employee ownership as financial investment. In J. A. Pearce & R. B. Robinson (Eds.), *Academy of Management proceedings* (pp. 339-342). Boston: Academy of Management.

French, J. L., & Rosenstein, J. (1984b). Employee ownership, work attitudes, and power relationships. *Academy of Management Journal, 27,* 861-869.

Fried, Y. (1991). Meta-analytic comparison of the Job Diagnostic Survey and Job Characteristics Inventory as correlates of work satisfaction and performance. *Journal of Applied Psychology, 76,* 690-697.

Fried, Y., & Ferris, G. R. (1987). The validity of the job characteristics model: A review and meta-analysis. *Personnel Psychology, 40,* 287-322.

Frost, C. F., Wakeley, J. H., & Ruh, R. A. (1974). *The Scanlon plan for organizational development: Identity, participation and equity.* East Lansing: Michigan State University Press.

Furubotn, E. G. (1985). Codetermination, productivity gains, and the economics of the firm. *Oxford Economic Papers, 37,* 22-39.

Furubotn, E. G. (1988). Codetermination and the modern theory of the firm: A property-rights analysis. *Journal of Business, 61*(2), 165-181.

Gabor, C. (1986, September). Special project task teams: An extension of a successful quality circle program. *Quality Circles Journal, 9*(3), 40-43.

Gaetan, M. (1988). The cell production process. *Bobbin, 30*(1), 24, 28.

Ganster, D. C., & Fusilier, M. R. (1989). Control in the workplace. In C. L. Cooper & I. Robertson (Eds.), *International review of industrial and organizational psychology* (pp. 235-280). Chichester, UK: John Wiley.

Garcia, J. E., & Haggith, C. (1989, June). OD interventions that work. *Personnel Administrator,* pp. 90-94.

Gardell, R. (1977). Autonomy and participation at work. *Human Relations, 30,* 515-533.

Gardner, D. G. (1990). Task complexity effects on non-task-related movements: A test of activation theory. *Organizational Behavior and Human Performance, 45,* 209-231.

Gardner, D. G., & Cummings, L. L. (1988). Activation theory and job design: Review and reconceptualization. In L. L. Cummings & B. M. Staw (Eds.), *Research in organizational behavior* (Vol. 10, pp. 81-122). Greenwich, CT: JAI.

Gates, M. (1989). American Airlines: Do people make the difference? *Incentive, 163*(5), 16-18, 138-139.

Geare, A. (1976). Productivity from Scanlon-type plans. *Academy of Management Review, 1*(3), 99-108.

Geber, B. (1986). Quality circles: The second generation. *Training, 23*(12), 54-61.

General Accounting Office (GAO). (1981). *Productivity sharing programs: Can they contribute to productivity improvement?* (AFMD-81-22). Gaithersburg, MD: Author.

General Accounting Office (GAO). (1986). *Employee stock ownership plans: Benefits and costs of ESOP tax incentives for broadening stock ownership* (GAO/PEMD-87-8). Washington, DC: Author.

General Accounting Office (GAO). (1987). *Employee stock ownership plans: Little evidence of effects on corporate performance* (GAO/PEMD-88-1). Washington, DC: Author.

Gerber, B. (1987). Herman Miller: Where profits and participation meet. *Training, 24*(11), 62-66.

Gerhart, B. (1987). How important are dispositional factors as determinants of job satisfaction? Implications for job design and other personnel programs. *Journal of Applied Psychology, 72,* 366-373.

Gerhart, B. (1988). Sources of variance in incumbent perceptions of job complexity. *Journal of Applied Psychology, 73,* 154-162.

Giallourakis, M. (1989). Reforming corporate loyalty. *Small Business Reports, 14*(2), 17-19.

Gilson, T. Q., & Lefcowitz, M. J. (1957). A plant-wide productivity bonus in a small factory: Study of an unsuccessful case. *Industrial and Labor Relations Review, 10,* 284-296.

Glass, G. V., McGaw, B., & Smith, M. L. (1981). *Meta-analysis in social research.* Beverly Hills, CA: Sage.

Glick, W. H., Jenkins, G. D., & Gupta, N. (1986). Method versus substance: How strong are underlying relationships between job characteristics and attitudinal outcomes? *Academy of Management Journal, 29,* 441-464.

Glines, D. (1987). What's new at the zoo?—A joint union-management quality circle program. *Quality Circles Journal, 10*(2), 50-55.

Goetschy, J. (1991). An appraisal of French research on direct worker participation. In R. Russell & V. Rus (Eds.), *International handbook of participation in organizations* (Vol. 2, pp. 232-247). Oxford, UK: Oxford University Press.

Goldmann, R. (1976). *A work experiment: Six Americans in a Swedish plant.* New York: Ford Foundation.

Goldstein, S. (1978). Employee share ownership and motivation. *Journal of Industrial Relations, 20,* 311-330.

Golembiewski, R. T., & Sun, B. (1989). Positive-finding bias in quality of work life research: Public-private comparisons. *Public Productivity and Management Review, 13*(2), 145-154.

Golembiewski, R. T., & Sun, B. (1990a). Positive-finding bias in QWL studies: Rigor and outcomes in a large sample. *Journal of Management, 16,* 665-674.

Golembiewski, R. T., & Sun, B. (1990b). Testing the positive-finding bias in QWL studies: Rigor and outcomes by major classes of applications. *Organization Development Journal, 8*(2), 49-57.

Goodman, P. K., Wakeley, J. H., & Ruh, R. H. (1972). What employees think of the Scanlon plan. *Personnel, 49*(2), 22-29.

Goodman, P. S. (1982). The Rushton quality of work life experiment: Lessons to be learned. In R. Zager & M. P. Rosow (Eds.), *The innovative organization: Productivity programs in action* (pp. 222-259). New York: Pergamon.

Goodman, P. S., & Dean, J. W. (1983). Making productivity programs last. In B. E. Graham-Moore & T. L. Ross (Eds.), *Productivity gain sharing* (pp. 122-140). Englewood Cliffs, NJ: Prentice-Hall.

Goodman, P. S., & Moore, B. E. (1976). Factors affecting acquisition of beliefs about a new reward system. *Human Relations, 29,* 571-588.

Graen, G. B., Scandura, T. A., & Graen, M. R. (1986). A field experimental test of the moderating effects of growth need strength on productivity. *Journal of Applied Psychology, 71,* 484-491.

Graham-Moore, B. E. (1983). Improshare: The fastest growing productivity gain-sharing plan in the 1980s. In B. E. Graham-Moore & T. L. Ross (Eds.), *Productivity gain sharing* (pp. 89-94). Englewood Cliffs, NJ: Prentice-Hall.

Graham-Moore, B. E., & Ross, T. L. (1983). *Productivity gain sharing.* Englewood Cliffs, NJ: Prentice-Hall.

Graham-Moore, B. E., & Ross, T. L. (1990). *Gainsharing: Plans for improving performance.* Washington, DC: Bureau of National Affairs.

Granrose, C. S., Applebaum, E., & Singh, V. (1986). Saving jobs through worker buyouts: Economic and qualitative outcomes for workers in worker-owned, QWL, and non-QWL supermarkets. *IRRA 38th annual proceedings* (pp. 196-204). Madison, WI: Industrial Relations Research Association.

Greenbaum, H. H., Kaplan, I. T., & Metlay, W. (1988). Evaluation of problem-solving groups: The case of quality circle programs. *Group and Organization Studies, 13,* 133-147.

Greenberg, C. I., Wang, Y., & Dossett, D. L. (1982). Effects of work group size and task size on observers' job characteristics ratings. *Basic and Applied Social Psychology, 3*(1), 53-66.

Greenberg, E. S. (1980). Participation in industrial decision making and work satisfaction: The case of producer cooperatives. *Social Science Quarterly, 60*(4), 551-569.

Greenberg, E. S. (1984). Producer cooperatives and democratic theory: The case of the plywood firms. In R. Jackall & H. M. Levin (Eds.), *Worker cooperatives in America* (pp. 171-214). Berkeley: University of California Press.

Grenier, G. J. (1988). *Inhuman relations: Quality circles and anti-unionism in American industry.* Philadelphia: Temple University.

Griffeth, R. W. (1985). Moderation of the effects of job enrichment by participation: A longitudinal field experiment. *Organizational Behavior and Human Decision Processes, 35,* 73-93.

Griffin, R. W. (1982). *Task design: An integrative approach.* Glenview, IL: Scott, Foresman.

Griffin, R. W. (1983). Objective and social sources of information in task redesign: A field experiment. *Administrative Science Quarterly, 28,* 184-200.

Griffin, R. W. (1987). Toward an integrated theory of task design. In L. L. Cummings & B. M. Staw (Eds.), *Research in organizational behavior* (Vol. 9, pp. 79-120). Greenwich, CT: JAI.

Griffin, R. W. (1988). Consequences of quality circles in an industrial setting: A longitudinal assessment. *Academy of Management Journal, 31,* 338-358.

Griffin, R. W. (1991). Effects of work redesign on employee perceptions, attitudes, and behaviors: A long-term investigation. *Academy of Management Journal, 34,* 425-435.

Griffin, R. W., Bateman, T. S., Wayne, S. J., & Head, T. C. (1987). Objective and social factors as determinants of task perceptions and responses: An integrated perspective and empirical investigation. *Academy of Management Journal, 30,* 501-523.

Griffin, R. W., & Wayne, S. J. (1984). A field study of effective and less-effective quality circles. In J. A. Pearce & R. B. Robinson (Eds.), *Academy of Management proceedings* (pp. 217-221). Boston: Academy of Management.

Griffin, R. W., Welsh, A., & Moorhead, G. (1981). Perceived task characteristics and employee performance: A literature review. *Academy of Management Review, 6,* 655-664.

Guest, D., Williams, R., & Dewe, P. (1980). Workers' perceptions of changes affecting the quality of working life. In K. D. Duncan, M. M. Gruneberg, & D. Wallis (Eds.), *Changes in working life* (pp. 499-519). Chichester, UK: John Wiley.

Guest, R. H. (1979). Quality of work life—Learning from Tarrytown. *Harvard Business Review, 57*(4), 76-87.

Guest, R. H. (1982a). The Sharonville story: Worker involvement at a Ford Motor Company plant. In R. Zager & M. P. Rosow (Eds.), *The innovative organization: Productivity programs in action* (pp. 88-106). New York: Pergamon.

Guest, R. H. (1982b). Tarrytown: Quality of work life at a General Motors plant. In R. Zager & M. P. Rosow (Eds.), *The innovative organization: Productivity programs in action* (pp. 44-62). New York: Pergamon.

Gunderson, S. (1991, October 21). Archaic rules foul innovative labor strategies. *Wall Street Journal*, p. A18.

Gurdon, M. A., & Rai, A. (1990). Codetermination and enterprise performance: Empirical evidence from West Germany. *Journal of Economics and Business, 42,* 289-302.

Gustavsen, B., & Hunnius, G. (1981). *New patterns of work reform: The case of Norway.* Oslo, Norway: Universitetsforlaget.

Guzzo, R. A., Jackson, S. E., & Katzell, R. A. (1987). Meta-analysis. In L. L. Cummings & B. M. Staw (Eds.), *Research in organizational behavior* (Vol. 9, pp. 407-442). Greenwich, CT: JAI.

Guzzo, R. A., Jette, R. D., & Katzell, R. A. (1985). The effects of psychologically based intervention programs on worker productivity: A meta-analysis. *Personnel Psychology, 38,* 275-291.

Gwynne, S. C. (1990, October 29). The right stuff. *Time,* pp. 74-84.

Gyllenhammar, P. G. (1977a, July/August). How Volvo adapts work to people. *Harvard Business Review,* pp. 102-113.

Gyllenhammar, P. G. (1977b). *People at work.* Reading, MA: Addison-Wesley.

Hackman, J. R. (1975, September/October). Is job enrichment just a fad? *Harvard Business Review, 53,* 129-138.

Hackman, J. R., & Lawler, E. E. (1971). Employee reactions to job characteristics. *Journal of Applied Psychology Monograph, 55,* 259-286.

Hackman, J. R., & Oldham, G. R. (1975). Development of the Job Diagnostic Survey. *Journal of Applied Psychology, 60,* 159-170.

Hackman, J. R., & Oldham, G. R. (1976). Motivation through the design of work: Test of a theory. *Organizational Behavior and Human Performance, 16,* 250-279.

Hackman, J. R., & Oldham, G. R. (1980). *Work redesign.* Reading, MA: Addison-Wesley.

Hackman, J. R., Oldham, G., Janson, R., & Purdy, K. (1975). A new strategy for job enrichment. *California Management Review, 17*(4), 57-71.

Hackman, J. R., Pearce, J. L., & Wolfe, J. C. (1978). Effects of changes in job characteristics on work attitudes and behaviors: A naturally occurring quasi-experiment. *Organizational Behavior and Human Performance, 21,* 289-304.

Halcrow, A. (1988). Employee participation is a sign of the times in LA. *Personnel Journal, 67*(1), 1011.

Hallett, G. (1990, June). Devolve to evolve. *Management Today,* p. 31.

Hammer, T. H. (1986). The history of the Rath buyout: A role expectations analysis. *IRRA 38th annual proceedings* (pp. 205-213). Madison, WI: Industrial Relations Research Association.

Hammer, T. H., Currall, S. C., & Stern, R. N. (1991). Worker representation on boards of directors: A study of competing roles. *Industrial and Labor Relations Review, 44,* 661-680.

Hammer, T. H., Landau, J. C., & Stern, R. N. (1981). Absenteeism when workers have a voice: The case of employee ownership. *Journal of Applied Psychology, 66,* 561-573.

Hammer, T. H., & Stern, R. N. (1980). Employee ownership: Implications for the organizational distribution of power. *Academy of Management Journal, 23,* 78-100.

Hammer, T. H., & Stern, R. N. (1983). Worker representation on company boards of directors. In K. H. Chung (Ed.), *Academy of Management proceedings, 1983* (pp. 364-368). Dallas: Academy of Management.

Hammer, T. H., & Stern, R. N. (1986). A yo-yo model of cooperation: Union participation in management at the Rath Packing Company. *Industrial and Labor Relations Review, 39*, 337-349.

Hanford, T. J., & Grasso, P. G. (1991). Participation and corporate performance in ESOP firms. In R. Russell & V. Rus (Eds.), *International handbook of participation in organizations* (Vol. 2, pp. 221-231). Oxford, UK: Oxford University Press.

Hanlon, M. D., & Nadler, D. A. (1986). Unionists' attitudes toward joint union-management quality of work life programmes. *Journal of Occupational Behaviour, 7*, 53-59.

Hanlon, S. C., & Taylor, R. R. (1991). An examination of changes in w rk group communication behaviors following installation of a gainsharing plan. *Group and Organization Studies, 16*, 238-267.

Harders, D., & Wisniewski, J. (1989). Chase Manhattan manages HRIS implementation. *Personnel Journal, 68*(1), 120-124.

Harris, M. E., & Nicholson, R. N. (1989, August). *Interventions to successfully chip out of team building "sandtraps."* Paper presented at the Academy of Management National Meeting, Washington, DC.

Harrison, R. (1977, June). The European experience and what Bullock left out. *Personnel Management, 8*, 27-29.

Harvey, R. J., Billings, R. S., & Nilan, K. J. (1985). Confirmatory factor analysis of the Job Diagnostic Survey: Good news and bad news. *Journal of Applied Psychology, 70*, 461-468.

Haskew, M. (1985). Improshare and quality circles: Teamwork at John F. Kennedy Medical Center. *Quality Circles Journal, 8*(3), 24-26.

Hass, M. E., & Philbrick, J. H. (1988). The new management: Is it legal? *Academy of Management Executive, 2*, 325-329.

Hatcher, L. L., & Ross, T. L. (1985). Organization development through productivity gain sharing. *Personnel, 62*(10), 42-50.

Hatcher, L. L., & Ross, T. L. (1986). Gainsharing plans—How managers evaluate them. *Business, 36*(4), 30-37.

Hatcher, L. L., Ross, T. L., & Collins, D. (1989). Prosocial behavior, job complexity, and suggestion contribution under gainsharing plans. *Journal of Applied Behavioral Science, 25*, 231-248.

Hauck, W. C., & Ross, T. L. (1983). Is productivity gainsharing applicable to service sector firms? In B. E. Graham-Moore & T. L. Ross (Eds.), *Productivity gain sharing* (pp. 111-121). Englewood Cliffs, NJ: Prentice-Hall.

Hauck, W. C., & Ross, T. L. (1988). Expanded teamwork at Volvo through performance gainsharing. *Industrial Management, 30*(4), 17-20.

Head, T. C., Molleston, J. L., Sorensen, P. F., & Gargano, J. (1986). The impact of implementing a quality circles intervention on employee task perceptions. *Group and Organization Studies, 11*(4), 360-373.

Heath, P. M. (1990). Quality—And how to achieve it. *Management Decision, 28*(8), 42-46.

Heckscher, C. (1988). *The new unionism: Employee involvement in the changing corporation.* New York: Basic Books.

Hegland, D. E. (1991, January). Saturn assembly lifts off. *Assembly*, pp. 14-17.
Helfgott, R. B. (1988). *Computerized manufacturing and human resources: Innovation through employee involvement.* Lexington, MA: Lexington.
Heller, F. A., Drenth, P. J. D., Koopman, P., & Rus, V. (1977). A longitudinal study in participative decision-making. *Human Relations, 30*(7), 567-587.
Heller, F. A., Drenth, P. J. D., Koopman, P., & Rus, V. (1988). *Decisions in organizations: A three-country comparative study.* London: Sage.
Helmer, F. T., & McKnight, P. (1989). Management strategies to minimize nursing turnover. *Health Care Management Review, 14*(1), 73-80.
Henkoff, R. (1991a, February 25). Make your office more productive. *Fortune*, pp. 72-84.
Henkoff, R. (1991b, September 9). Some hope for troubled cities. *Fortune*, pp. 121-128.
Henkoff, R. (1991c, October 21). For states: Reform turns radical. *Fortune*, pp. 137-144.
Herbst, P. G. (1962). *Autonomous group functioning.* London: Tavistock.
Herbst, P. G. (1974). *Socio-technical design: Strategies in multidisciplinary research.* London: Tavistock.
Herrick, N. Q. (1983a). *Improving government: Experiments with quality of working life systems.* New York: Praeger.
Herrick, N. Q. (1983b). Institutional issues: Societal diffusion in the United States. In N. Q. Herrick (Ed.), *Improving government: Experiments with quality of working life systems* (pp. 154-170). New York: Praeger.
Herrick, N. Q. (1985). Parallel organizations in unionized settings: Implications for organizational research. *Human Relations, 38*, 963-981.
Herzberg, F. (1966). *Work and the nature of man.* New York: World.
Herzberg, F. (1968). One more time: How do you motivate employees? *Harvard Business Review, 46*(1), 53-62.
Herzberg, F., Mausner, B., & Snyderman, B. (1959). *The motivation to work.* New York: John Wiley.
Hespe, G., & Wall, T. (1976). The demand for participation among employees. *Human Relations, 29*(5), 411-428.
Hill, F. M. (1989). What British management can reasonably expect from a quality circle programme. *International Journal of Quality and Reliability Management, 6*(3), 59-75.
Hill, R. (1986). Harnessing "worker power" at a U.S. Cadillac plant. *International Management, 41*(11), 91-96.
Hinton, B. L. (1968). An empirical investigation of the Herzberg methodology and the two-factor theory. *Organizational Behavior and Human Performance, 3*, 286-309.
Hirschman, A. O. (1970). *Exit, voice, and loyalty: Responses to decline in firms, organizations, and states.* Cambridge, MA: Harvard University Press.
Hochner, A., & Granrose, C. S. (1985). Sources of motivation to choose employee ownership as an alternative to job loss. *Academy of Management Journal, 28*, 860-875.
Hodgson, G. M., & Jones, D. C. (1989). Codetermination: A partial review of theory and evidence. *Annals of Public and Cooperative Economy, 60*(3), 329-340.
Hoerr, J. (1987, December 14). Blue collars in the boardroom: Putting business first. *Business Week*, pp. 126-128.

Hoerr, J. (1988, November 28). Work teams can rev up paper-pushers too. *Business Week*, pp. 64-72.

Hoerr, J. (1989, July 10). The payoff from teamwork. *Business Week*, pp. 56-62.

Hoerr, J. (1990a, April 30). The strange bedfellows backing workplace reform. *Business Week*, p. 57.

Hoerr, J. (1990b, December 17). Sharpening minds for a competitive edge. *Business Week*, pp. 72-78.

Hoerr, J., & Collingwood, H. (1987, May 18). We're not going to sit around and allow management to louse things up. *Business Week*, p. 107.

Hoerr, J., Pollock, M. A., & Whiteside, D. E. (1986, September 29). Management discovers the human side of automation. *Business Week*, pp. 70-75.

Hoerr, J., Stevenson, G., & Norman, J. R. (1985, April 15). ESOPs: Revolution or ripoff? *Business Week*, pp. 94-108.

Holley, W., Field, H., & Crowley, J. (1981). Negotiating quality of work life, productivity, and traditional issues: Union members' preferred roles of their union. *Personnel Psychology, 34,* 309-329.

Honeycutt, A. (1989). The key to effective quality circles. *Training and Development Journal, 43*(5), 81-84.

Honeycutt, A. (1990). How important is quality circle training? *International Journal of Quality and Reliability Management, 7*(1), 64-69.

Hopkins, S. A. (1989). Have U.S. financial institutions really embraced quality control? *National Productivity Review, 8*(4), 407-420.

House, R. J., & Wigdor, L. A. (1967). Herzberg's dual-factor theory of job satisfaction and motivation: A review of the evidence and a criticism. *Personnel Psychology, 20*(4), 369-389.

Huff, S. L. (1986). Computer impacts on organizations—unanswered questions. *Business Quarterly, 51*(3), 16-17.

Hulin, C. L., & Blood, M. R. (1968). Job enlargement, individual differences, and worker responses. *Psychological Bulletin, 69,* 41-55.

Hunter, J. E., Schmidt, F. L., & Jackson, G. B. (1982). *Meta-analysis: Cumulating research findings across studies.* Beverly Hills, CA: Sage.

Huszczo, G. E. (1990, February). Training for team building. *Training and Development Journal*, pp. 37-43.

Idaszak, J. R., Bottom, W. P., & Drasgow, F. (1988). A test of the measurement equivalence of the revised Job Diagnostic Survey: Past problems and current solutions. *Journal of Applied Psychology, 73,* 647-656.

Idaszak, J. R., & Drasgow, F. (1987). A revision of the Job Diagnostic Survey: Elimination of a measurement artifact. *Journal of Applied Psychology, 72,* 69-74.

IDE International Research Group. (1979). Participation: Formal rules, influence, and involvement. *Industrial Relations, 18*(3), 273-294.

IDE International Research Group. (1981a). *European industrial relations.* Oxford, UK: Clarendon.

IDE International Research Group. (1981b). *Industrial democracy in Europe.* Oxford, UK: Clarendon.

IDE International Research Group. (1981c). Industrial democracy in Europe: Differences and similarities across countries and hierarchies. *Organization Studies, 2,* 113-129.

Ingle, S. (1987). Past, present and future training. *Journal for Quality and Participation, 10*(4), 4-6.

Ingle, S., & Ingle, N. (1983). *Quality circles in service industries: Comprehensive guidelines for increased productivity and efficiency.* Englewood Cliffs, NJ: Prentice-Hall.

Institute of Industrial Engineers. (1991). How to succeed brilliantly . . . *Managing for Continuous Improvement, 2, 1, 3.*

Isaac, M. J. (1989). The implementation of a quality circle programme at Cosalt Holiday Homes. *International Journal of Quality and Reliability, 6*(5), 30-36.

Ishikawa, K. (1985). *What is total quality control?* (D. J. Lu, Trans.). Englewood Cliffs, NJ: Prentice-Hall.

Jackall, R., & Levin, H. M. (1984). *Worker cooperatives in America.* Berkeley: University of California Press.

Jackson, S. E. (1983). Participation in decision making as a strategy for reducing job-related strain. *Journal of Applied Psychology, 68,* 3-19.

Jacob, R. (1992, May 4). Trust the locals, win worldwide. *Fortune,* pp. 76-77.

Jain, H. C. (1990). Human resource management in selected Japanese firms, their foreign subsidiaries and locally owned counterparts. *International Labour Review, 129*(1), 73-89.

Jain, H. C., & Giles, A. (1985). Workers' participation in Western Europe: Implications for North America. *Relations Industrielles, 40*(4), 747-774.

Janis, I. L. (1972). *Victims of groupthink.* Boston: Houghton Mifflin.

Jansen, M. A. (1986). Emotional disorders and the labour force: Prevalence, costs, prevention and rehabilitation. *International Labour Review, 125,* 605-615.

Jensen, M. C., & Meckling, W. H. (1979). Rights and production functions: An application to labor-managed firms and codetermination. *Journal of Business, 52*(4), 469-505.

Jex, S. M., & Spector, P. E. (1989). The generalizability of social information processing to organizational settings: A summary of two field experiments. *Perceptual and Motor Skills, 69,* 883-893.

Johannesen, J. (1979). VAG: A need for education. *Industrial Relations, 18*(3), 364-369.

Johnson, A. G., & Whyte, W. F. (1977). The Mondragon system of worker production cooperatives. *Industrial and Labor Relations Review, 31,* 18-30.

Jones, D. (1979). U.S. producer cooperatives: The record to date. *Industrial Relations, 18,* 342-357.

Jones, D. C. (Ed.). (1985). *Advances in the economic analysis of participatory and labor-managed firms* (Vol. 1). Greenwich, CT: JAI.

Jones, D. C. (1987). The productivity effects of worker directors and financial participation by employees in the firm: The case of British retail cooperatives. *Industrial and Labor Relations Review, 41*(1), 79-92.

Jones, D. C., & Pliskin, J. (1991). The effects of worker participation, employee ownership, and profit-sharing on economic performance: A partial review. In R. Russell & V. Rus (Eds.), *International handbook of participation in organizations* (Vol. 2, pp. 43-63). Oxford, UK: Oxford University Press.

Jones, D. C., & Svejnar, J. (1982a). The economic performance of participatory and self-managed firms: A historical perspective and a review. In D. C. Jones & J. Svejnar (Eds.), *Participatory and self-managed firms* (pp. 3-13). Lexington, MA: Lexington.

Jones, D. C., & Svejnar, J. (Eds.). (1982b). *Participatory and self-managed firms: Evaluating economic performance.* Lexington, MA: Lexington.

Juralewicz, R. S. (1974). An experiment on participation in a Latin American factory. *Human Relations, 27*(7), 627-637.

Kantrowitz, B., Wingert, P., McDaniel, A., McCormick, J., Barrett, T., & Cerio, G. (1991, April 22). Playing catch-up. *Newsweek,* pp. 28-31.

Kapstein, J., & Hoerr, J. (1989, August 28). Volvo's radical new plant: "The death of the assembly line"? *Business Week,* pp. 92-93.

Kapstein, J., Riemer, B., & Melcher, R. A. (1990, October 29). Workers want their piece of Europe, Inc. *Business Week,* pp. 46-47.

Karasek, R. (1990). Lower health risk with increased job control among white collar workers. *Journal of Organizational Behavior, 11,* 171-185.

Karasek, R. A. (1979). Job demands, job decision latitude, and mental strain: Implications for job design. *Administrative Science Quarterly, 24,* 404-416.

Kassalow, E. M. (1989, September). Employee representation on U.S., German boards. *Monthly Labor Review, 112,* 39-42.

Katerberg, R., Hom, P. W., & Hulin, C. L. (1979). Effects of job complexity on the reactions of part-time employees. *Organizational Behavior and Human Performance, 24,* 317-332.

Katz, D., & Kahn, R. L. (1978). *The social psychology of organizations* (2nd ed.). New York: John Wiley.

Katz, H. C., Kochan, T. A., & Gobeille, K. R. (1983). Industrial relations performance, economic performance, and QWL programs: An interplant analysis. *Industrial Relations and Labor Review, 37*(1), 3-17.

Katz, H. C., Kochan, T. A., & Weber, M. R. (1985). Assessing the effects of industrial relations systems and efforts to improve the quality of working life on organizational effectiveness. *Academy of Management Journal, 28,* 509-526.

Katzell, R. A., & Guzzo, R. A. (1983). Psychological approaches to productivity improvement. *American Psychologist, 38,* 468-472.

Kaufman, R. T. (1992). The effects of Improshare on productivity. *Industrial and Labor Relations Review, 45,* 311-322.

Kavcic, B., & Tannenbaum, A. S. (1981). A longitudinal study of the distribution of control in Yugoslav organizations. *Human Relations, 34,* 397-417.

Kaye, A. R., & Sutton, M. J. D. (1985). Productivity and quality of working life for office principals and the implications for office automation. *Office: Technology and People, 2*(4), 267-286.

Kelley, M. R., & Harrison, B. (1992). Unions, technology, and labor-management cooperation. In L. Mishel & P. Voos (Eds.), *Unions and economic competitiveness.* New York: M. E. Sharpe.

Kelly, J. (1985). Quality circles in Fort Collins: A municipal perspective and experience. *Public Personnel Management, 14*(4), 401-408.

Kelly, J. E. (1978). A reappraisal of sociotechnical systems theory. *Human Relations, 12,* 1069-1099.

Kelso, L., & Adler, M. J. (1958). *The capitalist manifesto.* New York: Random House.

Kemp, N. J., & Cook, J. D. (1983). Job longevity and growth need strength as joint moderators of the task design-job satisfaction relationship. *Human Relations, 36*(10), 883-898.

Kemp, N. J., Wall, T. D., Clegg, C. W., & Cordery, J. L. (1983). Autonomous work groups in a greenfield site: A comparative study. *Journal of Occupational Psychology, 56,* 271-288.

Khan, S. (1986). Quality circles in India: A review and assessment of the participative management movement in Indian industry. *Quality Circles Journal, 9*(3), 51-55.

Kiechel, W. (1992, March 9). When management regresses. *Fortune*, pp. 157-162.

Kiggundu, M. N. (1983). Task interdependence and job design: Test of a theory. *Organizational Behavior and Human Performance, 31*, 145-172.

Kilduff, M., & Regan, D. T. (1988). What people say and what they do: The differential effects of informational cues and task design. *Organizational Behavior and Human Decision Processes, 41*, 83-97.

King, N. (1970). Clarification and evaluation of the two-factor theory of job satisfaction. *Psychological Bulletin, 74*, 18-31.

Kirkpatrick, D. (1988, December 5). How the workers run Avis better. *Fortune*, pp. 103-106, 110-114.

Kissler, L. (1989). Co-determination research in the Federal Republic of Germany: A review. In C. J. Lammers & G. Szell (Eds.), *International handbook of participation in organizations: For the study of organizational democracy, co-operation, and self-management* (Vol. 1, pp. 74-90). Oxford, UK: Oxford University Press.

Klein, J. (1984, September/October). Why supervisors resist employee involvement. *Harvard Business Review, 62*, 87-95.

Klein, J. A. (1988). *The changing role of first-line supervisors and middle managers* (U.S. Department of Labor, Bureau of Labor and Management, BLMR 126). Washington, DC: Government Printing Office.

Klein, J. A., & Posey, P. A. (1986). Good supervisors are good supervisors—anywhere. *Harvard Business Review, 46*(6), 125-128.

Klein, K. J. (1987). Employee stock ownership and employee attitudes: A test of three models. *Journal of Applied Psychology, 72*, 319-332.

Klein, K. J., & Hall, R. J. (1988). Correlates of employee satisfaction with stock ownership: Who likes an ESOP most? *Journal of Applied Psychology, 73*, 630-638.

Kleyn, J. D., & Perrick, S. (1990, February). Netherlands. *International Financial Law Review*, (Special suppl.), 51-56.

Knowles, D. W. (1989, May). Employee councils: An important human relations tool. *Small Business Reports, 14*, 17-19.

Kochan, T. A., & Cutcher-Gershenfeld, J. (1988). *Institutionalizing and diffusing innovations in industrial relations* (U.S. Department of Labor, Bureau of Labor and Management, BLMR 128). Washington, DC: Government Printing Office.

Kochan, T. A., & Dyer, L. (1976). A model for organizational change in the context of labor-management relations. *Journal of Applied Behavioral Science, 12*, 56-78.

Kochan, T. A., Katz, H. C., & Mower, N. A. (1984). *Worker participation and American unions: Threat or opportunity?* Kalamazoo, MI: UpJohn Institute.

Koenig, R. (1990, March 28). Quality circles are vulnerable to union tests. *Wall Street Journal*, pp. B1, B4.

Konrad, W. (1991, December 9). Nobody is resting easy at Simmons. *Business Week*, p. 35.

Konrad, W. (1992, March 2). This is some way to build employee loyalty. *Business Week*, p. 84.

Koopman, P. L., Drenth, P. J. D., Bus, F. B. M., Kruyswijk, A. J., & Wierdsma, A. F. M. (1981). Content, process, and effects of participative decision making on the shop floor: Three cases in the Netherlands. *Human Relations, 34*(8), 657-676.

Kopelman, R. E. (1985). Job redesign and productivity: A review of the evidence. *National Productivity Review, 4*(3), 237-255.

Kornhauser, A. (1965). *Mental health of the industrial worker.* New York: John Wiley.

Kotter, J. P., & Schlesinger, L. A. (1979, March/April). Choosing strategies for change. *Harvard Business Review, 57,* 106-114.

Kovach, K. A., Sands, B. F., & Brooks, W. W. (1980, Winter). Is codetermination a workable idea for U.S. labor-management relations? *MSU Business Topics,* pp. 49-55.

Kraiger, K., Billings, R. S., & Isen, A. M. (1989). The influence of positive affective states on task perceptions and satisfaction. *Organizational Behavior and Human Decision Processes, 44,* 12-25.

Krigsman, N., & O'Brien, R. M. (1987). Quality circles, feedback and reinforcement: An experimental comparison and behavioral analysis. *Journal of Organizational Behavior Management, 9*(1), 67-82.

Krim, R. M., & Arthur, M. B. (1989, Spring). Quality of work life in city hall: Toward an integration of political and organizational realities. *Public Administration Quarterly, 13,* 14-30.

Kuhn, T. S. (1970). *The structure of scientific revolutions* (2nd ed.). Chicago: University of Chicago Press.

Kuhne, R. J. (1976). Co-determination: A statutory re-structuring of the organization. *Columbia Journal of World Business, 11*(2), 17-25

Kulik, C. T., Oldham, G. R., & Hackman, J. R. (1987). Work design as an approach to person-environment fit. *Journal of Vocational Behavior, 31,* 278-296.

Kulik, C. T., Oldham, G. R., & Langner, P. H. (1988). Measurement of job characteristics: Comparison of the original and the revised Job Diagnostic Survey. *Journal of Applied Psychology, 73,* 462-466.

Kunst, P., & Soeters, J. (1991). Works council membership and career opportunities. *Organization Studies, 12*(1), 75-93.

Kuttner, R. (1985, November/December). Sharing power at Eastern Airlines. *Harvard Business Review, 63,* 91-101.

Lammers, C. J., Meurs, P. L., & Mijs, T. A. (1987). Direct and indirect participation in Dutch firms and hospitals. *Organization Studies, 8*(1), 25-38.

Landy, F. J. (1989). The early years of I/O: J. D. Houser and J. D. I. *The Industrial-Organizational Psychologist, 26*(2), 63-64.

Lansing, R. L. (1989). The power of teams. *Supervisory Management, 34*(2), 39-43.

Lavy, C. (1984). Perceived effect of direct and indirect participation by employees. *Perceptual and Motor Skills, 59,* 215-218.

Lawler, E. E. (1971). *Pay and organizational effectiveness: A psychological view.* New York: McGraw-Hill.

Lawler, E. E. (1978). The new plant revolution. *Organizational Dynamics, 6*(3), 2-12.

Lawler, E. E. (1981). *Pay and organization development.* Reading, MA: Addison-Wesley.

Lawler, E. E. (1986). *High-involvement management: Participative strategies for improving organizational performance.* San Francisco: Jossey-Bass.

Lawler, E. E. (1988a). Choosing an involvement strategy. *Academy of Management Executive, 2*(3), 197-204.

Lawler, E. E. (1988b). Gainsharing theory and research: Findings and future directions. In W. A. Pasmore & R. W. Woodman (Eds.), *Research in organizational change and development* (Vol. 2, pp. 323-344). Greenwich, CT: JAI.

Lawler, E. E. (1990). The new plant revolution revisited. *Organizational Dynamics,* *19*(2), 5-14.

Lawler, E. E. (1991). The new plant approach: A second generation approach. *Organizational Dynamics, 20*(1), 5-14.

Lawler, E. E., & Drexler, J. A. (1978, March). Dynamics of establishing cooperative quality-of-work-life projects. *Monthly Labor Review, 101,* 23-28.

Lawler, E. E., Hackman, J. R., & Kaufman, S. (1973). Effects of job redesign: A field experiment. *Journal of Applied Social Psychology, 3,* 49-62.

Lawler, E. E., Jenkins, G. D., & Herline, G. E. (1974). *Initial data feedback to General Foods, Topeka pet foods plants: Selected survey items.* Unpublished manuscript. Institute for Social Research, Ann Arbor, MI.

Lawler, E. E., & Ledford, G. E. (1981/1982, Winter). Productivity and the quality of work life. *National Productivity Review, 1,* 23-27.

Lawler, E. E., & Ledford, G. E. (1985). Skill based pay. *Personnel, 62*(9), 30-37.

Lawler, E. E., & Mohrman, S. A. (1985). Quality circles after the fad. *Harvard Business Review, 85*(1), 64-71.

Lawler, E. E., & Mohrman, S. A. (1987). Quality circles: After the honeymoon. *Organizational Dynamics, 15*(4), 42-54.

Lawler, E. E., & Mohrman, S. A. (1989). With HR help, all managers can practice high-involvement management. *Personnel, 66*(4), 26-31.

Lawrence, P. R., & Smith, P. C. (1955). Group decision and employee participation. *Journal of Applied Psychology, 39,* 334-337.

Leana, C. R. (1987). Power relinquishment versus power sharing: Theoretical clar- ification and empirical comparison of delegation and participation. *Journal of Applied Psychology, 72,* 228-233.

Leana, C. R., Locke, E. A., & Schweiger, D. M. (1990). Fact and fiction in analyzing research on participative decision making: A critique of Cotton, Vollrath, Froggatt, Lengnick-Hall, and Jennings. *Academy of Management Review, 15,* 137-146.

Ledford, G. E., Lawler, E. E., & Mohrman, S. A. (1988). The quality circle and its variations. In J. P. Campbell & R. J. Campbell (Eds.), *Productivity in organiza- tions: New perspectives from industrial and organizational psychology* (pp. 255- 294). San Francisco: Jossey-Bass.

Ledford, G. E., & Mohrman, S. A. (1988, August). *Attitudinal effects of employee participation groups: How strong, how persistent?* Paper presented at the Acad- emy of Management Annual Meeting, Anaheim, CA.

Lee, C. (1990). Beyond teamwork. *Training, 27*(6), 25-32.

Lee, C., & Schuler, R. S. (1982). A constructive replication and extension of a role and expectancy perception model of participation in decision making. *Journal of Occupational Psychology, 55,* 109-118.

Lee, J., & Dale, B. G. (1988). Quality circles in service industries: A study of their use. *Service Industries Journal, 8*(2), 143-154.

Lehnert, D. (1991, November 26). ESOP's fable, an unhappy one. *Wall Street Journal,* p. A14.

Lengnick-Hall, M. L. (1991, August). *Increasing employee involvement through em- ployee stock ownership plans (ESOPs).* Paper presented at the National Meetings of the Academy of Management, Miami Beach, FL.

Lesieur, F. G. (1958). *The Scanlon plan: A frontier in labor-management cooperation.* Boston: MIT Press.

Lesieur, F. G., & Puckett, E. S. (1969, September/October). The Scanlon plan has proved itself. *Harvard Business Review,* pp. 109-118.

Letize, L., & Donovan, J. M. (1986). Expanding employee involvement through the use of focused task forces. *Quality Circles Journal, 9*(3), 33-39.

Levine, D. I. (1990). Participation, productivity, and the firm's environment. *California Management Review, 32*(4), 86-100.

Levine, M. F. (1983). Self-developed QWL measures. *Journal of Occupational Behaviour, 4,* 35-46.

Levitan, S. A., & Werneke, D. (1984). Worker participation and productivity change. *Monthly Labor Review, 107*(9), 28-33.

Lewin, K. (1947). Frontiers in group dynamics. *Human Relations, 1,* 5-42.

Lewin, K. (1948). *Resolving social conflicts.* New York: Harper.

Lewin, K. (1951). *Field theory in social science.* Chicago: University of Chicago Press.

Lewin, K. (1952). Group decision and social change. In T. M. Newcomb & E. L. Hartley (Eds.), *Readings in social psychology* (pp. 459-473). New York: Holt, Rinehart & Winston.

Lewin, K., Lippitt, R., & White, R. K. (1939). Patterns of aggressive behavior in experimentally created "social climates." *Journal of Social Psychology, 10,* 271-299.

Lippitt, R. (1940). An experimental study of authoritarian and democratic group atmospheres. *University of Iowa Studies in Child Welfare, 16*(3), 43-195.

Liverpool, H. (1990). Employee participation in decision-making: An analysis of the perceptions of members and nonmembers of quality circles. *Journal of Business and Psychology, 4,* 411-422.

Locke, E. A., Feren, D. B., McCaleb, V. M., Shaw, K. N., & Denny, A. T. (1980). The relative effectiveness of four methods of motivating employee performance. In K. D. Duncan, M. M. Gruneberg, & D. Wallis (Eds.), *Changes in working life* (pp. 363-388). Chichester, UK: John Wiley.

Locke, E. A., & Latham, G. P. (1990). *A theory of goal setting and task performance.* Englewood Cliffs, NJ: Prentice-Hall.

Locke, E. A., & Schweiger, D. M. (1979). Participation in decision-making: One more look. In L. L. Cummings & B. M. Staw (Eds.), *Research in organizational behavior* (Vol. 1, pp. 265-339). Greenwich, CT: JAI.

Locke, E. A., Sirota, D., & Wolfson, A. D. (1976). An experimental case study of the successes and failures of job enrichment in a government agency. *Journal of Applied Psychology, 61,* 701-711.

Loher, B. T., Noe, R. A., Moeller, N. L., & Fitzgerald, M. P. (1985). A meta-analysis of the relation of job characteristics to job satisfaction. *Journal of Applied Psychology, 70,* 280-289.

Long, R. J. (1978a). The effects of employee ownership on organizational identification, employee job attitudes, and organizational performance: A tentative framework and empirical findings. *Human Relations, 31,* 29-48.

Long, R. J. (1978b). The relative effects of share ownership vs. control on job attitudes in an employee-owned company. *Human Relations, 31,* 753-763.

Long, R. J. (1980). Job attitudes and organizational performance under employee ownership. *Academy of Management Journal, 23,* 726-737.

Long, R. J. (1981). The effects of formal employee participation in ownership and decision making on perceived and desired patterns of organizational influence: A longitudinal study. *Human Relations, 34,* 847-876.

Long, R. J. (1982). Worker ownership and job attitudes: A field study. *Industrial Relations, 21*, 196-215.

Long, R. J. (1989). *Employee ownership and organizational performance: Exploring the linkages.* Paper presented at the ASAC Conference, Montreal, Quebec, Canada.

Long, R. J. (1990, August). *Worker ownership in North America and Western Europe: Can China learn from our experience?* Paper presented at the Canada-China International Management Conference, XI'an, China.

Long, R. J., & Warner, M. (1987). Organizations, participation and recession. *Industrial Relations (Canada), 42*, 65-90.

Looise, J. C. (1989). The recent growth in employees' representation in the Netherlands: Defying the times? In C. J. Lammers & G. Szell (Eds.), *International handbook of participation in organizations: For the study of organizational democracy, co-operation, and self-management* (Vol. 1, pp. 268-284). Oxford, UK: Oxford University Press.

Lowin, A. (1968). Participative decision making: A model, literature critique, and prescriptions for research. *Organizational Behavior and Human Performance, 3*, 68-106.

Lund, R. (1987). Industrial democracy in Denmark. *International Studies in Management and Organization, 17*(2), 17-26.

Luthans, F., Kemmerer, B., Paul, R., & Taylor, L. (1987). The impact of a job redesign intervention on salespersons' observed performance behaviors. *Group and Organization Studies, 12*, 55-72.

Luzon, M. D. M. (1988). Quality circles and organization culture. *International Journal of Quality and Reliability Management, 5*(4), 46-55.

MacStravic, R. S. (1986, Fall/Winter). Marketing circles in practice development. *Journal of Professional Services Marketing, 2*, 47-54.

Macy, B. A. (1979). The Bolivar quality of work life program: A longitudinal behavioral and performance assessment. *Proceedings of the thirty-second annual meeting* (pp. 83-93). Madison, WI: Industrial Relations Research Association.

Macy, B. A. (1982). The Bolivar quality of work life program: Success or failure? In R. Zager & M. P. Rosow (Eds.), *The innovative organization: Productivity programs in action* (pp. 184-221). New York: Pergamon.

Macy, B. A., Bliese, P. D., & Norton, J. J. (1991, August). *Organizational change and work innovation: A meta-analysis of 131 North American field experiments—1961-1990.* Paper presented at the Academy of Management National Meetings, Miami, FL.

Macy, B. A., & Mirvis, P. H. (1976). A methodology for assessment of quality of work life and organizational effectiveness in behavioral-economic terms. *Administrative Science Quarterly, 21*, 212-226.

Macy, B. A., & Mirvis, P. H. (1982). Organizational change efforts: Methodologies for assessing organizational effectiveness and program costs versus benefits. *Evaluation Review, 6*, 301-372.

Macy, B. A., Peterson, M. F., & Norton, L. W. (1989). A test of participation theory in a work re-design field setting: Degree of participation and comparison site contrasts. *Human Relations, 42*(12), 1095-1165.

Magnet, M. (1992, May 4). The truth about the American worker. *Fortune*, pp. 48-65.

Maher, J. R., & Overbagh, W. B. (1971). Better inspection performance through job enrichment. In J. R. Maher (Ed.), *New perspectives in job enrichment* (pp. 79-89). New York: Van Nostrand Reinhold.

Maletz, M. C. (1990). KBS circles: A technology transfer initiative that leverages Xerox's leadership through quality programs. *MIS Quarterly, 14*(3), 323-329.

Mallory, M. (1991, September 9). How can we be laid off if we own the company? *Business Week*, p. 66.

Manz, C. C., Keating, D. E., & Donnellon, A. (1990). Preparing for an organizational change to employee self-management: The managerial transition. *Organizational Dynamics, 19*(2), 15-26.

Manz, C. C., & Sims, H. P. (1986). Leading self-managed groups: A conceptual analysis of a paradox. *Economic and Industrial Democracy, 7*, 141-165.

Manz, C. C., & Sims, H. P. (1987). Leading workers to lead themselves: The external leadership of self-managing work teams. *Administrative Science Quarterly, 32*, 106-128.

Margolis, B. L., Kroes, W. H., & Quinn, P. R. (1974). Job stress: An unlisted occupational hazard. *Journal of Occupational Medicine, 16*, 654-661.

Margulies, N., & Black, S. (1987). Perspectives on the implementation of participative approaches. *Human Resource Management, 26*(3), 385-412.

Markham, S. E., Scott, K. D., & Little, B. L. (1992, January/February). National gainsharing study: The importance of industry differences. *Compensation and Benefits Review, 24*, 34-45.

Marks, M. L. (1986). The question of quality circles. *Psychology Today, 20*, 36-46.

Marks, M. L., Mirvis, P. H., Hackett, E. J., & Grady, J. F. (1986). Employee participation in a quality circle program: Impact on quality of work life, productivity, and absenteeism. *Journal of Applied Psychology, 71*, 61-69.

Marsh, R. M. (1992). The difference between participation and power in Japanese factories. *Industrial and Labor Relations Review, 45*, 250-257.

Marsh, T. R., & McAllister, D. E. (1981). ESOPs tables: A survey of companies with employee stock ownership plans. *Journal of Corporation Law, 6*, 551-623.

Martin, A. W. (1988). Work restructuring in the 1980s: The view from PEWS. *ILR Report, 26*(1), 6-11.

Masi, D. A., & Bowler, M. H. (1988). Managing mental health benefits: The changing role of the EAP. *Compensation and Benefits Management, 4*(2), 129-132.

Masternak, R. L., & Ross, T. L. (1992, January/February). Gainsharing: A bonus plan or employee involvement? *Compensation and Benefits Review, 24*, 46-54.

Mazzolini, R. (1978). The influence of European workers over corporate strategy. *Sloan Management Review, 19*(3), 59-81.

McCormick, C. P. (1938). *Multiple management.* New York: Harper.

McFarlin, D. M., Sweeney, P. D., & Cotton, J. L. (in press). Attitudes toward employee participation in decision making: A comparison of European and American managers. *Human Resource Management Journal.*

McGregor, D. (1957). The human side of enterprise. *Management Review, 46*(11), 22-28, 88-92.

McIsaac, G. S. (1977, September/October). What's coming in labor relations. *Harvard Business Review, 55*, 22-24, 30, 34-36, 190.

McKenna, T. F. (1985). Midwest Steel moves from confrontational to cooperative labor relations. In Y. K. Shetty & V. M. Buehler (Eds.), *Productivity and quality through people: Practices of well-managed companies* (pp. 103-110). New York: Quorum.

Mears, J. M., & Brunet, L. (1983). Overview: QWL activities in Canada. In N. Q. Herrick (Ed.), *Improving government: Experiments with quality of working life systems* (pp. 5-11). New York: Praeger.

272   EMPLOYEE INVOLVEMENT

Menefee, M. L., & Owens, S. L. (1988). Safety circles. *Incentive, 162*(9), 160-161.
Metz, E. J. (1981a). Caution: Quality circles ahead. *Training and Development Journal, 35*(8), 71-76.
Metz, E. J. (1981b, November). Diagnosing readiness. *Quality Circles Journal, 4,* 16-20.
Meyer, G. W., & Stott, R. G. (1985). Quality circles: Panacea or Pandora's box? *Organizational Dynamics, 13*(4), 34-50.
Miller, C. S., & Schuster, M. H. (1987a). A decade's experience with the Scanlon plan: A case study. *Journal of Occupational Behaviour, 8,* 167-174.
Miller, C. S., & Schuster, M. H. (1987b). Gainsharing plans: A comparative analysis. *Organizational Dynamics, 16*(1), 44-67.
Miller, E. J. (1975). Socio-technical systems in weaving, 1953-1970: A follow-up study. *Human Relations, 28,* 349-386.
Miller, E. J., & Rice, A. K. (1967). *Systems of organization: The control of task and sentient boundaries.* London: Tavistock.
Miller, K. I., & Monge, P. R. (1986). Participation, satisfaction, and productivity: A meta-analytic review. *Academy of Management Journal, 29,* 727-753.
Miller, M. A. (1988). A sociotech approach to internal controls evaluation. *Internal Auditing, 3*(4), 38-44.
Miner, J. B. (1980). *Theories of organizational behavior.* Hinsdale, IL: Dryden.
Mirvis, P. H., & Lawler, E. E. (1977). Measuring the financial impact of employee attitudes. *Journal of Applied Psychology, 62,* 1-8.
Mirvis, P. H., & Lawler, E. E. (1984). Accounting for the quality of work life. *Journal of Occupational Behavior, 5,* 197-212.
Moch, M. K., & Bartunek, J. M. (1990). *Creating alternative realities at work: The quality of work life experiment at FoodCom.* New York: Harper Business.
Mohrman, A. M., Resnick-West, S. M., & Lawler, E. E. (1989). *Designing performance appraisal systems: Aligning appraisals and organizational realities.* San Francisco: Jossey-Bass.
Mohrman, S. A., & Cummings, T. G. (1989). *Self-designing organizations: Learning how to create high performance.* Reading, MA: Addison-Wesley.
Mohrman, S. A., & Lawler, E. E. (1984). Quality of work life. In K. Rowland & G. Ferris (Eds.), *Research in personnel and human resources management* (Vol. 2, pp. 219-260). Greenwich, CT: JAI.
Mohrman, S. A., Ledford, G. E., Lawler, E. E., & Mohrman, A. M. (1986). Quality of worklife and employee involvement. In C. L. Cooper & I. Robertson (Eds.), *International review of industrial and organizational psychology* (pp. 189-215). Chichester, UK: John Wiley.
Mohrman, S. A., & Novelli, L. (1985). Beyond testimonials: Learning from a quality circles programme. *Journal of Occupational Behaviour, 6,* 93-110.
Morse N. C., & Reimer, E. (1956). The experimental change of a major organizational variable. *Journal of Abnormal and Social Psychology, 52,* 120-129.
Moskal, B. S. (1989, January 16). Quality of life in the factory: How far have we come? *Industry Week,* pp. 12-15.
Mroczkowski, T. (1983). Japanese and European systems of industrial relations— Which model is more applicable for the U.S.? *Industrial Management, 25*(4), 26-31.
Mroczkowski, T., & Champagne, P. (1984). Job redesign in two countries: A comparison of the Topeka and Kalamar experiences. *Industrial Management, 26*(6), 17-22.

References

273

Munchus, G. (1983). Employer-employee based quality circles in Japan: Human resource policy implications for American firms. *Academy of Management Review, 8*, 255-261.

Muthukrishnan, A. V., & Sethuraman, T. V. (1985). Job design and job satisfaction as moderators of financial incentives—Labour performance relationship. *Indian Journal of Social Work, 46*(1), 125-134.

Nadler, D. A., Hanlon, M., & Lawler, E. E. (1980). Factors influencing the success of labour-management quality of work life projects. *Journal of Occupational Behaviour, 1*, 53-67.

Nadler, D. A., & Lawler, E. E. (1983). Quality of work life: Perspectives and directions. *Organizational Dynamics, 11*(3), 20-30.

Nale, R. D. (1989). Satisfied—yes, consultant use—low. *Journal for Quality and Participation, 12*(2), 68-72.

Nasar, S. (1989, September 25). The foolish rush to ESOPs. *Fortune,* pp. 141-150.

Nassau, M. J., & Schwartz, M. J. (1989). ESOPs as financing tools. *CFO, 5*(10), 56-58, 71.

National Commission on Productivity and Work Quality. (1975). *A plant-wide productivity plan in action: Three years of experience with the Scanlon plan.* Washington, DC: Government Printing Office.

Neuman, G. A., Edwards, J. E., & Raju, N. S. (1989). Organizational development interventions: A meta-analysis of their effects on satisfaction and other attitudes. *Personnel Psychology, 42*, 461-489.

Neumeier, S. (1992, March 9). Companies to watch: Vans. *Fortune,* p. 63.

Newman, B. (1987, March 25). Yugoslavia's workers find self-management doesn't make paradise. *Wall Street Journal,* pp. 1, 16.

Newton, T., & Keenan, T. (1991). Further analyses of the dispositional argument in organizational behavior. *Journal of Applied Psychology, 76*, 781-787.

New York Stock Exchange. (1982). *People and productivity: A challenge to corporate America.* New York: Author.

Nicholas, J. M. (1982). The comparative impact of organization development interventions on hard criteria measures. *Academy of Management Review, 7*, 531-542.

Nickel, J. E., & O'Neal, S. (1990, March/April). Small-group incentives: Gain sharing in the microcosm. *Compensation and Benefits Review, 1*, 22-29.

Nirenberg, J. (1986). The quality of work life issue: The corporation as the next political frontier. *International Journal of Manpower, 7*(3), 27-36.

Norrgren, F. (1990). Designing and implementing the software factory—A case study from telecommunications. *R & D Management, 20*(3), 263-273.

Nurick, A. J. (1982). Participation in organizational change: A longitudinal field study. *Human Relations, 35*, 413-430.

Nurick, A. J. (1985). The paradox of participation: Lessons from the Tennessee Valley Authority. *Human Resource Management, 24*, 341-356.

Nykodym, N., Rudd, W., & Liverpool, P. (1986). Quality circles: Will transactional analysis improve their effectiveness? *Transactional Analysis Journal, 16*(3), 182-187.

O'Boyle, T. F. (1992, June 5). Working together: A manufacturer grows efficient by soliciting ideas from employees. *Wall Street Journal,* pp. A1, A5.

Obradovic, J. (1970). Participation and work attitudes in Yugoslavia. *Industrial Relations, 9*, 161-169.

Obradovic, J. (1975). Workers' participation: Who participates. *Industrial Relations, 14*, 32-44.

O'Brien, G. E. (1983). Skill-utilization, skill-variety and the job characteristics model. *Australian Journal of Psychology, 35*(3), 461-468.

O'Connor, E. J., Rudolf, C. J., & Peters, L. H. (1980). Individual differences and job design: Where do we go from here? *Academy of Management Review, 5*(2), 249-254.

Oldham, G. R. (1976). Job characteristics and internal motivation: The moderating effect of interpersonal and individual variables. *Human Relations, 29*, 559-564.

Oldham, G. R., & Hackman, J. R. (1980). Work design in the organizational concept. In B. M. Staw & L. L. Cummings (Eds.), *Research in organizational behavior* (Vol. 2, pp. 247-278). Greenwich, CT: JAI.

Oldham, G. R., & Hackman, J. R. (1981). Relationship between organizational structure and employee reactions: Comparing alternative frameworks. *Administrative Science Quarterly, 26*, 66-83.

Oldham, G. R., Hackman, J. R., & Pearce, J. (1976). Conditions under which employees respond positively to enriched work. *Journal of Applied Psychology, 61*, 395-403.

Oliver, N. (1990). Work rewards, work values, and organizational commitment in an employee-owned firm: Evidence from the U.K. *Human Relations, 43*, 513-526.

Olkewicz, A. W. (1981). Productivity experiment at Maxwell House-Hoboken. In V. M. Buehler & Y. K. Shetty (Eds.), *Productivity improvement: Case studies of proven practice* (pp. 101-107). New York: AMACOM.

Once the ESOP is established, then what? (1990). *Employee Benefit Plan Review, 44*(11), 39-42.

Ondrack, D. A., & Evans, M. G. (1987). Job enrichment and job satisfaction in greenfield and redesign QWL sites. *Group and Organization Studies, 12*, 5-22.

O'Reilly, C., Parlette, G., & Bloom, J. (1980). Perceptual measures of task characteristics: The biasing effects of differing frames of reference and job attitudes. *Academy of Management Journal, 23*, 118-131.

Orly, C. (1988). Quality circles in France: Accor's experiment in self-management. *Cornell Hotel and Restaurant Administration Quarterly, 29*(3), 50-57.

Orpen, C. (1979). The effect of job enrichment on employee satisfaction, motivation, involvement, and performance: A field experiment. *Human Relations, 32*, 189-217.

Orpen, C. (1983). Westernization as a moderator of the effect of job attributes on employee satisfaction and performance. *Humanitas, 9*(3), 275-279.

Orsburn, J. D., Moran, L., Musselwhite, E., & Zenger, J. H. (1990). *Self-directed work teams: The new American challenge.* Homewood, IL: Irwin.

Ost, E. J. (1989). Gain sharing's potential. *Personnel Administrator, 34*(7), 92-96.

Ost, E. J. (1990). Team-based pay: New wave strategic incentives. *Sloan Management Review, 31*(3), 19-27.

O'Toole, J. (1979, November/December). The uneven record of employee ownership. *Harvard Business Review, 57*, 185-197.

Overman, S. (1990). Workers, management, unite. *HRMagazine, 35*(5), 8-41.

Owens, T. (1988). Gainsharing. *Small Business Reports, 13*(10), 19-28.

Pace, L. A., & Argona, D. R. (1989). Participatory action research: A view from Xerox. *American Behavior Scientist, 32*, 552-565.

Park, C., & Rosen, C. (1990). The performance record of leveraged ESOP firms. *Mergers and Acquisitions, 25*(3), 64-68.

Parker, M., & Slaughter, J. (1988). *Choosing sides: Unions and the team concept.* Boston: South End.

Pascarella, P. (1982, June 26). Quality circles: Just another management headache? *Industry Week, 213,* 50-55.

Pasewark, W. R. (1991). Implementing quality circles in internal audit departments. *Internal Auditing, 6*(4), 10-15.

Pasmore, W. A. (1978). The comparative impacts of sociotechnical system, job-redesign, and survey-feedback interventions. In W. A. Pasmore & J. J. Sherwood (Eds.), *Sociotechnical systems: A sourcebook* (pp. 291-301). La Jolla, CA: University Associates.

Pasmore, W. A., Francis, C., & Haldeman, J. (1982). Sociotechnical systems: A North American reflection on empirical studies of the seventies. *Human Relations, 35,* 1179-1204.

Patchin, R. (1981, February). Facilitators, facilitation and ownership. *Quality Circles Journal, 4,* 13-14.

Pati, G. C., Salitore, R., & Brady, S. (1987). What went wrong with quality circles? *Personnel Journal, 61*(12), 83-87.

Paul, R. J., Ebadi, Y. M., & Dilts, D. A. (1987). Commitment in employee-owned firms: Involvement or entrapment? *Quarterly Journal of Business and Economics, 26*(4), 81-99.

Paul, W. J., Robertson, K. B., & Herzberg, F. (1969, March/April). Job enrichment pays off. *Harvard Business Review, 47,* 61-79.

Pearce, J. A., & Ravlin, E. C. (1987). The design and activation of self-regulating work groups. *Human Relations, 40,* 751-782.

Penzer, E. A. (1990). Keeping team spirit alive. *Incentive, 164*(4), 86-87.

Perlman, S. L. (1990a, June). Employee-centered work redesign. *Journal for Quality and Participation,* pp. 64-69.

Perlman, S. L. (1990b). Employees redesign their jobs. *Personnel Journal, 69*(11), 37-40.

Peters, M., & Robinson, V. (1984). The origins and status of action research. *Journal of Applied Behavioral Science, 20,* 113-124.

Peters, T. (1988). *Thriving on chaos: Handbook for a management revolution.* New York: Knopf.

Peterson, R. B., & Tracy, L. (1988, Fall). Lessons from labor-management cooperation. *California Management Review, 31,* 40-53.

Pfeffer, J. (1981). Four laws of organizational research. In A. H. Van De Ven & W. F. Joyce (Eds.), *Perspectives on organizational design and behavior* (pp. 409-418). New York: John Wiley.

Phillips, J. S., & Freedman, S. M. (1984). Situational performance constraints and task characteristics: Their relationship to motivation and satisfaction. *Journal of Management, 10,* 321-331.

Pierce, J. L. (1984). Job design and technology: A sociotechnical systems perspective. *Journal of Occupational Behaviour, 5,* 147-154.

Pierce, J. L., & Dunham, R. B. (1976). Task design: A literature review. *Academy of Management Review, 1,* 83-97.

Pierce, J. L., & Dunham, R. B. (1978). The measurement of perceived job characteristics: The Job Diagnostic Survey versus the Job Characteristics Inventory. *Academy of Management Journal, 21,* 123-128.

Pierce, J. L., & Furo, C. A. (1990). Employee ownership: Implications for management. *Organizational Dynamics, 18*(3), 32-43.

Pierce, J. L., Rubenfeld, S. A., & Morgan, S. (1991). Employee ownership: A conceptual model of process and effects. *Academy of Management Review, 16*, 121-144.

Pipkin, A. (1989). The controller's role en route to the 21st century. *CMA Magazine, 63*(3), 10-18.

Platt, J. R. (1964). Strong inference. *Science, 146*, 347-353.

Poole, M. (1979). Industrial democracy: A comparative analysis. *Industrial Relations, 18*(3), 262-272.

Porter, L. W., & Lawler, E. E. (1968). *Attitudes and performance.* Homewood, IL: Irwin-Dorsey.

Preiwisch, D. F. (1981). GAO study of productivity-sharing programs. In V. M. Buehler & Y. K. Shetty (Eds.), *Productivity improvement: Case studies of proven practice* (pp. 177-200). New York: AMACOM.

Prokesch, S. (1991, July 14). Kinder, gentler plant a failure. *Chicago Tribune,* Sec. 17, p. 5.

Puckett, E. S. (1958). Productivity achievements—A measure of success. In F. G. Lesieur (Ed.), *The Scanlon plan: A frontier in labor-management cooperation* (pp. 109-117). Boston: MIT Press.

Putti, J. M., & Cheong, W. K. (1990). Singapore's positive experience with quality circles. *National Productivity Review, 9*(2), 193-200.

Quality control circles: Implementation key to success—Part 2. (1986, August). *Small Business Report, 11*, 30-35.

Rafaeli, A. (1985). Quality circles and employee attitudes. *Personnel Psychology, 38*, 603-615

Rahman, W. (1987). Software quality by management. *Information and Software Technology, 29*(9), 511-516.

Ram, J. (1989). Quality circles in Silicon Glen. *Asian Business, 25*(11), 54-55.

Ramondt, J. (1987). Managing dualism in Dutch employee representation. *International Studies of Management and Organization, 17*(2), 78-85.

Ramsing, K. D., & Blair, J. D. (1982). An expression of concern about quality circles. In K. H. Chung (Ed.), *Academy of Management proceedings, 1982* (pp. 323-327). New York: Academy of Management.

Reilly, B. J., & DiAngelo, J. A. (1988). From hard work to smart work: A look at job redesign. *Personnel, 65*(2), 61-65.

Rhodes, S. R., & Steers, R. M. (1981). Conventional vs. worker-owned organizations. *Human Relations, 34*, 1013-1035.

Rice, A. K. (1953). Productivity and social organization in an Indian weaving shed. *Human Relations, 6*, 297-329.

Rice, A. K. (1958). *Productivity and social organization: The Ahmedabad experiment.* London: Tavistock.

Riley, G. W., & McSweeny, T. A. (1987). Leveraged ESOPs: Fable or favorable financing tool? *Price Waterhouse Review, 31*(2), 39-45.

Roberts, K. H., & Glick, W. (1981). The job characteristics approach to task design: A critical review. *Journal of Applied Psychology, 66*, 193-217.

Roethlisberger, F. J., & Dickson, W. J. (1939). *Management and the worker—An account of a research program conducted by the Western Electric Company, Chicago.* Cambridge, MA: Harvard University Press.

Rollins, T. (1989, May/June). Productivity-based group incentive plans: Powerful, but use with caution. *Compensation and Benefits Review, 21,* 39-50.

Ronchi, D., & Morgan, W. R. (1983). Springfield, Ohio: Persisting and prevailing. In N. Q. Herrick (Ed.), *Improving government: Experiments with quality of working life systems* (pp. 42-52). New York: Praeger.

Rooney, P. M. (1988). Worker participation in employee-owned firms. *Journal of Economic Issues, 22*(2), 451-458.

Rosen, C. M. (1983). Employee stock ownership plans: A new way to work. *Business Horizons, 26,* 48-54.

Rosen, C. M. (1987). Supervising in an employee-owned company. *Management Solutions, 32*(2), 5-11.

Rosen, C. M. (1990). An introduction to employee stock ownership plans. In K. M. Young (Ed.), *The expanding role of ESOPs in public companies* (pp. 1-10). New York: Quorum.

Rosen, C. M., & Klein, K. J. (1983). Job-creating performance of employee-owned firms. *Monthly Labor Review, 106*(8), 15-19.

Rosen, C. M., Klein, K. J., & Young, K. M. (1986a). *Employee ownership in America: The equity solution.* Lexington, MA: Lexington.

Rosen, C. M., Klein, K. J., & Young, K. M. (1986b, January). When employees share the profits. *Psychology Today, 20,* 30-36.

Rosen, C. M., & Quarrey, M. (1987). How well is employee ownership working? *Harvard Business Review, 65*(5), 126-132.

Rosenbach, W. E., & Zawacki, R. A. (1989). Participative work redesign: A field study in the public sector. *Public Administration Quarterly, 13,* 112-121.

Rosenberg, R. D., & Rosenstein, E. (1980). Participation and productivity: An empirical study. *Industrial and Labor Relations Review, 33*(3), 355-368.

Rosenthal, R. (1979). The "file drawer problem" and tolerance for null results. *Psychological Bulletin, 86,* 638-641.

Rosow, J. M., & Zager, R. (1990). *Management involvement for high commitment.* Scarsdale, NY: Work in America Institute.

Ross, T. L. (1983). Why productivity gainsharing fails in some firms. In B. E. Graham-Moore & T. L. Ross (Eds.), *Productivity gain sharing* (pp. 141-156). Englewood Cliffs, NJ: Prentice-Hall.

Ross, T. L., & Collins, D. (1987, Autumn). Employee involvement and the perils of democracy: Are management's fears warranted? *National Productivity Review, 6,* 348-359.

Ross, T. L., Hatcher, L. L., & Adams, D. B. (1985). How unions view gainsharing. *Business Horizons, 28*(4), 15-22.

Ross, T. L., Ross, R. A., & Hatcher, L. (1986). The multiple benefits of gainsharing. *Personnel Journal, 65*(10), 14-25.

Rousseau, D. M. (1977). Technological differences in job characteristics, employee satisfaction, and motivation: A synthesis of job design research and socio-technical systems theory. *Organizational Behavior and Human Performance, 19,* 18-42.

Rubinstein, S. P. (1987). Linking worker participation with quality and employment security. In S. P. Rubinstein (Ed.), *Participative systems at work* (pp. 25-67). New York: Human Sciences Press.

Ruffenach, G., & Anders, G. (1992, June 4). Big textile firm is accused in suit of "gutting" ESOP. *Wall Street Journal,* p. B2.

Ruh, R. A., Johnson, R. H., & Scontrino, M. P. (1973). The Scanlon plan, participation in decision making, and job attitudes. *Journal of Industrial and Organizational Psychology, 1*, 36-45.

Ruh, R. A., Wallace, R. L., & Frost, C. F. (1973). Management attitudes and the Scanlon plan. *Industrial Relations, 12*, 282-288.

Ruh, R. A., White, J. K., & Wood, R. R. (1975). Job involvement, values, personal background, participation in decision making, and job attitudes. *Academy of Management Journal, 18*, 300-312.

Rus, V. (1970). Influence structure in Yugoslav enterprise. *Industrial Relations, 9*, 148-160.

Russell, R. (1988). Forms and extent of employee participation in the contemporary United States. *Work and Occupations, 15*, 374-395.

Russell, R., Hochner, M., & Perry, S. E. (1979). Participation, influence, and worker ownership. *Industrial Relations, 18*(3), 330-341.

St. George, T. (1984). Quality of work life: Why things get tougher as you go. *Training, 21*(1), 70-72.

Salancik, G., & Pfeffer, J. (1977). An examination of need-satisfaction models of job attitudes. *Administrative Science Quarterly, 22*, 427-456.

Salancik, G., & Pfeffer, J. (1978). A social information processing approach to job attitudes and task design. *Administrative Science Quarterly, 23*, 224-253.

Sales, C. A., Levanoni, E., & Knoop, R. (1989). Employee performance as a function of job orientation and job design. *Industrial Relations (Canada), 44*(2), 409-419.

Samuel, H. (1987). A labor perspective on participative management. *Quality Progress, 20*(2), 38-39.

Sanderson, S. W., & Hayes, R. H. (1990). Mexico—Opening ahead of Eastern Europe. *Harvard Business Review, 68*(5), 32-42.

Saporito, B. (1986, July 21). The revolt against "working smarter." *Fortune*, pp. 58-65.

Sashkin, M. (1976). Changing toward participative management approaches: A model and methods. *Academy of Management Review, 1*(3), 75-86.

Sashkin, M. (1984, Spring). Participative management is an ethical imperative. *Organizational Dynamics*, pp. 5-22.

Sashkin, M. (1986). Participative management remains an ethical imperative. *Organizational Dynamics, 14*(4), 62-75.

Schlesinger, L. A. (1982). *Quality of work life and the supervisor.* New York: Praeger.

Schlesinger, L. A., & Oshry, B. (1984, Summer). Quality of work life and the manager: Muddle in the middle. *Organizational Dynamics, 13*, 5-19.

Schloss, S. (1990, September). Carrot or club? *Industrial Society Magazine (UK)*, pp. 9-13.

Schnabel, C. (1991). Trade unions and productivity: The German evidence. *British Journal of Industrial Relations, 29*(1), 15-24.

Scholl, W. (1987). Codetermination and the ability of firms to act in the Federal Republic of Germany. *International Studies of Management and Organization, 17*(2), 27-37.

Schrank, R. (1974). On ending worker alienation: The Gaines pet food plant. In R. Fairfield (Ed.), *Humanizing the workplace* (pp. 119-140). New York: Prometheus.

Schregle, J. (1970). Forms of participation in management. *Industrial Relations, 9*, 117-122.

Schroeder, M., & Hoerr, J. (1989, January 23). Has Weirton's ESOP worked too well? *Business Week*, pp. 66-67.

Schuler, R. S. (1980). A role and expectancy perception model of participation in decision making. *Academy of Management Journal, 23*, 331-340.

Schuster, M. H. (1983). Forty years of Scanlon plan research: A review of the descriptive and empirical literature. *Organizational Democracy and Political Processes, 1*(2), 53-71.

Schuster, M. H. (1984a). The Scanlon plan: A longitudinal analysis. *Journal of Applied Behavioral Science, 20*, 23-38.

Schuster, M. H. (1984b). *Union-management cooperation: Structure, process and impact.* Kalamazoo, MI: UpJohn Institute.

Schuster, M. H. (1985). Models of cooperation and change in union settings. *Industrial Relations, 24*, 382-394.

Schuster, M. H. (1987). Gain sharing: Do it right the first time. *Sloan Management Review, 28*(2), 17-25.

Schwab, D. P. (1980). Construct validity in organizational behavior. In B. M. Staw & L. L. Cummings (Eds.), *Research in organizational behavior* (Vol. 2, pp. 3-43). Greenwich, CT: JAI.

Schwab, D. P., & Cummings, L. L. (1976). A theoretical analysis of the impact of task scope on employee performance. *Academy of Management Review, 1*, 23-35.

Schwab, D. P., & Heneman, H. G. (1970). Aggregate and individual predictability of the two-factor theory of job satisfaction. *Personnel Psychology, 23*, 55-66.

Schweiger, D. M., & Leana, C. R. (1986). Participation in decision making. In E. A. Locke (Ed.), *Generalizing from laboratory to field studies* (pp. 147-166). Lexington, MA: D. C. Heath.

Scott, W. E. (1966). Activation theory and task design. *Organizational Behavior and Human Performance, 1*, 3-30.

Seashore, S. E. (1981). Quality of working life perspective. In A. H. Van De Ven & W. F. Joyce (Eds.), *Perspectives on organizational design and behavior* (pp. 89-120). New York: John Wiley.

Seeborg, I. S. (1978). The influence of employee participation in job redesign. *Journal of Applied Behavioral Science, 14*, 87-98.

Seelye, H. N., & Sween, J. A. (1982). Quality circles in U.S. industry: Survey results. *Quality Circles Journal, 5*(4), 26-29.

Sel, R. (1988, March). The human face of industry in Sweden. *Industrial Society Magazine*, pp. 30-32.

Sellers, P. (1990, June 4). What customers really want. *Fortune*, pp. 58-68.

Sharp, W. H. (1985). Case studies of successful cooperation: Preconditions and roadblocks. In Y. K. Shetty & V. M. Buehler (Eds.), *Productivity and quality through people: Practices of well-managed companies* (pp. 123-128). New York: Quorum.

Shea, G. P. (1986). Quality circles: The danger of bottled change. *Sloan Management Review, 27*(3), 33-46.

Sheridan, J. A. (1990). Are banks ready for employee participation? *Bankers Magazine, 173*(1), 73-77.

Siegel, I. H., & Weinberg, E. (1982). *Labor-management cooperation.* Kalamazoo, MI: UpJohn Institute.

Simmons, J., & Mares, W. (1982). *Working together: Employee participation in action.* New York: Knopf.

Simplify, then automate, for smoother flow. (1989). *Modern Materials Handling,* 44(4), 43-51.

Sims, H. P., & Szilagyi, A. D. (1976). Job characteristics relationships: Individual and structural moderators. *Organizational Behavior and Human Performance, 17,* 211-230.

Sims, H. P., Szilagyi, D. D., & Keller, R. T. (1976). The measurement of job characteristics. *Academy of Management Journal, 19,* 195-212.

Singer, J. N. (1974). Participative decision-making about work. *Sociology of Work and Occupations, 1,* 347-371.

Smeltzer, L. R., & Kedia, B. L. (1987). Training needs of quality circles. *Personnel,* 64(8), 51-55.

Smith, C. S., & Brannick, M. T. (1990). A role and expectancy model of participative decision-making: A replication and theoretical extension. *Journal of Organizational Behavior, 11,* 91-104.

Smith, M. J. (1985). Machine-paced work and stress. In C. L. Cooper & M. J. Smith (Eds.), *Job stress and blue collar work* (pp. 51-64). Chichester, UK: John Wiley.

Sockell, D. (1984). The legality of employee-participation programs in unionized firms. *Industrial and Labor Relations Review, 37,* 541-556.

Sockell, D. (1985). Attitudes, behavior, and employee ownership: Some preliminary data. *Industrial Relations, 24,* 130-138.

Sohal, A. S., Tay, G., & Wirth, A. (1989). Total quality control in an Asian division of a multinational corporation. *International Journal of Quality and Reliability,* 6(6), 60-74.

Sonnenstuhl, W. J. (1988). Contrasting employee assistance, health promotion, and the quality of work life programs and their effects on alcohol abuse and dependence. *Journal of Applied Behavioral Science, 24,* 347-363.

Soutar, D. H. (1973). Co-determination, industrial democracy and the role of management. *Industrial Relations Research Association proceedings* (pp. 1-7). Madison, WI: Industrial Relations Research Association.

Spector, B., & Lawrence, P. (1981). *General Motors and the United Auto Workers* (Case 9-481-142). Cambridge, MA: Harvard Business School.

Spector, P. E. (1985). Higher-order need strength as a moderator of the job scope-employee outcome relationship: A meta-analysis. *Journal of Occupational Psychology, 58,* 119-127.

Spector, P. E. (1986). Perceived control by employees: A meta-analysis of studies concerning autonomy and participation at work. *Human Relations, 39,* 1005-1016.

Spiers, J. (1992, March 9). Productivity looks promising. *Fortune,* pp. 21-22.

Stackel, L. (1985). Cultivating corporate culture. *Employment Relations Today, 12*(4), 355-361.

Staff. (1982, September). Research spotlight: Why quality circles failed at 21 firms. *Management Review, 71,* 56.

Staff. (1991a, January 7). ESOP plan assets increased rapidly, but many plans terminated, GAO finds. *Employee Relations Weekly, 9,* 26.

Staff. (1991b, August 26). NLRB set to examine employer domination of joint labor-management committees. *Employee Relations Weekly, 9,* 940-941.

Staff. (1991c, September 9). Unions ask NLRB to endorse traditional test on participation committees. *Employee Relations Weekly, 9,* 957-958.

Stanic, N. (1988). Yugoslavia's self-managed crisis. *International Management, 43*(1), 65-67.

Staw, B. M., Bell, N. E., & Clausen, J. A. (1986). The dispositional approach to job attitudes: A lifetime longitudinal test. *Administrative Science Quarterly, 31,* 56-77.

Staw, B. M., & Boettger, R. D. (1990). Task revisions: A neglected form of work performance. *Academy of Management Journal, 33,* 534-559.

Staw, B. M., & Ross, J. (1985). Stability in the midst of change: A dispositional approach to job attitudes. *Journal of Applied Psychology, 70,* 469-480.

Stayer, R. (1990, November/December). How I learned to let my workers lead. *Harvard Business Review, 68,* 66-83.

Stebbins, M. W., & Shani, A. B. (1988). Communications forum interventions: A longitudinal case study. *Leadership and Organization Development Journal, 9*(5), 3-9.

Steel, R. P., Jennings, K. R., & Lindsey, J. T. (1990). Quality circle problem solving and common cents: Evaluation study findings from a United States federal mint. *Journal of Applied Behavioral Science, 26,* 365-381.

Steel, R. P., & Lloyd, R. F. (1988). Cognitive, affective, and behavioral outcomes of participation in quality circles: Conceptual and empirical findings. *Journal of Applied Behavioral Science, 24*(1), 1-17.

Steel, R. P., Mento, A. J., Dilla, B. L., Ovalle, N. K., & Lloyd, R. F. (1985). Factors influencing the success and failure of two quality circle programs. *Journal of Management, 11*(1), 99-119.

Steel, R. P., & Shane, G. S. (1986). Evaluation research on quality circles: Technical and analytical implications. *Human Relations, 39,* 449-468.

Steers, R. M., & Mowday, R. T. (1977). The motivational properties of tasks. *Academy of Management Review, 2,* 645-658.

Stein, B. A., & Kanter, R. M. (1980). Building the parallel organization: Creating mechanisms for permanent quality of work life. *Journal of Applied Behavioral Science, 16,* 371-388.

Stern, R. N. (1988). Participation by representation: Workers on boards of directors in the United States and abroad. *Work and Occupations, 15*(4), 396-422.

Stern, R. N., & Hammer, T. (1978). Buying your job: Factors affecting the success or failure of employee acquisition attempts. *Human Relations, 31,* 1101-1117.

Stewart, T. A. (1991, June 3). Brainpower. *Fortune,* pp. 44-46, 50, 54-56, 60.

Stohl, C., & Jennings, K. (1988). Volunteerism and voice in quality circles. *Western Journal of Speech Communications, 52,* 238-251.

Stone, E. F. (1976). The moderating effect of work-related values on the job scope-job satisfaction relationship. *Organizational Behavior and Human Performance, 15,* 147-167.

Stone, E. F., & Gueutal, H. G. (1985). An empirical derivation of the dimensions along which characteristics of jobs are perceived. *Academy of Management Journal, 28,* 376-396.

Stone, E. F., Mowday, R., & Porter, L. (1977). Higher order need strengths as moderators of the job scope-job satisfaction relationship. *Journal of Applied Psychology, 62,* 466-471.

Stone, E. F., Stone, D. L., & Gueutal, H. G. (1990). Influence of cognitive ability on responses to questionnaire measures: Measurement precision and missing response problems. *Journal of Applied Psychology, 75,* 418-427.

Strauss, G. (1977). Quality of work life and the union. In J. R. Hackman, E. E. Lawler, & L. W. Porter (Eds.), *Perspectives on behavior in organizations* (pp. 479-486). New York: McGraw-Hill.

Strauss, G. (1982). Workers' participation in management: An international perspective. In L. L. Cummings & B. M. Staw (Eds.), *Research in organizational behavior* (Vol. 4, pp. 173-265). Greenwich, CT: JAI.

Sulzner, G. T. (1982). The impact of labor-management cooperation committees on personnel policies and practices at twenty federal bargaining units. *Journal of Collective Negotiations, 11*(1), 37-45.

Sundstrom, E., DeMeuse, K. P., & Futrell, D. (1990). Work teams: Applications and effectiveness. *American Psychologist, 45*, 120-133.

Supervisors, begone! (1988, June 20). *Industry Week*, p. 32.

Susman, G. I. (1973). Job enlargement: Effects of culture on worker responses. *Industrial Relations, 12*, 1-15.

Susman, G. I. (1976). *Autonomy at work: A sociotechnical analysis of participative management*. New York: Praeger.

Svejnar, J. (1982). Codetermination and productivity: Empirical evidence from the Federal Republic of Germany. In D. C. Jones & J. Svejnar (Eds.), *Participatory and self-managed firms* (pp. 199-212). Lexington, MA: Lexington.

Sweeney, P. D., McFarlin, D. B., & Cotton, J. L. (1991). Employee participation and mental health: A test of a mediational model. *IRRA 43rd annual proceedings* (pp. 390-396). Madison, WI: Industrial Relations Research Association.

Tang, T. L., Tollison, P. S., & Whiteside, H. D. (1987). The effect of quality circle initiation on motivation to attend quality circle meetings and on task performance. *Personnel Psychology, 40*, 799-814.

Tang, T. L., Tollison, P. S., & Whiteside, H. D. (1989). Quality circle productivity as related to upper-management attendance, circle initiation, and collar color. *Journal of Management, 15*, 101-113.

Tannenbaum, A. S. (1968). *Control in organizations*. New York: McGraw-Hill.

Tannenbaum, A. S. (1983). Employee-owned companies. In L. L. Cummings & B. M. Staw (Eds.), *Research in organizational behavior* (Vol. 5, pp. 235-268). Greenwich, CT: JAI.

Tannenbaum, A. S., Kavcic, B., Rosner, M., Vianello, M., & Wieser, G. (1974). *Hierarchy in organizations: An international comparison*. San Francisco: Jossey-Bass.

Taplin, P. T. (1989). Successful ESOPs include participatory management. *Employee Benefit Plan Review, 44*(2), 52-54.

Taylor, A. (1988, August 1). Back to the future at Saturn. *Fortune*, pp. 63-72.

Taylor, F. W. (1911). *The principles of scientific management*. New York: Harper.

Taylor, F. W. (1947). *Scientific management*. New York: Harper & Row.

Temple, A. E., & Dale, B. G. (1987). A study of quality circles in white collar areas. *International Journal of Operations and Production Management, 7*(6), 17-31.

Teulings, A. W. M. (1987). A political bargaining theory of co-determination—An empirical test for the Dutch system of organizational democracy. *Organization Studies, 8*(1), 1-24.

Thacker, J. W., & Fields, M. W. (1987). Union involvement in quality-of-worklife efforts: A longitudinal investigation. *Personnel Psychology, 40*, 97-111.

Thacker, J. W., & Kulick, N. (1986). The use of consultants in joint union/management quality of work life efforts. *Consultation, 5*, 116-126.

Thomas, H. (1982). The performance of the Mondragon cooperatives in Spain. In D. C. Jones & J. Svejnar (Eds.), *Participatory and self-managed firms: Evaluating economic performance* (pp. 129-151). Lexington, MA: Lexington.

Thomas, J., & Griffin, R. W. (1983). The social information processing model of task design: A review of the literature. *Academy of Management Review, 8,* 672-682.

Thomas, K. W., & Velthouse, B. A. (1990). Cognitive elements of empowerment: An "interpretive" model of intrinsic task motivation. *Academy of Management Review, 15,* 666-681.

Thompson, P. C. (1982). Quality circles at Martin Marietta Corporation, Denver Aerospace. In R. Zager & M. P. Rosow (Eds.), *The innovative organization: Productivity programs in action* (pp. 3-20). New York: Pergamon.

Thompson, T. (1981, February). Volvo's team manufacturing concept for assembly and test. *Assembly Engineering,* pp. 44-47.

Thorsrud, E., & Emery, F. E. (1970). Industrial democracy in Norway. *Industrial Relations, 9,* 187-196.

Tjosvold, D. (1986). *Working together to get things done: Managing for organizational productivity.* Lexington, MA: Lexington.

Tjosvold, D. (1987). Participation: A close look at its dynamics. *Journal of Management, 13,* 739-750.

Tolentino, A. L. (1984). Quality control circle practices in some selected Philippine companies. *Quality Circles Journal, 7*(4), 35-37.

Tortorich, R., Thompson, P., Orfan, C., Layfield, D., Dreyfus, C., & Kelly, M. (1981). Measuring organizational impact of quality circles. *Quality Circles Journal, 4*(4), 24-34.

Toscano, D. J. (1983a). *Property and participation: Employee ownership and workplace democracy in three New England firms.* New York: Irvington.

Toscano, D. J. (1983b). Toward a typology of employee ownership. *Human Relations, 36,* 581-602.

Tosi, H. (1970, Spring). A reexamination of personality as a determinant of the effects of participation. *Personnel Psychology, 23,* 91-99.

Treece, J. B. (1991, April 8). Are the planets lining up at last for Saturn? *Business Week,* pp. 32-34.

Trist, E. L. (1981). The sociotechnical perspective. In A. H. Van de Ven & W. F. Joyce (Eds.), *Perspectives on organization design and behavior* (pp. 19-75). New York: John Wiley.

Trist, E. L. (1986). Quality of working life and community development: Some reflections on the Jamestown experience. *Journal of Applied Behavioral Science, 22,* 223-237.

Trist, E. L., & Bamforth, K. W. (1951). Some social and psychological consequences of the long wall method of goal getting. *Human Relations, 4,* 3-38.

Trist, E. L., Higgin, G. W., Murray, H., & Pollock, A. B. (1963). *Organizational choice: Capabilities of groups at the coal face under changing technologies.* London: Tavistock.

Trist, E. L., Susman, G. I., & Brown, G. R. (1977). An experiment in autonomous working in an American underground coal mine. *Human Relations, 30,* 201-236.

Trump, L. D. (1985). Hercules' experiences from implementing QCs. In Y. K. Shetty & V. M. Buehler (Eds.), *Productivity and quality through people: Practices of well-managed companies* (pp. 275-279). New York: Quorum.

Tucker, J., Nock, S. L., & Toscano, D. J. (1989). Employee ownership and perceptions of work. *Work and Occupations, 16,* 26-42.

Turner, A. N., & Lawrence, P. R. (1965). *Industrial jobs and the worker.* Boston: Harvard University, Graduate School of Business Administration.

Tymoski, J. (1987). The new Postal Service. *Quality Circles Journal, 10*(2), 42-44.

Umstot, D., Bell, C. H., & Mitchell, T. R. (1976). Effects of job enrichment and task goals on satisfaction and productivity: Implications for job design. *Journal of Applied Psychology, 61,* 379-394.

Vanderslice, V. J., & Leventhal, R. B. (1987, February). Employee participation: A game plan for the real world. *Training and Development Journal,* pp. 34-35.

Van Fleet, D. D., & Griffin, R. W. (1989). Quality circles: A review and suggested future directions. In C. L. Cooper & I. Robertson (Eds.), *International review of industrial and organizational psychology* (pp. 213-233). Chichester, UK: John Wiley.

Verma, A. (1989). Joint participation programs: Self-help or suicide for labor? *Industrial Relations, 28,* 401-410.

Verma, A., & McKersie, R. (1989). Employee involvement: The implications of non-involvement by unions. *Industrial and Labor Relations Review, 40,* 556-568.

Versteeg, A. (1990). Self-directed work teams yield long-term benefits. *Journal of Business Strategy, 11*(6), 9-12.

Vogt, J. F., & Hunt, B. D. (1988). What really goes wrong with participative work groups? *Training and Development Journal, 42*(5), 96-100.

Voos, P. B. (1987). Managerial perceptions of the economic impact of labor relations programs. *Industrial and Labor Relations Review, 40,* 195-208.

Vroom, V. H. (1959). Some personality determinants of the effects of participation. *Journal of Abnormal and Social Psychology, 59,* 322-327.

Vroom, V. H. (1960). *Some personality determinants of the effects of participation.* Englewood Cliffs, NJ: Prentice-Hall.

Vroom, V. H. (1964). *Work and motivation.* New York: John Wiley.

Wagner, J. A., & Gooding, R. Z. (1987a). Effects of societal trends on participation research. *Administrative Science Quarterly, 32,* 241-262.

Wagner, J. A., & Gooding, R. Z. (1987b). Shared influence and organizational behavior: A meta-analysis of situational variables expected to moderate participation-outcome relationships. *Academy of Management Journal, 30,* 524-541.

Wall, T. D., & Clegg, C. W. (1981). A longitudinal field study of group work redesign. *Journal of Organizational Behavior, 2,* 31-49.

Wall, T. D., Corbett, J. M., Martin, R., Clegg, C. W., & Jackson, P. R. (1990). Advanced manufacturing technology, work design, and performance: A change study. *Journal of Applied Psychology, 75,* 691-697.

Wall, T. D., Kemp, N. J., Jackson, P. R., & Clegg, C. W. (1986). Outcomes of autonomous workgroups: A long-term field experiment. *Academy of Management Journal, 29,* 280-304.

Wall, T. D., & Martin, R. (1987). Job and work design. In C. L. Cooper & I. T. Robertson (Eds.), *International review of industrial and organizational psychology, 1987* (pp. 61-91). Chichester, UK: John Wiley.

Walters, R. W., & Associates. (1975). *Job enrichment for results.* Reading, MA: Addison-Wesley.

Walton, A. E., & Lodge, G. (1985). *Eastern Air Lines* (Case 9-385-244). Cambridge, MA: Harvard Business School.

Walton, R. E. (1973). Quality of working life: What is it? *Sloan Management Review,* 15, 11-21.

Walton, R. E. (1975). Criteria for quality of working life. In L. E. Davis & A. B. Cherns (Eds.), *The quality of working life* (Vol. 1, pp. 91-104). New York: Free Press.

Walton, R. E. (1977). Work innovations at Topeka: After six years. *Journal of Applied Behavioral Sciences,* 13, 422-433.

Walton, R. E. (1982). The Topeka work system: Optimistic visions, pessimistic hypotheses, and reality. In R. Zager & M. P. Rosow (Eds.), *The innovative organization: Productivity programs in action* (pp. 260-287). New York: Pergamon.

Walton, R. E., & Schlesinger, L. A. (1979, Winter). Do supervisors thrive in participative work systems? *Organizational Dynamics,* 7, 25-38.

Wanous, J. P. (1976). Who wants job enrichment? *S.A.M. Advanced Management Journal,* 41(3), 5-22.

Warner, M. (1976). Further thoughts on experiments in industrial democracy and self-management. *Human Relations,* 29, 401-410.

Warner, M. (1990). Management versus self-management in Yugoslavia. *Journal of General Management,* 16(2), 20-37.

Wartzman, R. (1992, May 4). Sharing gains: A Whirlpool factory raises productivity—and pay of workers. *Wall Street Journal,* pp. A1, A4.

Washington Post Service. (1990, August 5). People power falls victim to automation. *Milwaukee Journal,* p. D5.

Wayne, S. J., Griffin, R. W., & Bateman, T. S. (1986). Improving the effectiveness of quality circles. *Personnel Administrator,* 31(3), 79-88.

Weber, J. (1991, October 7). Offering employees stock options they can't refuse. *Business Week,* p. 34.

Weber, J. (1992, May 4). A big company that works. *Business Week,* pp. 124-132.

Weed, E. D. (1971). Job enrichment "cleans up" at Texas Instruments. In J. H. Maher (Ed.), *New perspectives in job enrichment* (pp. 55-77). New York: Van Nostrand Reinhold.

Weiler, P. C. (1990). *Governing the workplace.* Cambridge, MA: Harvard University.

Welbourne, T. M., & Gomez-Mejia, L. R. (1988). Gainsharing revisited. *Compensation and Benefits Review,* 20(4), 19-28.

Wellins, R. S., Byham, W. C., & Wilson, J. M. (1991). *Empowered teams: Creating self-directed work groups that improve quality, productivity, and participation.* San Francisco: Jossey-Bass.

Wells, D. M. (1987). *Empty promises: Quality of working life programs and the labor movement.* New York: Monthly Review.

Wever, K. R. (1989). Toward a structural account of union participation in management: The case of Western Airlines. *Industrial and Labor Relations Review,* 42(4), 600-609.

White, J. A. (1991, January 25). As ESOPs become victims of '90s bankruptcies, workers are watching their nest eggs vanish. *Wall Street Journal,* p. C1.

White, J. A. (1992, February 13). When employees own big stakes, it's a buy signal for investors. *Wall Street Journal,* pp. C1, C10.

White, J. B. (1991, May 24). GM struggles to get Saturn car on track after rough launch. *Wall Street Journal,* pp. 1, 12.

White, J. B., & Guiles, M. G. (1990, July 9). GM's plan for Saturn to beat small imports trails original goals. *Wall Street Journal,* pp. 1, 4.

White, J. K. (1978). Individual differences and the job quality-worker response relationship: Review, integration, and comments. *Academy of Management Review, 3*, 267-280.

White, J. K. (1979). The Scanlon plan: Causes and correlates of success. *Academy of Management Journal, 22*, 292-312.

White, J. K., & Ruh, R. A. (1973). Effects of personal values on the relationship between participation and job attitudes. *Administrative Science Quarterly, 14*, 506-514.

White, R., & Lippitt, R. (1960). *Autocracy and democracy.* New York: Harper.

White, S. E., & Mitchell, T. R. (1979). Job enrichment versus social cues: A comparison and competitive test. *Journal of Applied Psychology, 64*, 1-9.

Whiteside, D., Brad, R., Schiller, Z., & Gabor, A. (1985, January 28). How GM's Saturn could run rings around old-style carmakers. *Business Week*, pp. 126, 128.

Whyte, W. F., & Whyte, K. K. (1988). *Making Mondragon: The growth and dynamics of the worker cooperative complex.* Ithaca, NY: ILR.

Williams, D. R., & House, J. S. (1985). Social support and stress reduction. In C. L. Cooper & M. J. Smith (Eds.), *Job stress and blue collar work* (pp. 207-224). Chichester, UK: John Wiley.

Wilson, J. (1990, July/August). Investing in our future: Quality and participation for students and school staff. *Journal for Quality and Participation, 13*, 78-81.

Wilson, N., & Peel, M. J. (1991). The impact of absenteeism and quits of profit-sharing and other forms of employee participation. *Industrial and Labor Relations Review, 44*(3), 454-468.

Witt, L. A., & Brkovic, A. (1989, April). *Job attitudes among Yugoslav workers as a function of role in self-management.* Paper presented at the 1989 meeting of the Society of Industrial and Organizational Psychology, Boston, MA.

Wood, R. C. (1982). Squaring off on quality circles. *Inc., 4*(8), 98-100.

Wood, R. C., Hull, F., & Azumi, K. (1983). Evaluating quality circles: The American application. *California Management Review, 26*(1), 37-53.

Woodruff, D. (1991, December 2). At Saturn, what workers want is . . . fewer defects. *Business Week*, pp. 117-118.

Woodworth, W. P. (1984). The blue-collar boardroom: Worker directors and corporate governance. *New Management, 2*, 53-57.

Woodworth, W. P. (1986). Managing from below. *Journal of Management, 12*, 391-402.

Woodworth, W. P. (1988, February). Why success didn't take: The Hyatt Clark experience. *Management Review, 77*, 50-55.

Wright, M., Thompson, R. S., & Robbie, K. (1989). Privatization via management and employee buyouts: Analysis and U.K. experience. *Annals of Public and Co-Operative Economy, 60*, 399-429.

Young, K. M. (1990). Managing an employee ownership company. In K. M. Young (Ed.), *The expanding role of ESOPs in public companies* (pp. 157-188). New York: Quorum.

Zaccaro, S. J., & Stone, E. F. (1988). Incremental validity of an empirically based measure of job characteristics. *Journal of Applied Psychology, 73*, 245-252.

Zellner, W. (1989, March 27). The UAW rebels team up against teamwork. *Business Week*, pp. 110, 114.

Zenger, J. H. (1991). Supervisors of the future. *Small Business Reports, 16*(3), 16-21.

Zenger-Miller Company. (1990). *Report on self-directed work teams questionnaire*. San Jose, CA: Author.

Zwerdling, D. (1984). *Workplace democracy: A guide to workplace ownership, participation and self-management experiments in the United States and Europe*. New York: Harper Torchbooks.

Author Index

Subject Index

Ability, 83, 102, 120, 121, 163, 168-171, 197, 243, 244, 278, 281

Absenteeism, 14, 38, 39, 65, 99, 127, 143, 147, 151, 152, 154-156, 165, 168, 153, 179-182, 184, 187, 188, 190, 189, 212, 214, 220, 216, 238, 260, 271, 286

Acceptance, 20, 24, 23, 35, 98, 112, 134

Acceptance of change, 98, 112

Access, 27, 28, 30, 41, 115, 142, 210

Activation theory, 145, 257, 279

Adapt, 24, 57, 237

Adaptability or flexibility of the organization, 236

Adversarial, 50

Affiliation, 76

Africa, 61, 114

Age, 75, 109, 179, 219, 252

Air Force, 67

Alienation, 2, 130, 140, 147, 278

Amalgamated Clothing and Textile Workers Union, 50, 79

American Center for the Quality of Work Life, 48

Anecdotal case studies, 64

Arbitration, 122

Archival records, 65

Army, 64

Assembly line, 4, 5, 39, 74, 90, 102, 174, 179-181, 194, 195, 251, 262, 265, 283

Assessment center approach, 197

Associated Labour Act, 123

Assumptions, 11, 27, 78, 95, 137, 139, 240

AT&T, 142-144, 256

Attitude, 63, 65, 71, 187, 188, 211, 215, 223

Auditing, 60, 272, 275

Australia, 61, 187, 203

Austria , 118, 137, 115

Auto industry, 38, 40, 41, 50, 59, 181

Automation, 1, 11, 36, 263, 265, 285

Avis, 227, 266

Backlash, 243

Bank tellers, 156

Bankruptcy, 41, 92, 128

Banks, 60, 279

Belgium, 135

Benefits and Drawbacks of ESOPs, 6, 9, 52, 57, 62, 64, 66, 78, 98, 117, 166, 185, 192, 193, 202, 218, 221, 223-225, 241, 247, 250, 255, 257, 270, 271, 273, 277, 284, 285

Bias, 43, 72, 107, 146, 170, 188, 199, 247, 258

Blue-collar workers, 17, 73, 74, 174, 219, 220, 237, 286

Board of directors, 20, 28, 31, 41, 57, 114, 116-118, 126-129, 138, 139, 201, 204, 205, 206

Board representatives, 20, 114, 115, 120, 122, 126, 138-140, 115

Bolivar, 39, 270

Bonus formulas, 92, 95, 106, 107

Bottom-up approach, 166

Boundaries, 27, 86, 117, 118, 135, 138, 191, 193, 253, 272

About the Author

John L. _____ in the College of _____ ty, Milwau-
kee, Wi_____ sity of Iowa
and has _____ University,
and Pu_____ employee
involve_____ ployees. He
has pub_____ cs. In addi-
tion, he_____ a member
of the A_____ logical So-
ciety, an_____ chologists.